Archibald Simpson Architect

His Life and Times
1790 – 1847

Archibald Simpson
Architect

His Life and Times
1790 – 1847

by

David G. Miller Dip. Arch. Aberdeen

Librario

Published by

Librario Publishing Ltd.

ISBN 10: 1-904440-84-3
ISBN 13: 978-1-904440-84-0

Copies can be ordered via the Internet
www.librario.com

or from:

Brough House, Milton Brodie, Kinloss
Moray IV36 2UA
Tel/Fax No 00 44 (0)1343 850 617

Printed and bound by
4edge, Hockley, Essex

Typeset by 3btype.com

Contents

Introduction   7

Historical Background   11

The Age of Improvement   19

Apprenticeship   21

A Start is Made   29

Arcadian Dreams   61

A Fair Body of Work   159

The Simpson Achievement   307

The Complete Works of Archibald Simpson   325

Glossary of Terms   335

Acknowledgements   341

Index of Buildings   353

Introduction

Few people living in Aberdeen today can be unaware of the name of Archibald Simpson. Some of course might think that he is the proprietor of a pub, others might even think that he is some kind of restaurant entrepreneur, but the name and the work of the architect who more than anyone else stamped his personality and genius on Aberdeen and the North-east of Scotland during its golden age, is still happily very much around. Despite his relatively brief period of professional activity from 1813–1847, his impact on the city and surrounding region was remarkable, exploiting the inherent monumental qualities of the ever present natural granite building material with his own personal extremely restrained neoclassical flair, to produce built jewels of the very highest architectural quality.

Achieving even in his lifetime an almost legendary status, his many individual triumphs within the city itself, including the old North Bank, Union Buildings, the Medico Chirurgical Hall, the Assembly Rooms (Music Hall), the old High School (Harlaw Academy), St Andrew's Cathedral and the old Infirmary in Woolmanhill, still manage to survive more or less in the condition he left them in. His New Marischal College has been considerably overwhelmed in the interim, while even more unhappily his unique Triple Kirks has been unforgivably damaged now beyond any possible repair. Tragically also his august New Market Building is no more, carelessly sacrificed to other more 'modern' commercial interests. In the main however Aberdeen has been quite kind to her famous architectural son. Of course many of his lesser buildings, especially in Union Street, have been disfigured over time and internally stripped, again due mainly to commercial pressures, but even here impressively, much still remains. Aberdeen also still possesses numerous streets in Ferryhill and the west end, built or directly inspired by his personal involvement, and in Bon Accord Square and Crescent we retain in almost pristine condition, the most serene monuments to his remarkable planning genius.

When we consider his wider work from Lerwick to Rothesay, his achievement is all the more astonishing given the problems and difficulties of travel in those days, even despite the undoubted improvements to the road network during the period. Elgin's magnificent St Giles Church and Anderson Institution, Huntly's Gordon School and Clydesdale Bank, compete with an array of churches and great houses throughout the North-east region. Masterpieces as diverse as Park, Murtle, Thainstone and Stracathro still survive today, although most have been commandeered for institutional or some other commercial use. The demise of country house living (in the grandest style) during the twentieth century has resulted in the greatest loss of Simpson buildings being in this genre. Great mansions of the calibre of Scotstown, Castle Newe, and Carnousie, are unfortunately gone while many of his most interesting modernisations and extensions have been more recently swept away, prey to various attempts to reduce many houses back to a more manageable size. Lessendrum, Tillery and Leask have fallen victim to fire, while many more of course have been converted into Hotels, Residential Homes and sub-divided into apartments.

This study seeks to chronicle Simpson's great achievement by examining in order of execution all his known works, buildings generally attributed to him, and buildings also in the 'style of Simpson' which may in fact be by his hand. Each commission will be briefly described, and its merits discussed along with its subsequent history and present condition. In this endeavour, the information on his many lesser and more far-flung commissions, contained within the very excellent Illustrated Architectural Guides Series covering the North-east Region, Moray and Angus, has been invaluable. Armed with these little books I have been able to study in some detail, many mansions, which are relatively unknown, many stables and service buildings of an architectural importance far outweighing their relatively humble status, and many exquisitely considered gate lodges and gardener's cottages carried out in his cottage-orné style. Hopefully also the chronological approach will better illustrate his prodigious energy, while revealing something of the scope and diversity of his work as well as the sometimes rather haphazard nature of an architectural practice, dependent as it is on many external factors well beyond the architect's personal control. Alternating between early promise and sometimes dire disappointment, most of the time Simpson and his assistants were totally committed to extremely hard work and application, the foundation stones of all achievement. Archibald Simpson of course also remained unmarried, finding perhaps like Adam before him, little time for such diversion while otherwise totally absorbed in building up his young practice from virtually nothing. He was also therefore in the position throughout his career of being able to channel his whole energies into his work, without the competition of a wife and family. The very remarkable prosperity and expansion of Aberdeen and the North-east during the period of Simpson's lifetime was also crucial in creating the requirement for a vast array of necessary new buildings, to be designed and built within the city and surrounding area on a scale previously unknown.

Simpson of course never had the field entirely to himself, as the equally gifted work of his great rival John Smith so eloquently demonstrates. The two men however appear to have had a healthy and mutual respect for one another, very often competing for commissions, and both frequently consulted about the same project. On a number of occasions also they collaborated with each other when the possibility of creating a mutually advantageous architectural contribution to the city arose.

It has also been noted that his unforeseen early death in 1847 at the age of only fifty-seven at least spared Simpson the dreadful repercussions of the economic collapse of 1848, when the local textile industry imploded, never to fully recover. The shift also in the national consciousness of taste, away from the neoclassical and into an Abbotsford-inspired Historical Romanticism, increasingly witnessed the arrival of the Gothic and Baronial ascendancy, which eventually sidelined Simpson's severe restraint in any case. Archibald Simpson and more especially 'Tudor' Johnny Smith of course had never been blind to the possibilities of institutional Tudor, neo-Jacobean or even ecclesiastic Gothic, these styles in particular perhaps being more attuned to their own shared personal vision of cool classical order and restraint.

After 1850, despite taking a further twenty years to finally complete the entirety of Union Street, it was increasingly obvious however that the era of the neoclassical ideal was drawing to a close and that a freer and more eclectic order was in vogue, in the hands of a breed of new, younger architects, many actually trained in the offices of both Archibald Simpson and John Smith themselves. In this manner the tradition of suitability for purpose and respect for material survived undimmed, creating for the most part that remarkable sense of built monumentality and unity, whatever the style, which is still so very evident in Aberdeen's city centre even today, despite the vast intervening social and commercial changes which have brought about a very different modern world. Regrettably however, this world frequently demonstrates a still very casual disregard for its past, with too many of the remarkable buildings described in this study either ruinous, boarded up or half empty and neglected. For those of us who had thought that the bad old days were behind us, when even the great New Market building could be so easily swept away, perhaps we should keep the image of Simpson's desecrated Aberdeen Triple Kirks permanently before us, as an awful warning. Currently there are many more of his less prominent buildings either empty or quietly rotting away, in streets where owners and landlords seem increasingly content to exploit the commercial possibilities of only the very lucrative ground floors, leaving the remainder almost completely to its own devices.

Historical Background

In 1790, Aberdeen was at the start of what turned out to be a period of unprecedented change, witnessing the almost complete transformation of a small, yet still basically medieval Burgh at the mouth of the River Dee estuary, into what would become the subsequent basis of the great Victorian expansion, further leading to the later modern city. From a population of only five and a half thousand at the beginning of the eighteenth century, by its end the burgeoning little town of just over twenty thousand inhabitants was literally bursting at the seams of its ancient medieval constraints. Its population however was poised to treble in the next fifty years.

Aberdeen has always occupied an enviable position at the point where by natural good fortune the north-east channels out into the only really viable coastal route to the south. In addition, the excellent sheltered harbour created by the Dee estuary, provided an exit for the export of the region's considerable natural produce. Over time the Burgh had become the focus of the north-east, with the establishment of trading links with both the rest of Scotland and much of continental Europe. Its position and prosperity assured, and dependent on the exploitation of its many natural assets, the indigenous character and abilities of the local and regional hard working inhabitants ensured the rest. However the city would always very wisely look to the condition of its vital harbour and the sustainability of its expanding trading connections.

During the eighteenth century Britain, despite the tensions which would surface in 1715 and 1745 in two major political rebellions, was fully in the throes of enormous change, as the United Kingdom struggled to emerge as the leading country of Europe. Already experiencing a period of remarkable growth and prosperity following the religious and political turmoil of the previous century, the more settled times and peace at home favoured economic progress on all fronts, as early industrialisation and agricultural reform swept the entire country. Although remote, and not possessing ready access to any mineral wealth, Aberdeen was fortunate to benefit from the considerable improvements and more efficient land use of the north-east region, which naturally percolated increased wealth and activity into the Burgh. The attendant rise in production and the better quality of farm produce, as well as coming into the town for direct export from the busy harbour, also much encouraged the establishment of various related processing industries. In this manner many mills, granaries, brewing, distilling, and animal product processing establishments set up throughout the town and region. The coastal communities, Aberdeen included, combined all these activities with fishing, fish processing and shipbuilding. As the eighteenth century progressed, due to the abundance of suitable water supplies, textile manufacture made its appearance in the area with linen, cotton, wool and flax making being established along with various paper making mills. Aberdeen was most fortunate and well placed to benefit greatly from all these developments, as the Burgh continued to grow and expand with a marked increase in population and density. Whilst in the mid-century Aberdeen would be famous across Europe for her stockings, gloves and the quality of her salmon, by the beginning of the nineteenth century, cotton, linen, woollens, granite and paper would all be added to that list as well as whisky, beer and cattle exports.

The development of the granite industry in itself, following the opening up of the Loanhead Quarry in 1730, was of considerable importance as the requirement for building material increased. As the Burgh grew and the density of houses increased, demand encouraged the opening up of many more quarries within the region as far afield as Pitmuxton, Nigg, Ferryhill, Cove, Greyhope, Craiglug, Kincausie and Dyce, all at this time exploiting easily obtained basically surface deposits. The immediate results were impressive, as even visitors of the calibre of Doctor Johnson favourably commented on the neatness and cleanliness of the town as well as the excellence of the granite buildings. The continued increase in demand, the development of a very profitable export trade in pavement slabs and street cassies, combined with a marked increase in the quality of material as quarries began to exploit ever deepening deposits, resulted in considerable advances being made in the industry. Technological change in quarrying, as well as advances in the handling, cutting and finishing of the stone, progressed throughout the nineteenth century leading to a marked increase in quantity, quality and the ability to economically work the material. This in itself made savings possible and with the availability of cheaper stone, this also encouraged the development of more easily obtained elaborate decorative building effects. In tandem with a progressive change in the national mood as the country emerged as undisputed leader of the World, this would also inexorably lead to the eventual breakdown of the restrained neoclassical consensus – but we get ahead of ourselves.

As all the agricultural advances fuelled a natural increase in the population, happily the development of large scale industrial enterprises within the region created ready employment for the less fortunate who had been driven off the land by the various efficiencies and farm amalgamations of the time. The inexorable drift from the country into the towns and villages had commenced, and as a result all the towns and cities of Scotland experienced very remarkable growth in this period, the north-east included. This, and the new interest in improving mankind's lot as encouraged by the great thinkers of the enlightenment, also witnessed a marked increase in living standards and the development for the first time since Roman times, of new towns and villages throughout much of the country. In 1716 Sir Archibald Grant commenced laying out his planned village at Monymusk, to be swiftly followed by Lord Cockburn of Ormiston's more ambitious planned village in the Lothians in 1735. Shortly, new communities were appearing all over, encouraging better living and health standards as well as fostering trade, new economic opportunities and very desirable social improvements. Before long James Craig's plan for the New Town in Edinburgh materialised along with the almost parallel creation of Glasgow's Merchant City in the 1780s, stimulating various similar but smaller scale initiatives in various towns throughout the land.

In the north-east, Aberdeen in particular would benefit from the application of this thinking, as the Burgh struggled to accommodate its expanding population and new economic and industrial activity within what was ostensibly still a very inadequate medieval framework. The first great improvement was the building of Marischal Street in 1767, thereby greatly facilitating access from the Castlegate down to the harbour. This was quickly followed with the building of ten new, largely residential streets around the old Burgh, within the next decade. By

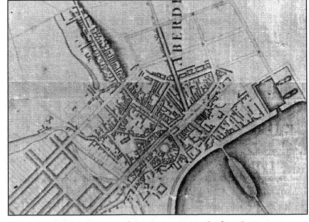

Abercrombie's over ambitious proposals for the extension of the Burgh.

the end of the eighteenth century Aberdeen had experienced a period of phenomenal change, which showed no signs of abating, indeed the prospects for the future seemed unlimited. New Turnpike roads being built throughout the country revolutionising travel, and the progressive development of Aberdeen harbour, simply underlined the Burgh's confidence and undoubted status as the region's natural centre. As the need for even more expansion became increasingly obvious, the citizens and the Town Council were beginning to deliberate on the most appropriate direction to take, as well as contemplating a programme of major new street building, which would hopefully address the inadequacies of the medieval road system once and for all.

Archibald Simpson was born into these exciting times on the 4th of May 1790, at No. 15 the Guestrow, the fourth son and ninth child to William Simpson and his wife Barbara Dauney. William had arrived into Aberdeen in 1770 from Kincardineshire with the intention of buying a clothiers business in Broad Street in partnership with his brother Joseph. It seems probable that he was already acquainted with his future wife Barbara Dauney, who was the eldest daughter of the minister of Banchory Ternan, the Reverend Francis Dauney. A distinguished local family, her brothers Alexander and Francis would both in due course become Sheriff Substitutes of the city, while her brother William became a notable builder-architect.

From the outset however Archibald was a weakly child, unfortunately also possessing a lame arm, much to the concern of his parents. Even into his manhood he would have a slight build and was not strong physically. In the event however at least he survived, his older brothers William, Francis and James all dying young. It was probably these personal family bereavements, which resulted in Archibald forming the closest bond with his seven year older surviving brother Alexander, a relationship which would sustain him throughout the rest of his life. Both his parents also died relatively young, his father William expiring in August 1804. He had the presence of mind to bequeath to Archibald a special legacy over his general share of his estate in "consideration of his being unable to prosecute any laborious business by means of the lameness in the left arm". It was at this difficult time that his mother's Dauney relatives gathered round to offer their support, and in particular her brother William.

He had built up a considerable reputation as a builder-architect within the city, having constructed the rather modest family dwelling in the Guestrow backlands for his sister, as well as erecting more notable efforts, including a very fine town house in the Gallowgate in 1789. He was also responsible for a number of houses flanking the western side of the newly built Marischal Street in 1799. He himself built and owned No. 32, and he also erected No. 30 for

Provost Young next door. Interestingly he must also have worked in close co-operation, as well as in competition with, his rival builder-architect, William 'sink em' Smith, the highly successful father of John Smith who, born earlier in 1781, was destined eventually to become Archibald's greatest architectural rival and the future City Architect of Aberdeen.

Initially Archibald had been sent to the Grammar School in Schoolhill to obtain his education and there, in the rather modest premises adjacent to Gordon's Hospital, he enrolled in January 1800. Apparently he was not particularly bright, getting there at the end of the day more by application and persistence. While at school however, the decision on the building of the Abercrombie Union Street proposals had been taken, works were being put in hand, and the programme of preparatory demolitions had been completed. These were interesting times indeed. Following Archibald's matriculation into Marischal College however in 1803, he had only completed one year by the time of his father's untimely death. As his mother had also died three years prior to this, Alexander immediately became titular head of the family. It seems extremely likely that at this juncture, William Dauney persuaded the young Archibald to give up his avowed ambition of becoming a merchant, doubtless drawing the young man's attention to the glowing prospects now associated with building and architecture. He might even have indicated as an example the prospects of John Smith, then still in training in London. He would return shortly in 1805 and have completed his first notable commission in Aberdeen by 1807 for Milne of Crimonmogate, as the first house built on Union Street at No. 202. Regrettably this very fine building is now all but a photographic memory.

Forced by circumstances to withdraw himself from the University, Archibald immediately entered the firm of James Massie, a local builder with premises on the Castlehill. The initial intention appears to have been the acquisition of necessary mason's skills. At this time, and with the construction phase of the work building the Union Street thoroughfare virtually complete, it must have appeared that the city's prospects in the field of building activity had never looked better. The further study of Architecture therefore, must simply have suggested itself.

'Architecture' was of course a fairly novel concept even at this time in the far-flung remote north-eastern shoulder of Scotland. For most of the eighteenth century, masons or wrights had been considered sufficiently skilled operatives for most building purposes, with architects, few and far between as they were, being employed on only the most elaborate or prestigious commissions, which were mainly in and around the Capital apart from aristocratic work. Aberdeen had even produced the redoubtable James Gibbs, a native born near Fittysmire, who after a local education and a period of apprenticeship with Carlo Fontana in Rome, returned to become one of the leading talents of his time. He still found it more expedient to establish himself in London however, thereby ensuring his lasting and international fame. He also gifted to the city an extremely distinguished Basilican design for the replacement of the ruinous West Church of St Nicholas. His only other, but attributed work in Aberdeen, was the astylar brick, but for him rather sober, extension of Seaton House, now tragically long burnt out and demolished. His departure from Scotland however rather left the field open for William Adam, father of the even more famous John, Robert and James. William, by his prodigious if slightly derivative efforts, could be said to have stamped the classical style across the face of Scotland, earning for himself the sobriquet of 'Universal Architect'. His major contribution to the Burgh of Aberdeen was the design and building of the Auld Hoose at Robert Gordon's Hospital, although his name has also been associated with the Back Hoose in Virginia Street as well, long removed to make way for the inner ring road. The requirements for greater sophistication in planning and design, coupled with the need to carry out and interpret the increasingly

Burn's Castlegate Bank at the head of Marischal Street introduced a more sophisticated neoclassical note into the City for the first time.

complex and more fashionable classically correct compositions and details, would quickly encourage the development of this new profession however across the length and breadth of the entire country.

In Aberdeen, John Jeans, the first recorded home grown 'architect' actually operating within the Burgh is recorded as rebuilding the Bow Brig over the Denburn in 1747, following the destruction of the previous structure by a spate. He was subsequently responsible for the construction of the Mealmarket, on a site immediately to the north of North Street. Other local practitioners were also active including Alexander and George Jaffray, both of whom had created many very fine houses in the immediate vicinity of the town. However it would be Gibbs' West Church of St Nicholas and Adam's Robert Gordon's Hospital, which would remain the main adornments of the period until the laying out of Marischal Street in 1767. This was however merely a prelude to a period of considerable and very necessary developments which would at last free the city from its medieval straight jacket.

The Age of Improvement

By 1794, in response to the very evident shortage of space within the still medieval confines of the Burgh, and the inadequacies of the increasingly congested ancient road system, Charles Abercrombie's Proposals for the improvement of the situation were being widely considered. These included two possible new routes to the south, a new east-west street and a new street to the north, as well as a proposal for an Edinburgh-inspired New Town on the Gilcomston Lands west of the Denburn valley itself. By this time, the necessity for something to be done had become glaringly obvious to all, as there was little easily available land for expansion in any direction. The Burgh was confined to the south by the Dee estuary, to the east by the Castlehill and Heading Hill, to the north by the old Lochlands, and to the west by the Denburn valley defile. The decision was therefore taken to build the east-west street, a new street south from that to the Bridge of Dee, and to construct a new street also to the north. The more ambitious scheme for the New Town however unfortunately failed to materialise, even although a very tentative start was actually made on it.

By July 1801, the foundation stone was laid for David Hamilton's ill-fated three-arched bridge design carrying the new street over the Denburn. At the same time, James Burn of Haddington commenced the construction of his new bank design for the Aberdeen Bank in the Castlegate at the head of Marischal Street. This most sophisticated neoclassical building was certainly a portent of things to come, being by far the most advanced design in town. Meanwhile things were not destined to run smoothly in the construction of the new bridge, as miscalculations in the contractor's price, coupled by serious errors in the levels as given by Hamilton, forced the work to an ignominious halt. After due deliberation and the hasty submission of four alternative schemes, the Trustees decided to entrust the construction of a completely new design to their own Superintendent of Works, Thomas Fletcher. William Ross, builder of the

Aberdeenshire Canal, was appointed the contractor for the work in November 1802, which now envisaged a noble 130ft single span arch supporting a roadway 50ft wide. With great speed the work progressed so that the keystone of the arch was driven by 25th August 1803, and by the 27th February 1805, the bridge was complete, including the fine granite balustrade and central decorative panels designed by James Burn. Union Bridge, with the street commemorating the Union of Great Britain and Ireland, was formally opened with considerable civic ceremony on the 4th June 1805, the King's birthday. Shortly afterwards, on one of his regular visits to the city, the Circuit Judge, Lord Medwyn famously observed that "he had come to Aberdeen when it was a city without an entrance but that recently it had become an entrance without a city".

Notwithstanding, the most difficult part of the jigsaw was now in place and the broad viaduct extending on either side of the bridge from the Adelphi in the east to what would become Diamond Street in the west was complete. The construction phase of the new modern buildings lining both sides of the magnificent new thoroughfare could now commence in earnest, and developments were eagerly awaited. In the event the Council and populace were to be sadly disappointed as initial progress was painfully slow. The high feu-duties imposed, the perceived excessive requirements of the very high building specification, and the increased costs associated with that and the necessary and sometimes very considerable under-building required, were all given as reasons for the difficulties and delays.

Apprenticeship

To the Dauney family however at this stage, it must have appeared that the prospects were absolutely limitless. It could not have escaped their notice either, that apart from one or two active locals, the major architectural practitioners of the new neoclassical style had only very recently arrived from the south in the form of David Hamilton and James Burn. Despite apparently very little evidence of any early predilection towards architecture, the decision to point Archibald in the direction of this career was eminently sensible, enabling him also the future possibility of exploiting the considerable local connections his uncle had built up during his own career as architect-builder within the city. The Smith Family of course had already stolen a march on them, having groomed their son John in the niceties of building practice within their own extensive building business. He was also currently in London, polishing up his own design talent, and to return in 1805, shortly also landing the extremely important post of Superintendent to the Trustees, a position just vacated by Thomas Fletcher who retired in 1807. This wonderful opportunity and the very considerable local and regional connections enjoyed by his father would ensure his immediate success. As already mentioned, almost at once he was employed erecting Milne of Crimonmogate's house in Union Street, while for the Trustees themselves he was actively considering various designs for many new commercial and residential buildings lining the recently broken through thoroughfare of King Street.

Archibald Simpson however, having just completed his apprenticeship as a mason in 1810, and no doubt fired at the prospect of vastly improving his prospects, somehow succeeded in obtaining a post in the Holborn office of Robert Lugar, a notable London-based country house architect. His greatest claim to fame nowadays are his books, two volumes published by him on Villa Architecture, Plans and Views of Buildings executed in England and Scotland in the Castellated and Other Styles, A Collection of Views with Plans of

The young Archibald Simpson's first portrait painted by his friend James Giles.

Buildings executed in England and Scotland, and Architectural Sketches for Cottages, Rural Dwellings and Villas. In consequence the experience the young Archibald gained in his office would prove invaluable to him in the future, both in his general approach to house design and in the necessary careful attention to detail. Lugar was particularly highly regarded at the time for his designs of various picturesquely inspired Gothic lodges and villas, which must have had a profound effect on some of Archibald's later experiments also in this field. Many of Lugar's most important large commissions too, were also erected in a castellated Gothic style, of which Balloch Castle, Tullichewan and Boturich beside Loch Lomond are his most typical and successful Scottish examples. The publication of these particular designs in 1811 would also do much to fuel the secular Gothic

Revival in Scotland. At the same time however Archibald had letters of introduction and was rubbing shoulders with most of the greatest talents of the day, being acquainted with such leading lights as Sir John Soane, George Dance, Robert Smirke and S. P. Cockerel. The latter was somewhat unhelpful to him however, suggesting perhaps rather realistically that the practice of architecture at that time "was hopeless without a connection of consequence".

Despite all the attendant problems still fresh in the memory following the French Revolution, and the ongoing political turmoil of the Napoleonic Wars, London at this moment was an extremely exciting and vibrant place to be in, particularly in architectural terms. The great danger to the very survival of the nation had, with the increasing success of its army and navy, created a universal mood throughout the entire island of national awareness and pride. Despite all the immediate problems, the quickly emerging new industrial towns and cities would bring in their wake an enormous change in patronage and scale, away from the old landowning order, towards the new urban centres and their civic and institutional bodies. In the capital itself, Dance who had personally ushered in the spirit of the Greek

NO. 15 THE GUESTROW, ABERDEEN
The Simpson's family home.

Revival with his Greek Doric portico at Stratton Park in 1803–04, was also erecting his great Ionic portico on the College of Surgeons Building in Lincoln's Inn Fields in 1806–13, the first such edifice in London. Nash's Regent Park and Regent Street Proposals too were actively under considera-tion. His Park Crescent, perhaps his greatest and most serene statement at

Nash's Park Crescent in the course of erection during
Simpson's stay in the Capital.

John Soane's remarkable house at Lincoln's Inn Fields, London

the head of his proposed Via Triumphalis, was itself underway in all its pristine neoclassical simplicity. Likewise Soane had just commenced his own very original house for himself in Lincoln's Inn Fields where, within the constraints of a London terrace, he achieved memorable interiors established above his inspired basement museum of personally acquired classical artefacts. His Bank of England work was also extremely influential, introducing internally as it did Soane's most personal and individual brand of smooth surface treatment, enlivened with linear-incised decoration. Smirke, who had also just built the rather lovely Covent Garden Theatre in 1808–09, and would go on to be arguably the greatest Greek Revivalist of them all, was also absorbed at this time in a very accomplished statement for the Royal Mint on the summit of Tower Hill. All this must surely have greatly stimulated Simpson's tender but provincial architectural imagination.

Meanwhile Archibald had removed from Lugar to the offices of David Laing, who was described at the time as Surveyor to the Custom House. At this juncture Archibald seemed to have been very happy to secure this post, even though it was only on a trial basis. Laing's immediate prospects for rebuilding the London Customs House even promised the possibility of permanent employment. It was from here in 1811 that in a letter home to his brother Alexander, he excitedly revealed that he was working on a proposal for a building in Union Street, Aberdeen. He goes on . . . "It was rather a curious coincidence that the first thing I got to do was make a drawing of Morrison of Auchentoul's House in Union Street, which I had made some plans of myself but did not send them, as somebody told me about three months ago it was half up, so I thought it would be useless. However, happening to go to him with Laing's drawings, he did not seem pleased with them, and I showed him a sketch I had made the idea of which pleased him, and I am now drawing it over in Laing's office who, although he scarcely overlooked them will be paid his thirty or forty guineas and I get nothing for fagging, I racing up and down from his office in Bloomsbury to Grosvenor Square three or four times a day . . . etc".

Shortly however Archibald departed on a study tour of Italy, travelling through Florence but concentrating his interest mainly on Rome, and no doubt making very good use of his father's legacy for the purpose. Drinking at the classical fountain at source, here he would have become familiar with the great monuments of the Roman past, the wonders of the High Renaissance, the glories of the Baroque and all the Italianate drama and smoothness of the presently highly fashionable neoclassical mode, which in French hands in particular had successfully conquered all of Europe.

Arriving back in London in due course armed with his new architectural appreciation, confidence and determination, and placing his design for Morrison of Auchintoul's Union Street scheme firmly under his arm, he decided to return home immediately and set up in practice in Aberdeen on his own account. Doubtless optimistic and secure in his own vastly expanded abilities, these were underpinned by an innate capacity for sound common sense married to complete dedication and application to hard work. He would of course eventually find just how golden his prospects actually were, but initially at least developments would prove to be painful, problematic and rather disappointingly slow.

The Scotland and Aberdeen he had returned to was, as we have seen at this time, experiencing a period of dramatic change. At long last the general population seemed to accept that its future was destined to be as a partner with its southern neighbour, the nation as a whole having become galvanised by the idea that the time was ripe for it to enjoy the glittering future promised by gloriously triumphant Protestant Imperialism. Enormous change, led in the

Irvine of Drum's famous 1805 view of the Castlegate, Aberdeen.

main by the four principal Scottish cities had filtered through to the smaller towns and villages throughout the land, as new roads, enterprises and opportunities spread outwards. Vast fortunes arriving back in the country from the expanding Empire, accompanied by their successful merchant owners, were all eager to be spent and built on many a country house and villa. The hugely expanding urban centres, increasingly attractive to the countryside poor, were urgently in need of hospitals, schools and various new institutions necessary to sustain their citizens, as populations expanded at an unprecedented rate. Enormous amounts of new houses were also required as the more well to do abandoned the old decaying centres for a better designed lifestyle, either in the planned new cities, on the edges of the old towns, or increasingly even in their own out of town country villas. The poorest as always simply inhabited the properties deserted by their former owners, which were subdivided up as necessary to house them as best they could.

These trends had encouraged almost for the first time in Scotland the development of an architectural profession, which was both national as well as local. The economic conditions now existed almost everywhere to sustain regional architects to serve their particular burgeoning areas, and Aberdeen was no exception to the rule. In tandem with the new Scottish awareness, the old idea of progress in harness with simplicity, order, economic, material and intellectual advance became increasingly modified by the new notion of historical romanticism encouraged by writers of the calibre of Sir Walter Scott. As the Roman inspired neoclassicism of the recent past in the hands of Adam and others, made way for the more modern new Grecian ascendancy, concepts

The just completed Union Bridge, over the Denburn defile Aberdeen in 1805.

such as the city as an entity became popular along with the idea of the city as a complete architectural whole. Scotland, being built almost completely of stone, was most fortunate that this material in its newly possible and popular ashlar form, was very readily available everywhere. This made the building of the extremely restrained smooth surfaces so essential to fully comply with the necessary Greek design requirements, a practical reality. As Archibald Simpson travelled back to Aberdeen, his mind must have been full to brimming of the new style with its heady promise of serene simplicity of form and elevational composition, its insistence on axial planning and trabeated rectilinear severity, and the attendant possibilities for introducing a noble Doric or Ionic portico as the occasion demanded. Most architectural observers have noted that Archibald Simpson was probably made for granite, although it is just as reasonable to suggest that granite was almost certainly also made for him, and this happy union of mind and material, in concert with his thoroughly Greek neoclassical philosophy and vision, had fully prepared him for his imminent entry on to the architectural stage. The early reality however as we have already noted, would prove to be rather slower, problematic and more difficult than he would have initially hoped.

A Start is Made

Initially Archibald Simpson commenced his practice working directly from his home at No. 15 the Guestrow. By all accounts even at this juncture he was a likeable young man, possessing an easy and natural charm, which coupled with his good sense and evident prodigious talent, soon drew him to the attention of prospective clients. His practicality, imaginative flair and capacity for hard work did all the rest, ensuring his eventual complete success. In addition to his architectural ability, he was also reputedly a fine singer and violinist, easily becoming a notable figure around town. However, although by nature quite shy and retiring, he was a man of very strong character and conviction who increasingly resented any interference in his designs and who could be extremely vigorous in his opinions and in his own defence when required. This tendency on occasion would lead him into some difficulty with clients. Perhaps it just took a little time for him to fully appreciate the truth of the old maxim that the customer is always right. Unfortunately also on a couple of occasions his structural ability may not have been quite as sound as it might have been, with problems occurring which would be the cause of considerable and understandable client difficulties at both the beginning and near the end of his career. His patience once lost however, his resulting exasperation could be total, even if on occasion this also led to his immediate professional disadvantage.

At this moment too, he must have been acutely aware that his rival John Smith was by this time extremely busy with the erection of tenement blocks in King Street and at Bremner's Corner on the Castlegate, both the result of the successful outcome of very protracted architectural and legal difficulties in the realisation of the new street. The building of Union Street was however to be another matter altogether, but here also initial progress proved to be still lamentably very slow.

Legend has it that the first property to be built at the bottom end of Union

George Washington Wilson's early 1895 view of lower Union Street showing Archibald Simpson's original Union Chambers design in the centre on the left as the town house with the five exceptionally long first floor windows.

Street was No. 64–66, a building named Union Chambers for the Duke and Duchess of Gordon, and to a design provided by Archibald Simpson. For this to be the case, Archibald must have obtained the commission subsequently to his Morrison scheme with the work starting almost immediately. In any event the building commenced in 1813, for his clients, in a relatively severe and sober

Union Chambers as subsequently reconstructed at the end of the nineteenth century with Morrison of Auchintoul's block beyond.

design embracing a commercial ground floor of arch-headed shop windows, an arched pend through McCombie's Court to the Netherkirkgate, and a two-storey plain ashlar, five-window wide arrangement under a bold horizontal cornice and low parapet, concealing the slated roof and dormers above. In particular the great ceiling height of the apartments of the first floor, expressed by architraved windows each provided with individual cornices, suggests interiors here of some consequence. Unfortunately all this is now no more, the upper floors remarkably having been removed altogether and the building almost completely rebuilt around 1900, to a redesign by James Henderson. Three new regular floors were thus squeezed in, virtually within the same old height, in a now six-window wide façade, with a cornice at second floor and paired Simpsonian style, blocked chimney heads above. All the new windows were given elegant architrave surrounds and linked vertically, successfully unifying the design. Given more recent deprivations in the form of dreadful shop fronts, removing even Simpson's rhythm of arch-headed shop windows, it may now be said that only the archway through to McCombie's Court represents his original design intentions, externally at least.

Slightly later in the same year, his London efforts of 1811 at last bore fruit, with a start being made also to Morrison of Auchintoul's building at 40–44 Union Street. The design bears all the signs of a young architect's exuberant first effort, full of action and busy with elements, all however basically within a well controlled ensemble. The three-bay ashlar central three-storey façade, is held between slightly advanced rusticated end bays, embracing segmental arched entrance doorways with flanking Corinthian pilasters, supporting boldly projecting decorative granite balconies at first floor. Above are windows within segmentally arched recessed panels, while over the continuous moulded string course which binds the entire façade at second floor level, a five-bay storey of windows is formed with plain architrave surrounds breaking down to the stringer. Above this a deep modillion cornice boldly breaks the façade, which continues into an attic storey of squared windows below a moulded parapet stringer. To the west, the block continues into a very plain two-window wide granite ashlar façade, matching its neighbour in scale, and set originally above an arcade of arch-headed shop windows. This of course has been subsequently removed in favour of a more 'modern' shopfront. In the mid-nineteenth century the centre of Simpson's main eastern section was somewhat altered when the double height central windows were given finely modelled spandrel panels. The central entrance doorway directly into the banking hall was also formed at this time. The now former banking hall with its spaciousness, good proportions and elaborate plasterwork, still clearly visible from the pavement outside, is presently occupied by a firm of opticians. Despite its obvious merits, it would be true to say that Archibald Simpson would never be quite so unrestrained in design terms again, having even in its western section and at Union Chambers next door, arrived at that severely monumental surface simplicity which would shortly be the hallmark of all his mature work and which so perfectly matched the innate strength and beauty of the granite material he was using. The building, initially occupied as the premises of the Town and County Bank, before their eventual removal to Simpson's subsequent new building for them at Nos. 93–95 Union Street, also accommodated the famous Song School of the period on one of the upper floors.

Morrison of Auchintoul's surviving Union Street property as viewed from the east. Unfortunately it has been subsequently damaged by the later attentions of others.

Commissions were still slow however, but it was in 1815 that we find Simpson embarked on the design of quite a considerable extension to the ancient and original Forbes seat at Druminnor, an old Scottish castle-house near Rhynie. The house as he found it dated back to 1430 when it was built as only part of a much larger castle by Alexander, 1st Lord Forbes. Attacked by the Gordons in 1449, sacked by the Douglases in 1452, refurbished in 1456, partly demolished in 1471–73, rebuilt in 1577, seized by the king in 1584 and raided by the Forbeses themselves in 1592, the history of the house could hardly be more colourful. In addition between 1645 and 1647 the property was held by the Royalists, probably necessitating the castle requiring considerable remodelling around 1660, and it was attacked yet again several times in 1689–90. Besieged by the Grants in 1745 and partially burned five years later, the Grants of Rothmaise finally succeeded in acquiring the property at the end of the eighteenth century and promptly proceeded to demolish the Lord's Tower situated at its south eastern end, in preparation for a new extension.

At that time the old castle was obviously much in need of 'modernisation' and Archibald Simpson was selected as the architect to carry it out. A new two-storey three-bay symmetrical and harled double block, referred to as the 'villa', was therefore erected, adjoining and overlapping the existing house, largely where the Lord's Tower had been, with slightly advanced end gables, stone stringers and first floor window hoods addressing the style of the older work. The new centrally placed doorway was set within an arch with an armorial panel above just below the central first floor window. To the east two high gables, a three-bay one just in advance of the other, with ogee-hooded first floor windows above the plain variety used on the ground floor, were set above a basement level underneath at the rear. At the same time Simpson re-floored the old basement, adjusting the floor levels at the same time, reorganised the old north staircase at

The now demolished 'Villa' end wing at Druminnor viewed from the garden.

33

its junction with his new ground floor link corridor, and set about enlarging many of the original window openings throughout the old structure. Sadly these widened windows are now giving problems with definite recent movement occurring. This interesting design effort still betrayed a certain Lugar influence however, as well as anticipating Simpson's own personal later version of the neo-Jacobean style. Simpson also used the high chimney design on top of his gables borrowed from the older house, setting the square stone chimney pots on the diagonal in the manner originally introduced in the 1660s' remodelling. This solution was of course itself originally inspired by those at Winton House near Edinburgh. This would not be the last time either that Simpson would resort to this chimney design, it becoming something of a signature in his Jacobean styled work.

Internally from the new front door of the extension, a long circulation hall traversed the villa wing, with a smoking room on the left and a dining room to the right. At the far end a new staircase was followed by the principal drawing room, which overlooked the valley and the very extensive flower garden developed at this end. The original vegetable garden occupied the more northerly end of valley,

The Simpson neo-Jacobean wing abutting the older house, viewed from the entrance side.

beyond a rather Chinese styled wooden bridge adjacent to the end of the old house. Above, on the first floor, was created a suite of fine new bedrooms, with staff accommodation placed in the attics above that. In all twelve very substantial new rooms were provided. In addition the ground floor vaults of the old castle were also employed to house the kitchen, various service rooms and stores. When this work was finally completed, the old castle was completely transformed, and was now rather more grandly referred to as Druminnor House. Subsequently in 1869 various bathrooms were installed and the dining room was also made into a library. A new dining room was at this time created out of one of the old stone vaults of the ancient castle wing.

All this survived until 1954 when the Grants were obliged to sell the property, which in the event returned again to the Forbeses in the form of the Hon. Margaret Forbes Semple of Craigievar. Almost at once she rather enthusiastically set about demolishing the Grant additions, returning the house back to its original scale and condition, during a refurbishment of the remaining fabric. This of course obviously involved the complete destruction of all of Archibald Simpson's neo-Jacobean work, which was unfortunate to say the least. The present incumbent, Mr Alexander Forbes of the Pitsligo and Monymusk branch of the family, bought the property in 1975 and has already commenced his own thorough programme of restoration within this much reduced but still absolutely fascinating ancient seat of the clan Forbes.

Interestingly also, just beyond the house and overlooking the beautiful small lake deeply embedded within the surrounding mature woodlands, a charming little two-storey L-shaped house now exists, very possibly built to a Simpson design.

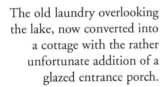

The old laundry overlooking the lake, now converted into a cottage with the rather unfortunate addition of a glazed entrance porch.

Intended to be rendered and complete with moulded stone hoods, chimneyed gables and spiky dormer window heads, its high simple blocky character certainly suggests Simpson, in a design originally intended as the Laundry.

This same year, Simpson was also fortunate to commence another commission, this time for the main branch of the same family, from Lord Forbes himself, a very important and considerable Donside landowner. A new replacement house had been under consideration for some time with various designs produced by various parties, one even for an extremely serene Adamesque classical mansion house, designed by John Patterson. Archibald was approached as early as 1814 and asked to create a large, castellated house absorbing the original existing Scotch mansion of 1731, which had a very controlling influence on the overall design. Carried out in a somewhat sober but still quite dramatic manner, and working in a faintly discernable Adam castle-style, the composition is rendered asymmetrical in the manner of his old mentor Robert Lugar. The basically two- and three-storey arrangement in squared granite, combines boxy corner towers with bartizans, crenellations, plainer elevations and a projecting entrance feature boasting a relieving arch and battlements. It is all held under the control of an imposing south-western angle four-storey crenellated corner tower, the fulcrum of the entire design. The inspiration and planning appears to have been considerably influenced by that of Lugar's Tullichewan (now demolished) in Dumbartonshire, near Loch Lomond. Simpson commenced work on the tower and the two-storey south-facing range which terminates in a higher three-storey crenellated square tower enlivened further with an advancing canted bay window. This extended backwards with a lower range including the service and kitchen wings facing eastwards, established on either side of a triumphal entry in a battlemented wall screening the service courtyard. Here and there, moulded hoods and round-headed windows were introduced for some additional interest. However, having also prepared the way for the construction of the northern extension wing to commence, the works apparently so seriously undermined the foundations of the existing house that serious cracks appeared in the fabric. At the end of the day the condition of the old mansion became so precarious that it had to be substantially demolished. Whether this disastrous occurrence was due to

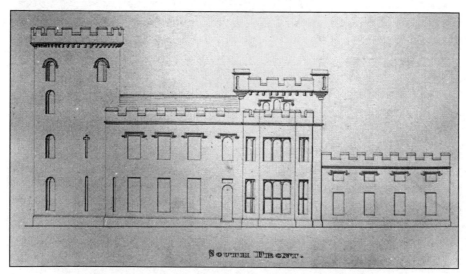

Simpson's principal elevation of Castle Forbes, Keig Aberdeenshire.

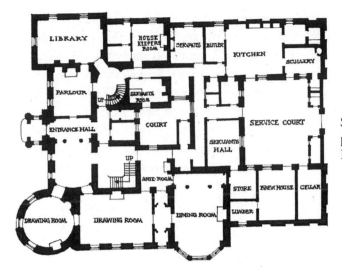

Simpson's final plan of the principal floor of Castle Forbes as executed.

Simpson's relative inexperience, or perhaps even to his over reliance on an over-enthusiastic local builder carrying out a contract quite far removed from his office in Aberdeen, the resultant debacle witnessed his dismissal, with him unfortunately shouldering most of the blame. The effect of this on Archibald Simpson was very considerable and he even seriously contemplated giving up the practice of architecture altogether. To make matters even worse, his great rival in Aberdeen John Smith was immediately called in to rectify matters and he is accredited with the completion of the north range, the west front and the decoration of the principal drawing room. Like the Adam Castle style before them however, this rather unhistorical, picturesque and for some very cavalier approach to castle design was not at all to everyone's liking, the redoubtable Lord Cockburn, (never one to keep his opinions to himself) observing that "Lord Forbes has lately built a new house in as bad taste as possible". Judged by the standards of Aberdeenshire's many original towers or even some of the more recent rather overblown dramas of the Tudor Gothic Revival in the south, this might well be supportable, but the end result at least achieves an undoubted simplicity of form quite in keeping with the original concept of the castle type, as well as building up into a carefully orchestrated arrangement boldly acknowledging the implicit drama of its magnificent site high on a shoulder overlooking the River Don. It might also be just sufficient to note however that Simpson never repeated this particular design experiment again, preferring to develop his own personal version of the neo-Jacobean style instead. This decision could of course also be explained by a desire not to revisit the far too painful memory of a commission that went so very badly wrong.

Internally however the castle contains an impressive arrangement of circulation and spacious, classically inspired, light and airy reception rooms on the ground floor commanding glorious views along the riverbank and beyond to the hills around Alford. The upper floors accommodate eighteen various sized bedrooms. A very notable feature also internally was the oval staircase with its Pantheon inspired coffered dome high overhead. Some necessary alterations have been made over time to the internal planning arrangements, with the dining room moved to the north-west corner along with an adjoining modern kitchen. This has allowed for the demolition of much of the now unnecessary former service and kitchen courtyard buildings, which has been sensitively achieved without damaging the external appearance to any great extent The old entrance porch which may have been designed by Smith, had also been previously removed but was restored to the building in 1992 using stonework and features salvaged from the demolition of the rear kitchen range of buildings. Adjacent to the service courtyard archway to the rear of the site and placed axially on it, is an inspired Y-shaped game store cum dairy larder cum laundry building, which very ingeniously combines three single-storey crow-stepped gabled arms with a two-storey central crenellated rotunda, in a manner which just has to be Simpson's own. This little tower is itself surmounted by a slated conical roof just visible above the parapet, and is preceded by a curved entrance porch inset between two of the flanking wings. This very delightful little building now serves as the wholly appropriate centre for the manufacture of a small range of perfumes.

The delightful Dairy cum Game Larder cum Laundry building at Castle Forbes.

Castle Forbes from the north-west showing John Smith's north wing.

Simpson's triumphal entry into his east kitchen court.

Castle Forbes viewed from the west showing Simpson's south front and tower.

Simpson's elegant drawing room as completed by John Smith.

On perhaps a happier note meanwhile, back in Aberdeen in 1816, work commenced on the erection of Simpson's successful competition winning design for a Chapel for the Episcopalians on an important central site on the new King Street, midway between the Castlegate and North Street on its eastern side. The Episcopalians had only very recently been freed from rather draconian penal laws, which were repealed in 1792, thereby allowing them for the first time since the beginning of the eighteenth century to establish a proper chapel for themselves. In the first instance meetings had taken place in John Skinner's house in Longacre, under the lea of old Marischal College, and actually it was here on the 14th November 1787 that he consecrated Samuel Seabury of Connecticut, the Bishop for America. The legal relaxation at last allowed the congregation to erect a small chapel next door which served well enough for a time but by 1816 it was felt that a move to the very much more prestigious location in King Street was eminently more desirable. Simpson, Smith and Young of London were all invited to submit designs, with Simpson's duly emerging as the winner. The new building would be called St Andrew's Chapel. Simpson completed the task by 1817, containing his design within a simple five-bay long rectangular box, with an internal gallery at the western end and down both sides, supported by crisply channelled piers with pointed arch arcades holding up the vaulted roof. The infill timber gallery balustrade was richly carved and stained matching the pews, which on the ground floor were arranged in a curving theatre-like manner successfully focusing on the preacher. He was actually accommodated in a pepper-mill style pulpit of some considerable height, designed to ensure that

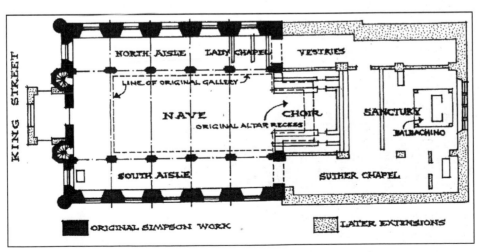

St Andrew's Chapel on King Street Aberdeen, showing Simpson's much altered building including various extensions by G E Street, Sir Robert Lorimer and Sir Ninian Comper.

everyone, including those at the furthest corners even at the back of the gallery, could clearly see him. Centred at the eastern end, an initially small apse contained the altar. Externally the entire architectural interest was concentrated on the front, where a dramatic perpendicular Gothic facade was realised in Craigleith freestone. Selected against Simpson's wishes only for its cheapness, its happy contrast with all the surrounding granite neighbouring buildings and its greater capacity for detail has resulted in a very notable statement in the street. Certainly influenced by Gillespie Graham's contemporary St Andrew's Cathedral, Glasgow and St Mary's Cathedral, Edinburgh, the sharply executed four bold piers and crocketed finials are contrasted with the smooth beige sandstone walls in between, themselves pierced by three noble and exquisitely traceried windows. A slightly pointed, fretted parapet completes the central

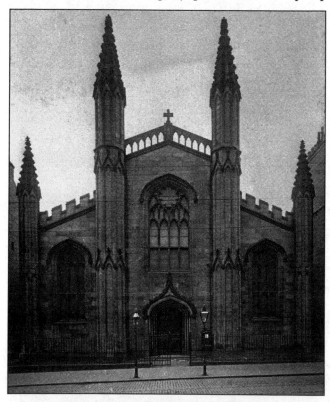

St Andrew's Chapel,
King Street Aberdeen
in its original condition.

section surmounted with a cross, while the lower flanking parapets are provided with a sloping crenellated version, probably introduced for added interest. Regrettably, and certainly due to cost limitations, the entire external interest of the building is concentrated to the street, the sides and rear being executed in

Simpson's original galleried interior of St Andrew's Chapel as provided with its much extended Chancel by Street. The galleries and curved pews have since been removed.

the most basic manner possible. This, with other similarly reduced designs, has in the past given rise to the rather unfair accusation of a certain tendency towards facadism. Unfortunately in this particular instance the back view is really now much more prominent following the slum clearances of the closes off the Castlegate with the opening up of the vista towards East North Street. The additional even later works of extension are also all mostly executed externally in a quite similarly impoverished manner, hardly worthy of a building now boasting Cathedral status. Notwithstanding in 1880, the famous London architect, G. E. Street extended the interior by adding the chancel, while in 1909 all the internal galleries were removed, creating an effect of considerably increased spaciousness. In 1911, Sir Robert Lorimer was engaged to add the entrance porch, designed in a wholly and very successfully compatible style. In 1914 the church was elevated to the status of a Cathedral. Following this, the congregation actively pursued the possibility of erecting a new and very magnificent building in Broad Street, to be placed immediately opposite Marischal College, thereby attempting to create a notable planning ensemble in the city centre. Unfortunately the repercussions of the Wall Street Crash dried up the very necessary American funds and it was decided therefore to further embellish the existing cathedral instead. In 1935, Sir Ninian Comper was employed to extend the building yet again, and it is he who was largely responsible also for the creation of the beautifully luminous interior. The finished work was famously visited on the 2nd September 1948 by Joseph Kennedy, the American Ambassador. The purpose was the inauguration of the Seabury Memorial, and for the occasion he was accompanied by his eldest son, the future President John F. Kennedy.

Meanwhile to the consternation and alarm of the general public, 1817 unfolded as perhaps the lowest point ever in municipal affairs when the Trustees were obliged to reveal that the city was bankrupt. The new street schemes, which had been completed were considerably over their anticipated cost (is anything new?), raising the city's overall debt to the sum of £225,710 14s 4d. As the Council's overall income of £10,042 10s 0d could not even service the interest on such a sum, the matter had to be made public. All manner of excuses were also circulated, varying from the expensive feu-duties, the high specification requirements for the new buildings, to the additional costs necessary for many sites requiring considerable under-building. In any event, the initial slowness of taking up sites along the new thoroughfares was plain enough for all to see. Between 1817 and 1825 a Board of twenty-one Trustees was appointed to represent the Council's Creditors while the financial position slowly managed to resolve itself. The more optimistic nature of the times following the upturn after the end of the Napoleonic Wars, and the continuing growth in the local economy as a result, quickly witnessed the increase in the pace of building activity. It is however to the eternal credit of the Town Council that despite all these difficulties, they remained resolute in the face of considerable pressure, and the high standards expected for the new buildings lining Union Street remained unaltered.

Simpson's now slightly damaged Union Street Hotel block frontage has subsequently lost its original elegant ground floor window arcade.

In 1817, Simpson embarked on the construction of his design for the Aberdeen Hotel Block at Nos. 136–144 Union Street, on a site adjoining the north abutment of the Union Bridge, and delineated by the late extension of Belmont Street through to Union Street with a last minute steep incline. This handsome block, obviously considerably indebted to

St Andrew's Cathedral, King Street, Aberdeen, complete with its later Lorimer porch.

THE INTERIOR OF ST ANDREW'S CATHEDRAL TODAY

The present interior's sense of spacious luminosity owes a considerable debt to
the refurbishment carried out by Sir Ninian Comper in the 1940's, dramatically uplifting
the framework he inherited from both Archibald Simpson and G E Street.

the multi-level planning approach pioneered by Robert Adam in London and Edinburgh somewhat earlier, has been given a fashionably discreet Grecian reinterpretation. It is notable that the considerable difference in levels between Union Street and its immediate environs, particularly on its southern side flanking the Green, encouraged this multi-layer planning solution on this side also. The hotel block is six windows wide to the front, with five-window wide side returns, very effectively forming a terminal pavilion to this side of the end of Union Street facing the Denburn. It has also been given a most distinguished return elevation to confront the valley itself and the Denburn Road below. Its almost cubic mass addresses Union Street and Belmont Street with the now obligatory series of arch-headed shop windows, stringer at first floor and two plain floors above that, below the cornice. This treatment actually continues on the Denburn façade where below at first basement level there is an additional

Simpson's Hotel, from across the Denburn with its sub-street levels and basement areas executed in rough bull-nosed granite for strength.

row of standard windows. Below this again however the entire weight is taken by a series of three bold, two-storey arches on massive piers in bull-nosed granite blocks, dramatically expressing the inherent strength of the design. Above the cornice however at the roof, the blocking course supports a broad chimney stack on the Union Street elevation, disguised as a panel retained by side scrolls. The Belmont Street and Denburn facades however support a continuous three-window wide attic and above its cornice, chimney pots betraying the ingenious introduction of flues threading through the walling below, with typical Simpson aplomb. Internally the central stairway and the upper floors have been most fortunate, although long used as the Victoria Restaurant and offices, but as usual the Union Street and Belmont Street commercial frontages have been most damaged by the introduction over time of plate glass windows by Jamieson & Carry and Bakers next door. However some arched-headed windows survive facing Belmont Street as well as the original windows with their astragals on the elevation above. Jamieson & Carry's row of five arch-headed windows complete with their original window frames on their return Denburn façade also still make a very fine sight indeed.

By the beginning of 1818, Simpson was very fortunate to obtain the commission to design a Library and Meeting Hall for Dr James McGrigor, on a site on the west side of King Street, immediately opposite St Andrew's Chapel. To be known as the Medico Chirurgical Hall, the Society which commissioned

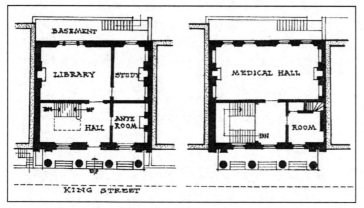

Simpson's Medico Chirurgical Hall plans, King Street, Aberdeen

it had been formed in 1789 by twelve medical students under the leadership of James McGrigor. They urgently required accommodation for their remarkable collection of medical books as well as rooms and a hall to conduct medical meetings. Within a simple rectangle Simpson arranged an august entrance with elegant cantilevered stair, giving access to the quite low library, study, and anteroom at ground floor, with the spacious main hall above, lit by four, slightly paired elegant windows, set against the back lane elevation shared by Queen Street. The basement area is basically made up of storage and toilet accommodation. On the King Street frontage, Simpson took advantage of the central importance of the site, to introduce the first giant tetrastyle portico into Aberdeen. Over a five-step plinth with base blocks, four plain drum granite columns soar upwards supporting Ionic capitals. Interestingly the volutes are all flat, even on the external corners. Above the plain entablature and frieze, a low Greek pediment completes the portico. The effect may be slightly on the heavy side, but the design is given extra strength by placing an additional pilaster alongside those of the back of the portico façade, on both sides. At this time also the opportunity was taken to write into the leases that when the sites on either side of the Hall were developed, the facades should be of two matching storeys above basement and balance, also being set back in line with the back of the portico. In the event it took some time before this ambitious undertaking was fully realised. It would be 1832 before John Smith embarked on his new Public Records Office, thereby realising a plain three-bay two storeys above basement block, set back behind a railinged-off sunken forecourt. This was skilfully linked by an arched porch to an apparently separate block brought forward to the back of the pavement line farther south, and boldly enlivened by Smith's favourite paired giant columned pilaster arrangement. It was 1870 however before the almost matching block to the north was built, thus successfully completing the Simpson-Smith ensemble. The buildings, including the now former Records Office next door (subsequently the HM Customs & Excise Offices, were totally restored and refurbished by Edmondson Properties Ltd as office suites available to let in the late 1980s. It should be noted that Sir James McGrigor, as he became, went on to establish the British Army Medical Corps. An impressive pink granite obelisk commemorating him and his achievements was erected in due course by the architect Alexander Ellis, in the centre of Simpson's Marischal College Quadrangle in 1860. Following however the commencement of A. Marshall Mackenzie's massive perpendicular Gothic extensions to the University complex at the turn of the twentieth century, the obelisk was removed to its current very prominent position overlooking the River Dee in the far-off Duthie Park.

Simpson's noble first giant portico in Aberdeen dramatically distinguishes his Medical Hall.

The following year, 1819, witnessed Simpson engaged in the design and erection of another church, this time the Parish Church of Kintore for his uncle, the Revd. John Shand. A petition had been placed before the Presbytory of Garioch in March of the previous year suggesting that the old church in Kintore was 'ruinous and unfit to accommodate the congregation'. Perhaps revealing within Simpson a rather cavalier attitude to the survival of old buildings, by March his plans for the total replacement of the old church were approved on condition that it could be achieved for the rather paltry sum of £1005, an amount even in those days insufficient to obtain a building of any real quality. Consequently a simple rectangular box would have to suffice, but despite the financial constraints, the three-bay granite ashlar building is none the less distinguished with an interesting early Gothic treatment. The three windows on both side elevations are hood-moulded, before the walls break back to form a narrower entrance vestibule end, a device becoming quite a favourite planning arrangement with him. The tall end-gable thus formed and the prominent corners were both provided with angled buttresses tapering up into elegant pinnacles. The axially placed central doorway and the three light tall arched window above are also provided with hooded mouldings, before the gable terminates upward, surmounted by a delicate granite bellcote placed at the apex. Internally the church is typically extremely restrained, the clean simple lines being relieved only by the presence of the upper gallery at the entrance end and side and end windows. Originally

Simpson's second Church design makes a small but nonetheless accomplished early Gothic statement in Kintore.

however the pews in the body of the church and the gallery, together with its front, were all arranged on the curve, imparting considerable life and interest to the interior, a feeling which unfortunately has subsequently been lost when everything was straightened up during a major later refurbishment. At the far end also at the same time, the chancel was extended outwards with a segmental arch-headed Gothic window making an imposing axial stop, albeit necessitating the removal of the original high, axially placed pulpit. Interestingly also, a sculptural relief from the 16th-century sacrament house from the previous building, was successfully incorporated into Simpson's front gallery staircase. More recent alterations include the rather unfortunate incorporation of dormers into the roof over the gallery to increase natural daylight there, and the much happier insertion of very beautiful stained glass into some of the church windows between 1956 and 1964.

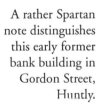
A rather Spartan note distinguishes this early former bank building in Gordon Street, Huntly.

Further north in Huntly in this same year, a distinctly early, sober but very Simpson-like building was erected at Nos. 23–25 Gordon Street to a design almost certainly by Simpson's own hand. Built for George Lawson, the result manages to be imposing and at the same time slightly unsatisfactory, lacking any expected central emphasis to the street. The broad granite ashlar two-storey three-window wide first floor façade sits boldly on a stringer over a seven-arch headed ground floor window arrangement, with three windows placed on either side of the central door. The design is skilfully turned round the corner with a quarter recessed curve, complete with arched headed window, stringer and first floor window all carried out on the turn. The matching two bay side elevation extends into a slightly lower scaled attached service wing. Above the continuous finishing cornice and parapet, the curved corner is further emphasised by a small granite shield supported by carved decorative brackets. The interior is unremarkable but still tolerably well preserved on the upper floor. The ground floor however, subsequently converted into the premises of a local bank, was fairly thoroughly transformed again more recently when the building was reinvented as Council Offices. Some original plasterwork still manages to survive here and there.

During his first decade of practice in Aberdeen work was steadily progressing on the building of Golden Square, the first planned residential development built on the west side of the Denburn defile, just to the north of Union Street. Unfortunately it was not yet practicable for the architectural treatment of the square to be completely uniform, but perhaps this is not surprising in a city which had rejected Charles Abercrombie's audacious proposal for a wholly planned new town on the Edinburgh model. Notwithstanding a gracious, if less than architecturally unified square quickly developed on the lands of the Hammermen Incorporated Trade, between 1810 and 1820. It would seem extremely likely that both Archibald Simpson and John Smith were active in the

NO. 15 GOLDEN SQUARE, ABERDEEN

A design usually attributed to Archibald Simpson. Note the very broad and characteristic chimney-head treatment of the return gable.

design of at least some of the houses within the square but evidence is now non-existent on this point. However at No.13 on the north side at its western corner with North Silver Street, a fine design exists where the overall treatment, the elegant proportions and the delicate balance of solid over void, very strongly suggest the hand of Simpson. The two-storey three-window wide granite ashlar façade is fairly typically set on a ground floor string course above a semi-suppressed basement and sunken forecourt set behind railings. As if this were not enough, the treatment of the return entrance three-bay gable elevation to North Silver Street, destined to become something of a signature element, is crowned with a block pediment and broad chimney-panel treatment, seeming to justify the long association with Simpson's name in itself. Happily the interior of this town house is more or less still intact, despite long being in commercial use. This property too, unusually still also retains its two original little roof dormers, just peeping over the low parapet and mocking various more aggressive later versions introduced elsewhere in the square.

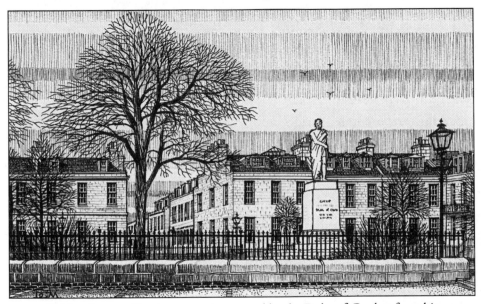

Golden Square, Aberdeen as now surveyed by the Duke of Gordon from his central car park position.

It seems extraordinary today that when these houses were being built and gracious, more civilised conditions were being made more generally available, (at least for the more affluent members of society), fundamentals such as drainage as we understand it today, hardly existed. Surface water might possibly be carried away, but soil had to be removed from a basement cesspit regularly by hand cart. A property might only boast a 'thunder-box' internally hidden away in an appropriate cupboard set aside for the purpose, and the contents had to be removed manually regularly by a servant. At this time also water was most usually delivered into a basement storage tank, from where it might be pumped up to the ground floor, by the use of a hand pump. It would be some time also before these rather primitive and unsatisfactory, not to say very insanitary arrangements, would substantially improve.

Notwithstanding, in the centre of the square, paradoxically a perfectly circular landscaped garden used to grace the area. In the middle of this the Hammermen placed a central well for the benefit of the residents, now to be found in the entrance hall of the most modern replacement Trinity Hall at the corner of Great Western Road and Holburn Street. In the 1950s the square became increasingly used as a car park as businesses and professionals progressively invaded the area. At this time, banished from his axial position in the Castlegate, the statue of George, 5th Duke of Gordon was placed in the centre on his high granite plinth, while tar and cars proliferated all around him. Archibald Simpson among others, had of course been instrumental originally in the setting up of the statue in the Castlegate in the first place, where interestingly enough Lord Cockburn on seeing it for the first time in 1844, observed that Gordon "was base and despicable, but a rather popular fellow. A bad statue, but still very ornamental of a street, so far as I am aware this is the first granite statue in Scotland". Happily the statue is also quite ornamental in Golden Square where it is very much in scale and keeping with its granite surroundings. Hopefully the day may not be too far off either, when the gardens might also be reintroduced into the centre, and the dreadfully over-fussy corner parking areas could be consigned to history, in order to restore this fine civic space to its original pristine simplicity.

Simpson was also actively engaged in 1819 on the problem of designing a completely new lunatic asylum just outside the city, to be built in the following year on a site at Barkmill at Berryden. He had been initially approached two years earlier with a view to restoring and extending the existing complex, which had become totally inadequate for its purpose. The asylum had been originally housed within the Infirmary itself in Woolmanhill, built in 1739, but this had been discontinued some thirty years later. Even in 1797 it had been recognised that accommodation for these poor afflicted individuals was urgently necessary, and a site was found at Barkmill for the purpose. At this stage, only fairly simple accommodation was erected upon it. It would be twenty-two years longer however, before the decision was taken to build a completely new institution. This determination was no doubt strongly influenced by the fact that Edinburgh, Glasgow and Dundee had all built for themselves new asylums. Both Simpson and Smith were invited to submit proposals, but the Managers, apparently not satisfied with either of their designs, sent them back for further amendment. Even the name of William Stark, the designer of Dundee's very advanced asylum, was put forward, but rather inconveniently he died before such a course of action could be put in hand. After a great deal of further consultation and alteration,

Simpson's rather diminished Lunatic Asylum design also shorn of its intended central portico failed by all accounts to bring any credit to either the Managers or their unfortunate Architect.

Simpson's proposals were finally accepted; however the relationship between the Managers and their architect seem to have always been rather strained even from the outset. For the moment however things initially went smoothly enough and shortly his severe, thoroughly neoclassical design emerged comprising a south facing H-shaped block with a five-bay two-storey central section, held between advanced flanking three-storey six-bay long wings, placed on either side. In the middle a small dome appeared over the low parapet. In the centre of the main front, a noble portico was proposed, and to the sides, single-storey east and west service wings extended out from this complete with projecting colonnades. These defined male and female exercise yards discreetly but resolutely hidden behind high surrounding walls. The commission however went badly very quickly, and what with incessant interference by the Managers and constantly required alterations during the course of the work, things went from bad to much worse for the young, still rather inexperienced architect. The portico was abandoned almost at once, various quite major internal changes were made, a feeble sundial was introduced into the frontage against the architect's advice, and even the front gate arrangement was altered beyond recognition. Opinion had it that the finished building cast little credit on either the Managers or their architect. Towards the end of the building works, Simpson's relationship with the Managers had deteriorated to such an extent that John Smith was engaged as architectural advisor to the Managers as his replacement. Although probably extremely glad to see the back of this dreadful commission it must have been a very disagreeable experience indeed to find his great rival installed in his place, particularly following the dreadful recent events at Castle Forbes. Smith immediately raised the chimneys, which seem to have been unacceptably smoky, resolved and repaired a very early outbreak of dry rot in one of Simpson's corridors, and made haste to erect additional accommodation for some of the more disturbed and noisy patients at the rear of the finished complex. It should be noted that by 1840 and 1845, Simpson, despite these circumstances, would be called upon again to carry out further major extensions to this work. How much of all this building activity however still remains is now extremely difficult to determine, although it is almost inconceivable that the entirety of this very substantial hospital complex was actually ever completely demolished.

In the heart of the city meanwhile, immediately opposite the Town House on the south side of Union Street, another opportunity presented itself with the possibility of achieving a unified palace façade design on this very prestigious site. Undoubtedly envisaged even from the outset as an integrated scheme, unfortunately for the moment the Castlegate end was occupied by a fairly ordinary three-storey building, enlivened only by raised attic gablets and chimneys. The property belonged to the Ferryhill laird, John Ewen, a notable Town Councillor of the time who operated a silversmith's shop from his premises. The site at the western end against the Shiprow at its corner with Union Street was available however and by the end of 1819 Simpson's design for Bailie Galen's Property was well up and almost complete. Interestingly Bailie Galen was the brother-in-law of Archibald's brother Sandy, and he would prove to be a very useful connection in the near future. The design obviously took its cue from Robert Adam as interpreted through various earlier precedents existing in the Castlegate and King Street, established by Burn, Fletcher and also Smith. Even here in this short façade however, Simpson managed to introduce his own special touch. The commercial ground floor of two shops between a centrally placed access serving the rear stairway to the residential accommodation above, was given an alternating rhythm of wider and narrower arch-headed window and door

The mansard and dormers are 1970's additions.

56

Union Buildings
with Bailie Galen's
House on the right.

openings, beneath a first floor broad stringer. Above this, three floors of elegant rectangular windows pierced the fine granite ashlar façade, broken only with a narrow string course at third floor window sill level in what would become quite a typical Simpson manner. The corner is very nicely turned into the Shiprow in the way he had already pioneered at Huntly, and the return gable repeats the Union Street arrangement in a four window wide plain façade. The first row of windows however, set vertically around the corner, are blanks. The crowning unifying cornice and block parapet complete the simple but effective design, taken round to the Shiprow gable where a broad chimney is placed on top of it. The low, slated and piended roof, complete with a few neat front and back dormer windows, is effectively concealed.

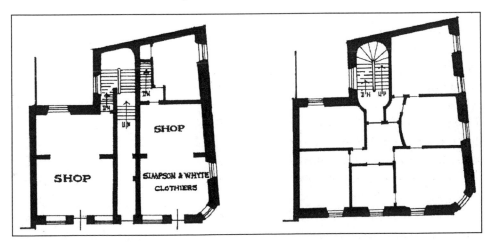

GROUND FLOOR PLAN   TYPICAL UPPER FLOOR PLAN

The rather elegant communal stone staircase combining straight sections with spiral winders on the external curve, rises up the whole four storeys of the block to the more modest roof attic flatted accommodation. The three floors below were laid out as individual town-apartments, the first floor one being initially occupied by Bailie Galen himself. The most important rooms faced Union Street, with the drawing room set on the Shiprow corner. Bedrooms and kitchen facilities completed the layout behind. Perhaps not surprisingly, given the family connection, the corner shop at the Shiprow, (presently a shoe shop), was originally occupied by the Clothiers, Simpson and Whyte, the Simpson concerned being none other than Archibald's elder brother Sandy. Bailie Galen's property however, now substantially complete, was destined to stand next to John Ewen's more modest buildings for a further three long years, before the remainder of Simpson's ambitious development would be finally realised.

It is fascinating to learn from the pages of the *Aberdeen Journal* of the time that in 1818 the Heritors of the Parish of Forgue in Aberdeenshire were inviting interested building contractors to submit estimates for the rebuilding of their old Parish Church there, and that their prices should be submitted either to the Heritors themselves or to A. Simpson, Architect of Aberdeen. The approved design, which actually commenced construction early in 1919, was very typical of its period, being a rather stark and rectangular axial box church provided with a U-plan upper gallery, all intended to seat a congregation of nine hundred. Its architectural treatment however is very singular with the centre of its entrance front slightly advanced to express the entrance doorway and three long and narrow windows above, while the feature tapers upward into the apex of the gable to support a delightfully elegant little bellcote. Two further lancet windows are placed within the remaining wall panels on either side. The even more remarkable south wall is enlivened with three impressively tall mullioned Gothic windows, which are further embellished by the introduction of four lovely circular windows placed above and between them in a most unusual and very striking combination. The opposite north wall is left entirely blank, while the west wall at the chancel end boasts also two further tall mullioned Gothic windows.

Internally the church is extremely light, elegant and spacious, with a double aisled arrangement of pews, reflecting the original U-plan layout of the upper gallery. Sadly the two side arms of the gallery were removed in 1929 but the stone access stair in the vestibule is still in place. The main axis terminates on the raised area of the chancel at the west gable end with a replacement off-centre pulpit, which was introduced rather more recently. The splendid organ was installed in 1872 by the firm of Connacher of Huddersfield, given as a most generous gift from the local Glendronach Distillery nearby. It was the first such installation apparently in the county. At the same time the opportunity was also taken to modify and refurbish the interior of the church. Interestingly parts of the Frendraugh pew of 1638 preserved from the original church on site are stiill also retained. Another very remarkable surviving feature of the interior is the beautiful eggshell-blue on white painterwork scheme of the flat plaster ceiling, which is sub-divided into large square panels across its area. A fine transition in the form of an all round moulded plaster cove completes the very elegant effect. The church today continues to serve the local area as a Community Project protected by a charitable trust, administered by the Friends of Forgue Kirk. Organ recitals, carol services and special concerts are regularly held.

THE PARISH CHURCH
Forgue, Aberdeenshire

Very worryingly at this juncture, Archibald Simpson along with his rival John Smith would have been acutely aware of the emergence of Edinburgh's Archibald Elliott's Damlands of Rubislaw scheme for the west end of Aberdeen. This had been produced on the instructions of James Skene of Rubislaw in order to facilitate the development of his substantial land holding in the area. The Skenes, having seen at first hand the serene elegance of the expanding later phases of the New Town of Edinburgh, were conscious of the fact that their lands lay rather similarly placed relative to Aberdeen at the western end of Union Street just beyond the West Prison. Anxious to realise both the full financial and architectural potential of their ground and hoping no doubt to make the most considerable early impression possible, a design inspired by the latest Edinburgh thinking by a famous Edinburgh architect was initially considered to be absolutely essential. The scheme, contemplated on a scale not equalled since the publication of Charles Abercrombie's unsuccessful New Town proposals, envisaged an extensively planned area embracing a major square, and a principal east – west thoroughfare centred on it with five north – south cross streets linking the new Alford Road (Albyn Place) with the new Skene Road in the north. This thoroughfare itself was to be given a fine frontage of terraced houses, terminating at its western end with a small crescent. To the south of the Alford Road, two extremely ambitious free-standing palace façade blocks in conjunction with a double crescent of individual but linked villas behind them were also proposed, centred on the southern side of the street where sporadic residential development had actually just commenced in any event. However, interest in the proposal within the city was at this stage merely polite. At this point in time an extremely ambitious and expensive planning undertaking a mile distant at its nearest point from the Castlegate, was simply just not on, certainly as far as the more affluent citizens of Aberdeen were concerned at any rate. However a seed was sown which would eventually bear some fruit, albeit in a quite different and altogether much diminished form at the end of the day. As a first step however the newly laid out Alford Road found itself much more grandly restyled Albyn Place acknowledging, as well as the name of James Skene's street of residence in the New Town of Edinburgh, almost certainly also its intended source of architectural inspiration.

Arcadian Dreams

Archibald Simpson's second decade opened with a marked increase in his workload in both City and County commissions, in no small part due to his early triumph with his County Buildings design. With a rush of superb country mansions such as Heathcot, Park, Murtle, Crimonmogate and Stracathro, Simpson's naturally extremely restrained perfectionist architectural personality responded to the style so eminently suited to it, especially in its most spartan phase. He of course was not alone, as something deep within the Scottish Presbyterian psyche has always tended to confuse great simplicity with great beauty. This country's rather prolonged allegiance to the Greek Revival is therefore completely understandable, in a style where simplicity and beauty are actually effortlessly combined. In the north-east in particular, Simpson with his very personal and inspirational neoclassical designs, may even have been said to have made the Greek manner his very own. He also managed to perfect the smaller house, which was obviously more suited to many of his general clients' more modest requirements and lesser means. However to complicate matters, the much better roads being completed throughout the country were to lead to some quite unforeseen architectural developments. As well as enabling Simpson to contemplate commissions well outside the natural orbit of Aberdeen, as far afield even as Forres, Elgin and Arbroath, it also encouraged the perhaps less welcome presence of southern-based architects into his natural local territory as well. The most obvious result of this particular tendency was however a speeding up of new building fashions across the length and breadth of the whole country.

All during the 1820s, the ascendancy of the great formal classical mansion was to be increasingly challenged as the desire for a more informal lifestyle made Simpson's smaller classical villa even more popular. Well aware of this trend, he often experimented with the plain classical box, now with or without a little Greek portico lingering at the entrance. Even this gesture would tend to disappear as service wings extending out under broad-eaved roofs anticipated more informal asymmetrical massing arrangements together with the removal of the need for a service basement. As architects of the calibre of Wilkins, Playfair and Burn explored Tudor, Jacobean and even Italianate solutions in the south, they also pioneered the introduction of reception rooms being grouped en suite around a central hall arrangement, with servants banished to linking corridors and the separate service wing beyond, in an increasingly hierarchical manner. The impression must be that things just happened, and the staff became virtually invisible. The implications of this trend were not lost on Archibald Simpson, where in his later mansions of this period he illustrated a full understanding of the new requirements. Another field where he was free to experiment was in the commissions for many service buildings, stables, outbuildings and gate lodges etc., where the omnipresent eye of the proprietor was perhaps a little more relaxed. Here he pioneered the classic cottage and the cottage-orné style where, particularly at Park, Crimonmogate and Caskieben he made excursions into this area to very great effect. In addition to work in the grand domestic field, Simpson also increasingly sought to gain civic and institutional commissions worthy of his talents. Indeed after the outstanding success of his Assembly Rooms and his Bon Accord Square

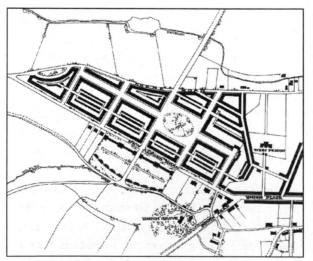

ARCHIBALD ELLIOTT'S DAMLANDS OF RUBISLAW SCHEME FOR THE WEST END OF ABERDEEN.
Clearly modelled on the latest West End of Edinburgh precedent, this extensive planned development on the Skene Lands was far too ambitious and premature. Even Archibald Simpson's very simplified alternative proposals of 1835 failed to attract the necessary interest for his scheme to materialise in anything like its anticipated form.

and Crescent planning achievement in Aberdeen, his hopes in this area must have been high. This particular tree would bear considerable fruit in the next decade with major institutional commissions. The 1820s would however prove to be Simpson's most exciting decade, and the one in which his particular architectural personality and genius seemed to be most completely at home.

As 1819 drew to a close with Archibald Simpson and John Smith no doubt more than a little put out by Archibald Elliott's unlooked for incursion into their territory, a most distinguished mansion house began to appear on the very lands in question, at No. 9 on the newly laid out New Alford Road (now Albyn Place). The first house to be built on the thoroughfare, it dominated the centre of a very generous plot of land. Unfortunately however there is no written, or planning evidence to suggest who the architect was, but he was definitely a man

NO. 9 ALBYN PLACE, ABERDEEN. Attributed to Archibald Simpson, this fine house is now the Royal Northern and University Club.

of consummate ability. Given the almost cubic mass, the slightly recessed centre supported by boldly expressed advanced ends treated almost as planes, the noble segmental high Tuscan portico, and evidence of an early and original use of contrasting granite textures, the man responsible must surely be Archibald Simpson himself. The bold use of squared rubble, outlined with smooth dressed margins, ashlar bands set prominently at ground floor and first floor window sill levels, and a strong cornice and low parapet with a broad panel introduced over the central first floor window, also strongly suggest his personal involvement. The main windows either side of the portico, tall and elegant within their ashlar surrounds, are also recessed into the relieving arches which so effectively reflect the portico and impart such a strong sense of movement to the composition. Originally the short eastern wing, still very noticeable on the left, was balanced by a similar version on the right. Unfortunately when the site was split up later in the nineteenth century to allow A. Marshall Mackenzie to introduce No. 11 into the space next door, the site was not wide enough for his purposes so the west wing had to go. This loss has undoubtedly spoiled the delicate balance of this most accomplished neoclassical design.

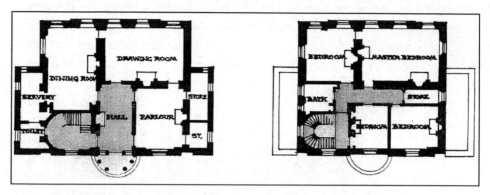

GROUND FLOOR PLAN   FIRST FLOOR PLAN

Internally the villa remains remarkably intact with a suite of very fine reception rooms above a fully suppressed service basement, and various spacious bedrooms on the floor above. Taking full advantage of the originally open views to the south, all the principal apartments are on the garden side. Perhaps surprisingly, the symmetry suggested on the outside is not maintained within, with the elegantly curving cantilevered stair situated immediately on the left of the rather chaste entrance hall on entering, balanced by the little family parlour on the right. Beyond, the drawing room and the dining room impress with their high, elegant proportions and fine plaster and woodwork detailing. Upstairs, bedrooms are all still original, created in a lower and more charming scale, very typical of Simpson. The house was lived in until well after the Second World War when it was acquired and made into the Royal Northern Club. At this time a major series of extensions began to the rear, mainly single-storey, and happily not very damaging to the original fabric. Since the incorporation of the University Club, forming the Royal Northern and University Club premises, the property continues to be immaculately maintained and very beautifully furnished.

The following year in 1820, the Regency was officially over and the new decade opened with Simpson now quite well established and eager to obtain the kind of important local commissions he longed for. His initial overtly Greek statement in King Street had been a success despite its rather forlorn setting standing alone on a side of the street, which would not attract further building until some ten years later. His dramatically striking perpendicular Gothic church statement directly opposite was further proof, if proof were needed, of his ability. He had also just secured the commission, in the face of direct competition from John Smith, to erect a Public Waterhouse in St Nicholas Street (now demolished), to a simple pedimented classic design. The city, which was steadily recovering from its bankruptcy, was spreading out in all directions as the new turnpike roads reached out far into the countryside. With the resultant reduction in travelling times, it was now perfectly feasible to travel considerable distances, making possible the building of many more out-of-town villas, and encouraging also the county to come more conveniently into town. As a result, and anxious to create a new, appropriately 'modern' and magnificent setting for polite society to gather and mingle, designs for new County Buildings were invited from all and sundry. In the event ten submissions were received from various parts of the country, and one design had even been specifically asked of his local rival, John Smith. Archibald Simpson however actually took the precaution of sending in his design anonymously, probably due to the unwelcome notoriety following his Castle Forbes and Lunatic Asylum debacles. After due consideration, the designs of George Smith of the Aberdeen Academy, James Raeburn of Edinburgh, and Archibald Simpson were all selected as worthy of more detailed consideration. In due course and after much thought, Simpson found his proposals selected winner of the competition.

THE COUNTY
BUILDINGS
(Assembly Rooms)
Aberdeen:
circa 1860

In the following two years Simpson carried out what was to be one of his most important commissions in the erection of these County Buildings, or Assembly Rooms as they were more usually called even at the time. The complete success of the design, and its very considerable prominence in the city, literally made his reputation overnight. The site occupied an important corner on the north side of Union Street immediately west of South Silver Street, and taking up more than two thirds of that street in depth. Conceived even from the outset as the most important statement at this end of the new thoroughfare, Simpson freely acknowledged this by incorporating a dramatic portico. His august main front, seen by some to be 'rather academic' is none the worse for that. The plan allows a central vestibule with east and west cloakrooms on either side, honestly

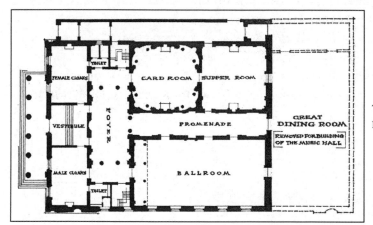

THE PRINCIPAL
FLOOR PLAN

expressed externally in a finely proportioned, immaculately detailed and executed elevation of considerable elegance. The stylobate supports the powerful giant hexastyle Ionic portico, this time with the proper corner volutes to the capitals set at 45 degrees, and made up of six plain columns constructed each of six massive granite drums. These support an architrave, a plain frieze and low Greek plain pediment, with the architrave and frieze treatment taken across the front and down the side of the building. Plain corner pilasters contain the design at either end, sitting on a low plinth base. Unfortunately for as long as anyone can remember public notice boards under the flanking eared-architrave windows have been allowed to disturb the powerful all pervading sense of monumental civic dignity. This has been further eroded more recently by the now almost permanent fixing of jolly banners between the upper columns. None the less the Assembly Rooms or Music Hall as most Aberdonians would now recognise it, still makes its august presence felt on a much altered Union Street, just as Archibald Simpson had originally intended.

The Assembly Rooms today, the prelude to Aberdeen's Music Hall.

Simpson's beautifully domed ceiling central in his Foyer corridor.

The promenade corridor terminating on the statue of the young Queen Victoria.

The Round (Card) Room and the Square (Supper) Room.

Once inside, the very restrained but dignified vestibule effects a considerable change in level up five full width steps into the foyer beyond which gives access to the main accommodation. This, a basically broad cross corridor, has been given a thoroughly chaste Grecian treatment of exceptional purity, enlivened by a coffered oval-shaped ceiling dome, held between flanking broad flat arches and further screens of exquisite Ionic columns, boldly dramatising the farthest ends. In the centre, opposite a marble statue of the young Queen Victoria, a further Ionic screen introduces the pilastered and vaulted promenade corridor running off at right angles to it. This served the remainder of the Graeco-Roman reception rooms originally terminating in the magnificent treble-cube principal dining room, now replaced by the Music Hall itself, built subsequently in 1858 by James Matthews, one-time apprentice to Archibald Simpson somewhat in the future. For the moment however, a gorgeous suite was arranged comprising also the lovely Round Card Room with its exquisite shallow dome held aloft above walls pierced with recesses for sofas flanked by in-antis Corinthian columns; the Square Supper Room complete with full height wall pilasters supporting a finely detailed almost Soanean compartmented ceiling; and the double-cube Ballroom with its high dado, long elegant windows and delicate musicians' gallery supported by elegant Composite columns. In addition to the east and west front cloakrooms already mentioned there are adjoining toilets, and overhead by means of very understated stairs, a number of top lit private rooms were discreetly tucked away for the playing of billiards. This additional floor had the happy effect externally of justifying the full monumental height of the Union Street frontage. The entire building also sits up on a basement originally lit by pavement lights, with at this lower level, many service rooms, kitchen accommodation and various necessary storage rooms. The entire building cost was a remarkable £11,500. On its completion Aberdeen at last could proudly boast a major neoclassical public building of the very highest design and quality, executed with a thoroughly metropolitan sophistication.

The eventual building of the Music Hall, replacing the dining room on the expanded site flanking the south western corner of Golden Square and South Silver Street, almost certainly resulted in the saving of this Assembly Rooms complex for posterity, providing appropriate accommodation and mingling space for the main hall itself. Indeed the ballroom quite quickly found itself being converted into a subsidiary hall, with the gallery removed and a stage incorporated at one end. By the 1960s changing fashions and the perceived need for more shops and supermarkets resulted in the western neighbours of the Assembly Rooms being consigned to history. The loss of Crimonmogate, Smith's rather sober first exercise in the street, (albeit later extended and much enriched), was particularly unfortunate. However

The Assembly Rooms today, now the splendid introduction to the Music Hall.

Despite considerable architectural change to its setting, with various more modern buildings imposing themselves dramatically on to the scene, Simpson's giant Ionic Greek portico still manages to hold its own even at the beginning of the 21st century.

even Simpson's magnificent rooms and portico were for a time placed in the greatest peril as the Council contemplated the removal of the portico and vast internal alterations. Following the outcome of a successful Public Enquiry, and thanks mainly to the Herculean efforts of the Civic Society, the Assembly Rooms were eventually saved. At the end of the day the Council put in hand a programme of magnificent restoration resulting in the brilliant re-emergence of the interior from its rather drab and gloomy condition, into a sparkling reaffirmation of Simpson's genius. What a pity though that the budget could not have run to crystal chandeliers. Regrettably however, the ballroom cum secondary hall was destined not to survive this transformation, having been converted into very necessary modern cloakroom and toilet accommodation, designed to meet the increased requirements of the 1980s. The entire complex, including a refurbished Music Hall as well, was reopened in May 1986 in perhaps better condition and appearance than at any time since it had been originally built.

In the midst of this great work which dominated fully two years of his professional life, a number of other extremely important opportunities were simultaneously to present themselves in both county and town. In quick succession in 1822, commissions were coming in at last, thick and fast. Refreshing his relationship with the very important Gordon Family, he was engaged to extend Huntly Lodge, (now Huntly Castle Hotel), for the Duchess of Gordon herself, adding to the rear of the original quite extensive house. The Lodge had already been much extended around 1800 with an extremely severe granite ashlar three-storey block boasting broad projecting canted bays at both ends, erected under

Simpson's extension and new entrance at Huntly Lodge, Huntly, for the Duchess of Gordon.

its previously known name of Sandiestone. A further rendered wing containing the Library was subsequently attached to the eastern end, before Simpson was asked to design a new entrance, additional mainly bedroom accommodation, and a new imposing timber main staircase within a spacious entrance hall. This he did by extending out an extremely plain but matching two-storey harled block to the end and rear of the existing mansion, enlivened only with ashlar stringers and exposed granite margins. The design was completed with a centrally placed and extremely understated projecting box-like entrance porch. The new wing adjoined the existing north facing kitchen block, which it successfully screened from view. At the western end of this an additional but balancing lower scaled two-storey building containing further service rooms with staff accommodation above was also erected in a matching rendered style with exposed margins and stringers.

In a much more substantial commission he was also engaged by Lord

Aberdeen, to rationalise the internal arrangements of Haddo House near Methlick, and almost certainly build the stables and other necessary estate accommodation at the same time. Haddo had been the Palladianesque brain child of William Adam, who had created the mansion in terms of a central block with lower kitchen and stables wings on either side, connected back to the main house by

Simpson's offices and private wing entry, Haddo House, Methlick.

Simpson's Stable block range, Haddo House.

curved single-storey quadrant link corridors in the then almost obligatory architectural manner. Undoubtedly visually very effective, the inconvenience of such an arrangement had long been only too apparent. Simpson was required to create upper corridors at the main piano nobile level of the state rooms, and in consequence two entirely new two-storey quadrants had to be built, unfortunately simultaneously severely reducing the bold drama and powerful sense of movement of the original main front. In addition internally, he replaced the staircase from the ground to the first floor. To the immediate south of the existing Adam south wing he expanded the block quite considerably and around a charming service court built various offices, accessed through a pend under a tall delightful cupola with clock-tower and weather vane. A range of these office buildings had to be demolished in the 1930s following an unfortunate fire. Some little distance off, Simpson is also attributed with the design of the rather splendid pinned rubble U-shaped two-storey stable block which, relieved by stone dressings at openings and windows, sits under a broad-eaved all embracing piended slated roof. It is now the most effectively and sensitively restored tea room, shop and toilet block for the Country Park and the National Trust for Scotland. The eight-bay centre is effectively held between advancing ends with high architraved surround doorways to the stabling, while in the middle of the range, a pend gives access through to an additional single-storey block behind, enclosing a spacious elongated courtyard for the horses.

Mains of
Haddo Farm,
Haddo Estate.

Within the Estate also at Mains of Haddo, Archibald Simpson must surely have built the still memorable but very much altered ensemble, combining an originally symmetrical arrangement of storey and a half farm buildings about a segmentally arched pend set between flanking ranges of houses, a usual and favourite Simpson device. The buildings, all harled with granite margins, are also accommodated under a typically Simpsonian heavy piended slated roof.

They effectively function now as the Factor's offices for the Haddo Estate. The courtyard range behind has been much less fortunate however for while most of it still survives, the southern range has been substantially broken through, and the centre has been largely infilled with a large corrugated asbestos cowshed,

The Factor's House, Haddo Estate

completely ruining the original architectural concept. (It should be noted also that this complex has been attributed by some to John Smith in the past, despite its considerable stylistic affinity with Simpson's other work in this genre). In the absence of drawings or written confirmation to the contrary however, it would appear to be the case that these buildings were erected before Smith's own personal involvement at Haddo which was in the 1840s. The adjacent distinguished two-storey three-bay harled Home Farmhouse to the north of the complex is similarly also attributed to Archibald Simpson, with its heavy-eaved slated roof contained by chimneyed gables, and a central single-storey gabled porch. The very charming single-storey Gardener's cottage also on the estate, is a delightful composition with heavy eaves, a Tudor porch and incorporating diagonal chimneys, most probably also by Simpson's hand. Although tantalisingly various drawings of all these buildings are still held at Haddo, unfortunately they are all unsigned, and given sometimes a certain similarity between Simpson's and Smith's more cheap and cheerful styles, which they both developed mainly for farm buildings, a problem can exist in separating out their involvements. This is particularly the case where both men worked for the same client as at Haddo. It would however appear to be the case that within the Haddo Estate, John Smith was responsible only for the later work, including the Laundry, the South Lodge, the Golden Gates and the Stag and Urn. In the very near vicinity he was also responsible for the Tarves and Udny Manses and the Methlick Bridge, which has just been beautifully restored.

In addition to this considerable achievement, the opportunity also presented itself to complete Simpson's august Adamesque palace block design for Union Buildings at the east end of Union Street. Alexander Brown, the local bookseller who had just become Provost, had acquired John Ewen's Castlegate premises with a view to building a new Library and Reading Room there, replacing his rather more humble premises which were due for demolition, immediately next door to Burn's 1801 Bank premises at the top of Marischal Street. The two plots which were necessary for the erection of the magnificent new building had a very high feu-duty, and combined with building costs of almost £12,000, and the establishment of the rival Union Club Newsroom in the County Buildings further west, poor Brown's enterprise understandably failed to thrive. However, in the heat of the moment, and possibly carried away with the prestige of his project in his first year as Provost, Brown instructed Archibald Simpson to complete his design and supervise the erection of the work. Whilst repeating a mirrored version of Bailie Galen's House on the Union Street frontage, at the eastern end of the composition, the centre is dominated with a five-window wide, slightly advanced block, very effectively terminating the axis of Broad Street opposite. The four-storey building, unified by taking a wide first floor stringer, and a continuous third floor sill stringer all round the three external facades, is given extra presence by a wide central Simpson panel placed above the cornice, held by decorative brackets and enlivened by sculptural swags and drops.

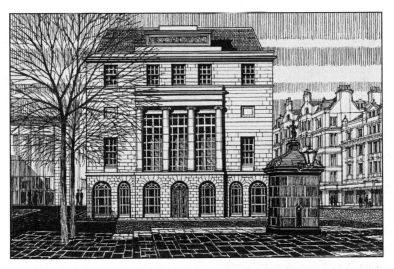

The Royal Athenaeum Castlegate elevation today, restored as offices.

On the return Castlegate elevation however, after toying with something altogether simpler, Simpson pulled out all the stops by incorporating into his design at first floor, a boldly advanced two-storey high tripartite window, expressing the great Reading Room behind, and held between three giant Ionic columns and a flat architrave and cornice overhead. Above this over the third floor, further central emphasis is given by a broad panel enlivened by continuous scrolls, placed over a blocking course. A four-bay further plain return elevation completes the design along Exchequer Row, subsequently extended into an adjoining three-storey matching building. This monumental composition, a most appropriate and noble introduction to Union Street, contained a typical ground storey comprising, behind subtle rhythms of arch-headed windows and doors, various commercial premises and two entries to the floors above. The principal accommodation was situated on the first floor where the library and the reading room were located with their associated facilities. Unfortunately Simpson's first intentions seem to have been either too ambitious or expensive, for the Reading Room was eventually completed in a diminished, if still extremely impressive manner. Legend recalls that at the end of the day Alexander Brown actually sold the now failing newsroom to his attendant for £5, and whatever the truth of the story, James Blake (the attendant until 1842), certainly successfully took over the business in that year. The Athenaeum Newsroom remained in operation until 1867, when it was temporarily pressed into service as the City Courthouse, during the construction phase of the Municipal Chambers and the Sheriff Courthouse opposite. At this time also the building housed on the ground floor, some famous city businesses including, A. & R. Milne, Booksellers; George Pegler, Greengrocer; Keith & Gibb, Lithographers; and Mrs McKilliam, Confectioners. In 1878 the redoubtable Jimmy Hay acquired Mrs McKilliam's shop and established his own Café there. Quickly prospering, he soon bought out the old Newsroom above, and with the upper storeys he established a rather splendid hotel, with the old reading room opening as the grand Athenaeum Restaurant. In due course, the fame of this particular establishment would spread far and wide. Eventually acquired and run very successfully by the Mitchell family, the business was sold in 1926 to a consortium of local businessmen who held it until it was eventually sold to a Brewery company. In 1965 Thomas Usher & Son bought the establishment, and at that time the premises were greatly refurbished, at the same time disastrously lowering the ceiling of the great room, to suit more 'modern' requirements of 'taste'. Gone forever were the chandeliers, the giant classical wall pilasters and the famous frieze which declared to all and sundry that "He that drinks well doth sleep well, He that sleeps well doth work well, He that works well doth eat well, and He that eats well doth drink well".

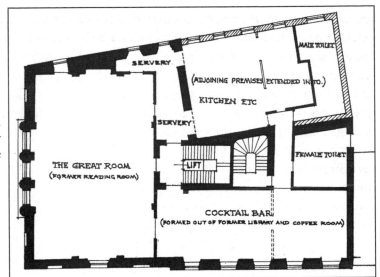

The Athenaeum immediately prior to the fire

On the night of August 13th 1973, the Athenaeum went up in flames, apparently due to an electrical fault somewhere above the dreaded suspended ceiling of the former great room. The end result was that overnight almost the entire premises were gutted and lay open, smouldering to the skies. After a period of considerable uncertainty, when even the total demolition of the ruins was contemplated, Corner House Hotels Ltd acquired the site with the express purpose of restoring the buildings as modern offices. Bailey Galen's House, surprisingly surviving absolutely intact next door, was incorporated into the scheme, which was duly completed, minus unfortunately the great room. In

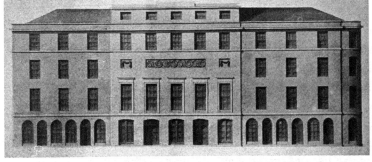

Simpson's initial thoughts for his Union Street frontage.

addition the former low piended roof was reinstated as a slated mansard with dormers matching the window arrangement below, which was taken all around. This allowed the addition of a further full floor of offices, whilst creating a not altogether unsuccessful but perhaps un-looked for French feel externally. More legend also had it that the Athenaeum was the first building in Aberdeen to be built on oak piles, due to the poor nature of the subsoil conditions. During the rebuilding works, when extensive foundations were required to be placed at basement level to support the necessary massive new internal steel structure, absolutely no evidence was found to support this. At first floor however there were indications of some change of intention during the original construction work with various inexplicable piers and brick infill exposed on the reverse of the Union Street façade at its eastern end.

Union Buildings immediately following its 1970's full restoration.

1822 however continued with a burst of further country house activity, and a number of extremely important opportunities for Simpson to develop his thoughts further in this particular field. Commencing with Heathcot situated on the Haugh of Ardoe on lower Deeside, the perfectionist in him created a very compactly planned villa within a tight rectangular block, enclosed within a chaste exterior of the most extreme elegance and restraint. The estate lay on the rising valley of the Shannaburn and had been originally carved out of the adjoining ancient lands of Auchlunies. Simpson was commissioned to erect the villa for John Garioch, who also acquired more land and greatly improved the general property. The mansion itself, built over an almost fully suppressed basement of kitchen and service rooms, emerging to a half basement at the rear, had the apparently single-storey main block effectively sandwiched between two-

The south front of Heathcot House with its subsequent extension wing on the left.

storey, only very slightly advanced wings placed at either end. This would develop into something of a favourite arrangement. In this particular instance the wings were provided with single long elegant windows at ground floor level with smaller almost square windows serving the lower scaled bedrooms on the floor above. The walls, except for granite margins and stringers, with recessed infill panels also under the main window sills, were entirely rendered and painted. The wings at roof level were additionally adorned at the front and at the rear with delicious low Greek pediments making their first appearance. At the centre of the high front linking facade, a tall segmentally bowed Doric portico proclaimed the entrance door with its own architrave, plain frieze and very low pitched leaded roof. On either side of this two long windows were centred on the remaining façade. The rear elevation was almost a full repeat of this composition, minus of course the portico, and with four long elegant windows substituted instead across the centre section. The exterior, very faithfully expressed the internal arrangement of the ground floor circuit of family rooms and reception rooms, with two end rows of first floor bedrooms facing east and west above. Some little distance off to the west, Simpson was also required to build a stable block and farm buildings as well as the original home farm. This typical U-shaped Simpson work with front stores supporting a monumental segmentally arched entry between them, was executed in coursed rubble, rendered with dressed margins. A dressed stringer was also provided at eaves level and the storey and a half main buildings sat on an ashlar base course. A low pitched slated roof all round completed the whole. On the opposite side of the access road round to the rear, the home farmhouse and additional farm buildings were aligned in a matching block.

On the death of Mr Garioch, the property passed to his sister, when on her demise it was purchased by James Fraser, an Aberdeen merchant. It may have been at this stage that a quite sensitive single-storey extension with basement was put out across the west reception room façade, creating a balcony at the same time for the first floor bedrooms. Shortly acquired by Adam Mitchell, the Aberdeen builder of among other things the Denburn Valley Railway and the Joint Station, Heathcot was transformed into a Hydropathic Establishment. For this purpose a rather dire block was moored alongside the most recent extension, with little architectural thought for the whole. In 1880 Mr Alexander Ogston of Ardoe acquired the entire estate and Hydropathic Centre, which of course lay contiguous to his property, across its eastern boundary.

Very regrettably, having successfully survived the Second World War, Heathcot was sold and the mansion, together with its extensions was demolished in 1958. In order to facilitate a business devoted to the growing of mushrooms, the old basement was actually retained with a thick, flat concrete slab set over it. The new proprietor immediately set about erecting a new house slightly to the south, rather indifferently designed, but constructed out of the old granite-work of Heathcot itself. Purchased again in 1996 by Mr and Mrs M. Dreelan, they immediately demolished this version and proceeded to erect a very much more impressive two-storey mansion house of their own, executed in a traditional but pleasantly rambling style, and again reusing old Heathcot's granite blocks. Indeed the new design builds up very nicely to the south in a series of well considered and receding broad gables. A new tunnel under the entrance forecourt allows all-weather access to Simpson's old basement, which has been extraordinarily glamorised with a riven slate surface and surround railings, together with a full internal opening up and

Heathcot House from the rear. The house was unnecessarily demolished in 1958.

refurbishment to accommodate Mr Dreelan's fine collection of vintage cars and motor cycles. The more distant stable block has received a similarly imaginative treatment with the considerable widening of the back leg of the original U-shape, all the better to store an impressive collection of farm implements and steam engines. By incorporating and reusing various elements from the demolitions, segmental arches, stringers, etc., a still very convincing Simpson-like building has been retained, albeit shorn of all its original render.

At this very same period Archibald Simpson was also appointed by a Mr Moir of Park, to design for him an even more palatial mansion on his newly acquired property beyond Drumoak. Unfortunately we have no evidence where Mr Moir actually came from, but it would seem reasonable to suppose that he was originally local and had probably returned from the Empire with a fortune gained as a

The south and west fronts of Park House today.

merchant, like so many others. Park had been a centre of habitation of course for some considerable time as the Pictish sculptured stone found around 1821 at East Park, (formerly Bakebare Farm) amply testifies. This stone, remarkably similar to one found at Dunvegan, is set up on a pedestal about a hundred yards from the house. The symbols comprise probably a flower, a crescent and a V-rod, and a mirror and comb with a divided rectangle above. Nearby the ruins of the ancient Church of Drumoak can also be found dating back to 1157 when Pope Adrian confirmed the See of Aberdeen. In 1323 King Robert the Bruce granted the original charter for the Lands of Drum to William de Irwine. The Park Estate as a separate entity goes back to 1348, when 'The Park' was reserved by King David II and given to Walter Moigne. Returned eventually to the Irvine family in 1389, they held them until the lands were eventually sold to Patrick Duff of Culter in 1737. By 1807 Thomas Burnett, a successful advocate of Aberdeen had acquired the property and fourteen years later he sold it to the aforesaid William Moir who intended to develop the estate and also build upon it.

Engaging Archibald Simpson at his most Grecian, between them they arrived at a villa of very considerable freshness and originality. The present owner, Mr John Foster, considers that since the construction of the new Deeside turnpike which actually traverses the estate, it was now perfectly possible for visitors from Aberdeen to travel out the twelve miles to Park from the city, stay while the horses rested, and then travel back before nightfall. For this reason, and perhaps also to prevent even the remotest possibility of large numbers of guests thinking of staying for the weekend, the mansion house was conceived from the outset as having only four really good bedrooms on the first floor. There was however by contrast a superb suite of reception rooms below for splendid daytime entertaining.

Simpson's front elevation of Park House.

Taking his cue from Heathcot's single bay two-storey bookend arrangement, this time minus the Greek pediments, the featured pavilion wings terminate a much expanded single-storey centre of three windows set at either side of a chaste tetrastyle Greek Doric portico. The result creates a serene and almost virginally pure front façade to the river. The dazzling off-white stucco finish exaggerates this powerful sense of still beauty and perfection, underlining the brilliant sharpness of this very pristine, but at the same time wholly monumental, neoclassical statement. Seen from any angle against the mature woodlands of the estate behind, or with the spreading green lawns sweeping down to the river in front, the mansion exerts a powerfully magnetic influence over the scene.

On entering, the impressive compartmentally domed entrance hall allows through a fine screen of scagliola columns, access to a magnificent suite of restrained but very elegant apartments set out on either side. The entire enfilade is obviously carefully arranged to capture the finest views across and up and down the valley of the River Dee, maximising the great intrinsic virtue of the site. The imaginatively interrelated reception rooms unfold with a particular emphasis to

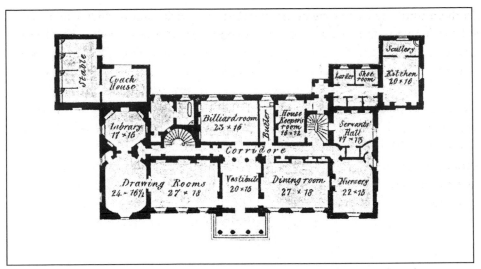

The original plan of Park House: the coach house and stable wing have been
subsequently altered along with various internal variations mainly to the
kitchen wing and the billiard room.

the western range, where the very august principal drawing room with its high
coved ceiling is placed, en suite with the second drawing room next door, now
used as a smoking room cum study. This room is enlivened with segmental ends
facing across at each other and a fine low relief plaster ceiling. Next door to the
north through further double doors, the old octagonal library can be found, a
delightful room now used as the morning room. From here a rear access corridor
connects back to the hall, with an extremely elegant half spiral staircase swelling
out in the middle. Sets of paired arched openings on either side of this
effectively reduce the apparent overall length of the passageway. To the east of
the entrance hall is the dining room, a room very similar in form to the drawing
room opposite, provided also with a high coved ceiling. Straight ahead is the old
billiard room, which is now used as the sole but still principal ground floor
bedroom. This eastern side of the house is also served by a slightly less grand rear
access corridor with a secondary stone staircase incorporated, beyond which is the
segmentally ended old nursery, now used as an office cum study. At this side of
the mansion also, the working part of the house developed, with accommodation
for the butler, housekeeper, pantry, servants' hall, kitchen and scullery. Meanwhile
below in the relatively small basement area, various cellars and stores were located.
Much of this service accommodation has of late been of necessity put to new and
different usage, including a modern kitchen complex and the gun room.

The tetrastyle Doric entrance portico at
Park House.

Although perhaps a little less grand than might have been expected, both stairs provide access up to a first floor arrangement where the principal bedroom suites of two rooms each have been located in the east and west terminal wings. Along the long interconnecting corridor on its north, further mainly staff bedrooms were placed, which over time has allowed the easy insertion of modern bathrooms without dramatically altering the plan. Like the corridor on the ground floor, Simpson skilfully controlled the length of the top passageway by the use of piers and top lighting, as well as the additional spatial drama created by both his staircases. To the rear of the east wing also, a small mezzanine floor was ingeniously introduced relatively recently with a suite of further small bedrooms and bathrooms.

Within the house the quality of the design, the variety of the room shapes, the understated plasterwork, and most especially the superb woodwork, is truly marvellous. There is as well a wonderful airy feeling throughout of lightness,

A screen of Doric
columns also enlivens
the entrance vestibule
at Park House.

The principal drawing Room, Park.

The Dining Room at Park.

The present day Morning Room at Park.

The top landing and spine corridor off the principal stair, Park.

elegance, restraint and space. The basic house plan also has been very little changed over the intervening period except for the use to which some rooms have been put. The most major change in fact has been the adaptation of the old stables and coach-house, which have been properly squared off and converted subsequently into a fine billiard and smoking room. This impressive space has been given a dentilled cornice and a Greek-key frieze with three matching decorative ceiling ovals, in a manner which would certainly have pleased Archibald Simpson himself. Apart from the very sensitive introduction of the additional toilet and bathroom facilities already mentioned, and the restoration by the present incumbent of the internal woodwork to many windows, the only really noticeable change to the house has been the recent addition of a well-designed glazed conservatory at the western end, in conjunction with its little formal landscaped garden area established immediately in front of it. Throughout also, the interiors have been beautifully maintained and furnished, the entire mansion being very appropriately decorated in a late Regency style.

Within the well-wooded estate, Simpson was also engaged this year in laying out all the major driveways and paths, together with the design and construction of the east and west lodges. Unfortunately only the west one now survives, the eastern version having been subsequently demolished probably to make way for the railway and then replaced in 1867 by a much busier Gothic version. The West Lodge, which is basically a simple gabled cottage with slated roof and two

The old West Lodge at Park.

narrow dormers reflecting the windows on the rendered rubble walls below, is distinguished by a central proto-Doric wooden flat topped distyle portico, anticipating that of the distant mansion house itself. This lodge has also been joined by a more Gothic style neighbour, built on the other side of the drive.

After this Simpson was engaged to complete much more at Park, which would keep him occupied on and off over the next full decade.

Meanwhile to the far north, directly off the main Inverness Road opposite Auldearn, Simpson was employed by the Dunbar family to create for them there a villa of a rather different type. The family had occupied an ancient tower on the site dating back to the early fifteenth century, and were anxious to enter into the modern era by building for themselves a house in the most up-to-date manner possible. Introducing what would become quite a favourite arrangement for his smaller country house designs, the very compact, rectangular plan created at Boath House a very elegant but understated exterior, lent considerable presence

Aerial view of Boath House, Auldearn.

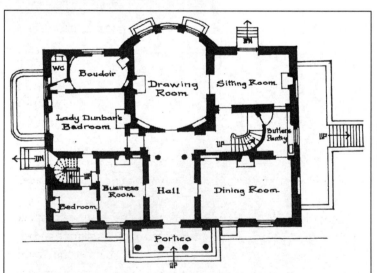

Simpson's original plan of Boath House.

by its simple massing and the storey and a half tetrastyle Ionic portico set centrally on the main front. The severely restrained two-storey façades, set over a fully suppressed kitchen and service basement, present a wide main south facing entrance frontage with pairs of typically long elegant windows on either side of the three-quarter height central portico. On the bedroom floor above, the reduced scale utilised created slightly squarer windows, set directly above those of the reception room suite below. The feeling of restraint is effortlessly carried round to the flanking gables where a four- and three-window wide arrangement is employed, with many of them being blank, particularly on the east side. On the rear facade, his first three-windowed full height segmental bow swells out, the better to view the surrounding estate and the delightful lake. Above this the design is totally unified by a bold cornice and low parapet allowing just the sight of the typically low slated piended roof and carefully positioned roof chimneys. On the centre of the front immediately above the portico, a broad wall-head panel sits on top of the blocking course, creating a further central emphasis. Narrower panels disguising chimneys, fulfil the same function centrally on both return elevations.

A tetrastyle Ionic portico dominates the serenely balanced entrance front at Boath House.

From the entrance hall with its delicate screen of Ionic columns, the compact plan unfolds with the bow-ended principal drawing room placed straight ahead, en suite with the sitting room next door. The very elegant half spiral main staircase and the fine old dining room complete that side of the house. Opposite this, accommodation is balanced by the business room with its adjoining bedroom, and Lady Dunbar's bedroom and en suite boudoir. At this side also, a secondary staff stair services all three levels. The top floor contains an arrangement of very elegantly designed bedrooms, each complete with a small adjoining dressing room, and laid out around the imposing galleried top of the half spiral staircase and along the main central cross-hall, itself enlivened by arches and a small domed cupola.

The rear elevation.

After the Dunbar family vacated the property in 1925, the house has operated since then very successfully as a small hotel. Recently magnificently restored and very beautifully refurbished throughout by the present owners Mr and Mrs Matheson, a basement Spa has been incorporated along with a kitchen supplying their dining room with very delicious food. Happily its superb accommodation, delightful interiors, its facilities, spreading lawns, encircling trees and lake are as memorable today as they were when Archibald Simpson successfully took leave of this commission.

In 1823, while still very active on the finishing of Park House itself, William Moir also employed Simpson to design for him the Home Farm on the estate, the even simpler Nether Farm complex and the great half-moon walled garden with its attached gardener's cottage. This latter element, enclosed within a great granite and brick lined wall incorporating fine gates, encompassed originally a large vegetable and fruit garden created to serve the requirements of the house. This is now mainly landscaped although the heated Peach House built in 1867 for the cost of £70, still exists. Less happily however the Home Farm, a very simple, understated, U-shaped arrangement carried out in his now quite typical most restrained manner, is set out on either side of the modest triumphal arched entry to the original screened-off yard, sadly more recently entirely filled with a large corrugated cowshed. The temptation to utilise Simpson's farmyards in this way by owners anxious to save themselves the cost of building enclosing walls is obviously considerable, as many such farm complexes have been overwhelmed in this manner. None the less at Park we can still just about appreciate yet another example of Simpson's philosophical sense of appropriateness and economy, married to great simplicity of classical form and function.

The original Dining Room, Boath House – now a sitting room.

The very elegant
Entrance Hall
and Ionic screen
at Boath House with
the impressive
Saloon (now the
dining room)
seen beyond.

The half-spiral principal
staircase at Boath House.

The Half-moon Walled Garden and gardener's cottage
at Park House.

In addition to all this, by 1835 Simpson had also created on site various other essential buildings including an Ice-house, Game Larder and probably also a Laundry, all of which sadly no longer exist, evidence of their situation only being now consigned to a fascinating portfolio of old plans and deeds retained at the house. In 1839 Mr A. J. Kinloch bought the House and Estate of Park and he continued to embellish and modernise the property as he required. With the laying down of the Deeside Railway however after 1854, immediately parallel to the turnpike road, this most probably necessitated his early Gothic rebuilding of the eastern gate lodge. Interestingly by 1867, a gasometer for the storage of a domestic supply of gas was also provided on site, located slightly behind the house. At this time also the Mausoleum appeared. In 1888 Andrew Penny acquired the estate, which he held until 1918 when Sir Robert Williams bought it, subsequently slightly remodelling the interior of the house and adding the African Room, together with additional on site staff houses and the garage. In 1946, following the loss of their family home near Pitlochry, which was submerged below a Hydro-electric Dam, Major H. F. B. Foster bought Park as his intended family home. Since his son John has inherited the property, he and his wife Clarinda have witnessed considerable changes to the Estate with sales and also land acquisitions on the south side of the River Dee. Both however have very enthusiastically expanded on Major Foster's initial programme of restoration at the mansion house, successfully recreating internally all the comfort, grace and elegance of the late Regency period in their memorable Deeside home.

Meanwhile, slightly nearer Aberdeen on a high bluff beyond Beildside overlooking the River Dee, Simpson was allowed by John Thorburn his client, to give full reign to his architectural imagination in the creation of Murtle House, another of his very original, dramatic and utterly beautiful Grecian statements. The estate, originally Murthill, had in the past been in the possession of many an Aberdeen Provost. Thorburn had made his fortune overseas as a merchant, and now in his retirement he was anxious to proceed with all haste. Fired by the sublime nature of the site, the full drama of the setting and the superb views over and west up the river valley, the romantic in Simpson realised one of his finest and most unequivocally Greek designs. Thoroughly classical both inside and out, he expanded his Heathcot type yet again, this time embracing two-window wide flanking terminal wings with balancing Greek pediments placed front and back within a sharp two-storey stuccoed block. To the entrance front in between, created as a high, apparently single-storey link, a Doric pilastrade was employed to control the central granite ashlar enclosed doorway and long narrow flanking inset windows. On the reverse where the mansion addresses the magnificent western sweep of the valley, Simpson boldly embedded a dramatically swelling semicircular bow, fronted by a colonnade of three-quarter height fluted Doric columns supporting a plain frieze, entablature and cornice, with a magnificent saucer dome above floating majestically over all. This very memorable ensemble, recalling something of the gravity of some ancient remembered Grecian Tholos, achieves a most powerful sense of dignity and serene monumentality, remarkable in such a relatively small mansion house.

The vestibule, which was originally adorned with very beautiful panels of low relief plasterwork, leads directly through to the delightful central saloon with its bow-fronted end, which was balanced on either side by the drawing room and dining room, typically now all interconnecting. The stair gives access to a long gallery/corridor, which serves the bedrooms on the first floor, but originally also the billiard room as well, which occupied the space immediately under the dome. Later this particular pursuit was removed to a more convenient position downstairs, slightly damaging the original Simpson arrangement. However by all accounts the original principal interiors were extremely spacious, elegant and very refined. The house also sits up upon a fully suppressed service and kitchen basement still typical of his usual manner at this time, but with its presence making itself known more towards the rear where the ground begins to fall away quite quickly to the edge of the valley below.

The mansion, long the centrepiece of the Camphill Rudolf Steiner School, sits within a beautifully maintained and wooded estate, which has managed over the years to absorb various neighbouring properties. Within these expanded policies a number of angular, interestingly conceived school buildings have been constructed, all with prominently shaped roofs in accordance with Rudolf Steiner's building design philosophy. A particularly bold and courageous accretion in this vein, comprising basically an auditorium and a chapel, is well tacked on to the north of the house. Extremely regrettably however, the interior quality of the mansion itself has been considerably compromised by the removal and covering up of much of the original fine plasterwork, many rooms having been subdivided, completely revamped and refurbished in a very plain and modern manner for use as offices, residential accommodation and classrooms. Notwithstanding these deprivations, it is still possible however when looking out of the elongated windows of the surviving central bow at the heart of this ensemble, to experience the full and wonderful impact of Simpson's Arcadian Grecian vision, built rather improbably on lower Deeside.

In town however at this same time, Simpson was also commissioned by the Incorporated Tailor Trade, to investigate the development possibilities of their

The east front of Murtle House with its elegant entrance pillastrade.

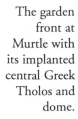

The principal floor plan of Murtle House

SALOON

DRAWING ROOM

DINING ROOM

VESTIBULE

BILLIARD ROOM (NOT ORIGINAL).

WC

PARLOUR

The garden front at Murtle with its implanted central Greek Tholos and dome.

lands, bordering the newly laid out Bon Accord Street to the west of the city. Fired no doubt by the success of the Hammermen's Golden Square equivalent, and even more recent incursions along Crown Street to the south of Union Street, Simpson was asked to prepare plans for the creation of a first class residential district. The roughly triangular site, considerably tapering towards its southern end, was controlled by the pre-existing back lane of Bon Accord Street and the edge of the valley rim to the west. Taking advantage of these constraints, Simpson realised the full potential of the land by creating a long rectangular Square, giving access to a one-sided terrace which itself introduced a magnificent crescent. It had been intended to turn the crescent in reverse beyond its present rather apologetic right angled end return, but difficulties with the levels and existing properties in Bon-Accord Street precluded the achievement of this solution which had envisaged a smooth link into Springbank Terrace and from there directly on to Crown Street itself. Disappointing as this might have been for the full integration of his scheme into the surrounding fabric, what Simpson did realise here with his very fine Square and even more sublime crescent, was undoubtedly the high point of his planning achievements and by far the finest piece of neoclassical street building in Aberdeen, before or since.

BON ACCORD CRESCENT, ABERDEEN.
The majestic sweep of Bon Accord Crescent creates the finest neoclassical street in Aberdeen.

Gracious living in a town house was of course a fairly new concept in Aberdeen, and available only to the few, rich enough to afford it or want it. Utilising a basically three-window wide fairly standard house type, of a reception suite over a full semi-suppressed service basement, family rooms and bedrooms were placed usually on the floor above with lesser bedrooms in the attics for children or live-in staff, situated within the roof space. These houses, contained securely within their granite enclosing walls, present ultra smooth ashlar front facades to the street, relieved only by a broad stringer at the slightly raised ground floor, and the finishing cornice and low parapet at roof level. Considerably more architectural control was however exercised on this site than in Golden Square, with the ten-house long north side, and the matching nine-house long south side of Bon Accord Square, achieving a total unity as the houses gently descend down the almost imperceptible slope, in steps hardly disturbing the elegant window rhythm. In addition, the railings protecting the basement sunken areas, the broad entrance steps, the original classical window fenestration and delightful over-door individually designed fanlights impart an all-embracing sense of very restrained and delightful simplicity. Simpson himself was to set up his home here at No. 15 in a house that he had originally designed himself, before removing himself latterly to the corner of the Square at No. 1 East Craibstone Street where he unexpectedly died in 1847. His office premises were however located separately at No. 1 Bon Accord Square.

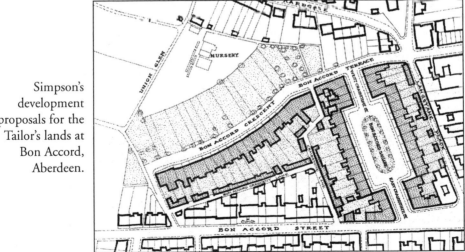

Simpson's development proposals for the Tailor's lands at Bon Accord, Aberdeen.

While East Craibstone Street gives access into the square from Bon Accord Street, West Craibstone Street effects a similar exit on to Bon Accord Terrace at its opposite western end. This terrace provides a very appropriate introduction to Simpson's Bon Accord Crescent, which hugging the very edge of the Holburn valley falling away to the west, suddenly unfolds in a magnificently serene sweep. Recalling perhaps something of Nash's extremely restrained Park Crescent in London but on a somewhat smaller scale, the apparently endless rhythm of elongated windows in a gracious curve of fifteen houses, is retained by slightly

A typical standard Bon Accord Town House.

returned, paired house terminal blocks at either end, completing the noble ensemble. The drama is further reinforced by insistent metal railings, sub-rhythms of entrance doors, entrance steps and roof dormers, in a design held between a continuous ground floor broad stringer and a bold overriding cornice and parapet. The crescent faces south-west, overlooking the valley, western Ferryhill, the Hardgate and Ruthrieston beyond. At the time of building, and with the greater agricultural landscape between these then suburban centres, residence here must have been something approximating to living in the country, whilst still being in town. On the other side of the retaining wall supporting the roadway in front of the houses, the west-facing valley slopes were subdivided into private gardens so that the residents could grow their own fruit and vegetables. Here indeed was the epitome of civilised living for the most affluent city dweller to enjoy. Despite the undoubted planning and architectural success of the development however, Simpson and the Tailors parted company acrimoniously, due to some modifications desired by the Tailors and Simpson's quickly inflamed temper resenting the interference. Initially the Incorporation attempted a reconciliation but to no avail, and subsequently the completion of the scheme was entrusted to other hands. The fact that the design was fairly resolutely pursued to completion with little alteration, perhaps says it all. Sadly, despite various future brave attempts, Simpson was never to achieve such a remarkable urban planning triumph again. It appears that Aberdeen at this time simply did not have either the impetus or the inclination to live in careful architecturally planned residential areas, preferring instead to reside in either individual villas, or in fairly piecemeal conceived terraces, allowing via the builder, the expression still of some individual personal taste and style.

Bon Accord
Square,
Aberdeen

Despite the building of a substantial garage in the 1930s, the almost universal loss of the Georgian window astragals, and further deprivations in the form of some dreadful roof dormers here and there, the original architecture of both the Square and the Crescent is very largely undisturbed. As well as the recent introduction of some dreadful signage, it is also quite difficult to forget the Council's very own proposal in the 1960s, to build an outrageously tiered multi storey car park all down the valley slopes. Having successfully seen this proposal off, the Aberdeen Civic Society presented its own landscaping proposals for the valley, which have now been happily executed, much to the considerable enhancement of the entire area. To commemorate European Heritage Year in 1975, the Society also designed a long awaited and very appropriate Archibald Simpson Memorial for the centre of Bon Accord Square, in the form of a wonderfully appropriate rough granite monolith. This was gifted by the City Council, apparently a leftover stone once intended to adorn the George VI Bridge, originally in the form of a carved lion.

It was also around this time that development in earnest started at the topmost end of Crown Street in a thoroughfare running parallel to the back of the Dee Street properties to the west. The prior existence of Windmill Brae forced an unfortunate early bend to avoid even greater difficulties with the levels involving bridging, but once straightened up, two very handsome rows of two-storey town houses with basements stepped leisurely down the slope towards the Dee Village at the bottom. It seems very likely that Archibald Simpson might have been active here, as many of the houses could easily have been by his hand, all very heavily indebted in any case to his pioneering work in the Bon Accord area. Whatever, numerous examples displaying stringers, recessed spandrels under principal windows, fanlights, railinged-off sunken forecourts and low parapets above broad flat stringers functioning as notional cornices, abound. Unfortunately also over time, the top-most end of this thoroughfare has been rather radically altered and overlaid with many later commercial buildings.

By 1824, Simpson was again fully committed with various country house designs, commencing with the considerable enlargement of Durris House situated on lower Deeside for John Innes. The original L-plan tower house had been restored after 1645, after being torched by the Marquis of Montrose's men during the religious strife of the times. Subsequently restored and progressively extended

Simpson's initial modest extension to old Durris House.

by the inclusion of an additional wing and a great hall, it was this arrangement on to which Simpson was asked to attach a more 'modern' wing allowing for the enjoyment of fashionably genteel standards of civilised late Georgian living. Executed in squared coursed rubble, and in consequence contrasting considerably with the original old harled building, a quite unremarkable no-nonsense, elongated two-storey wing was attached to the north of the old house. Containing for the moment the very best in up-to-date reception rooms with additional new bedrooms placed overhead, the design also revolved around a new staircase. More will be said however about this mansion later.

Meanwhile some two miles to the north of the Aulton in the lands of Scotstown opposite Perriwinies Moss, The Moirs of Scotstown and Spital instructed Simpson to design and erect what would be one of his most impressive mansions. The Moirs had been lairds since the fifteenth century, and whilst this was their principal land holding, they had also acquired the lands of Spital just south of the Aulton, allowing them the title of Spital and the right to erect their own Mausoleum in the St Peter's Cemetery there – more of that later, however. Simpson immediately got to work, realising perhaps too grand a mansion, for it was destined to survive only slightly in excess of one hundred years. Behind a magnificent giant tetrastyle Greek Ionic portico, no doubt acknowledging the Family's perception of their important social status, the drama unfolded with an initial two-storey, three-bay front with two-bay gable returns, capped with low Greek pediments. Beyond this, and in a slightly diminished scale, the main house extended backwards with a further two-storey block over a suppressed basement, enlivened by two three-windowed, Regency styled segmental bows, set either side of the flat three-bay centre. The construction, a relatively inexpensive and typical mix of rubble and brickwork, completely stuccoed throughout, unified the entire ensemble under an all embracing cornice and parapet which virtually hid the low slated roof overhead. The

The chaste stuccoed Grecian styled drama of Scotstown House just to the north of Aberdeen, immediately prior to its demolition.

interior, allegedly quite as grand as the exterior already suggested, immediately set out a cool and elegant suite of reception rooms on entering, created around a notable hall and staircase, whilst the more private family suite extended on either side beyond. The family and children's bedrooms with their nursery occupied the entire first floor with the principal guest provision being as always nearest the porticoed front. Kitchen, service rooms, staff and storage occupied the fully suppressed basement still necessary underneath.

Set amid spreading lawns dotted with magnificent trees, the estate, fully enclosed within encircling high rubble walls, was also provided with the obligatory stables, coach-house, gate-houses, game larder, and various other service buildings. Even an underground ice-house was considered necessary. Perhaps however housed over ambitiously, the mansion was abandoned by the Moirs and lay derelict for many years before finally being demolished in the 1930s. Even today, as the serried ranks of modern villas inexorably advance over the surrounding fields of the Bridge of Don just north of the city, some vestiges of gaunt rubble and brick walls remain, sufficient to recall the former grandeur of this very distinguished but now lost monument to the Moirs of Scotstown and Spital.

In the following year 1825, Simpson was completing a quite similar but slightly more manageable exercise for Sir Charles Bannerman on the far distant shoulder of Buchan near Lonmay. Called Crimonmogate, the new thoroughly neoclassical mansion house dominating the centre of a large triangular estate, immediately proclaims one of Archibald Simpson's most profoundly august Greek statements. Crimonmogate Estate once formed part of the vast Earldom of the Errols, the Hereditary High Constables of Scotland. The existence of the estate itself can be traced back to the fourteenth century. Despite having used John Smith to design and build his Union Street house in Aberdeen slightly earlier, Patrick Milne subsequently approached Archibald Simpson in 1820 to design a new house for himself on his estate, financed with the fortune he had acquired for himself trading in China and the West Indies. Unfortunately Milne died rather unexpectedly very shortly after this, the estate then passing to his kinsman Sir Charles Bannerman. The first thing therefore completed on site by Simpson was a delightful little obelisk erected in the park in 1821, commemorating the late Mr Patrick Milne.

The fine south and east fronts of Crimonmogate just prior to the imposition of a very overbearing mansard roof of additional bedroom accommodation in 1864. The portico lends the house a sense of scale which actually belies its actual size.

The very poised, originally serene design, built in finely executed Kemnay granite develops behind an extremely sober three-quarter height hexastyle Greek Doric portico firmly implanted into the centre of the main front, held by the terminal ends of both flanking wings, graced by elegant windows corniced and bracketed on the ground floor. The portico has been deliberately very simply designed with two Doric columns standing in-antis behind the principal outer rank. The capitals are also unusually small and this, together with the absence of any entasis on the columns themselves, suggests from any distance that the portico and indeed the house are actually larger than it initially appears. The shallow pediment, plain tympanum and the omission of any triglyphs or metopes also greatly contribute to the general air of simple august dignity. From the grassed avenue extending south in front of the mansion house, the pediment is seen to be crowned by the sight of the delicate little dome which illuminates the main hall immediately behind. Very unusually also the soffit of the portico is decorated with painted banded decoration in shades of violet and pink, contained within a continuous stylised floral repeat surround, which most probably dates from the time of the 1864 alterations.

Internally after a short vestibule, this gives immediate access into an extremely impressive central, perfectly cubic hall, which is dramatically enlivened with giant fluted marble painted Corinthian pilasters supporting a fine frieze, cornice and coffered ceiling. At its centre there is placed a glazed lantern dome allowing cascading vertical light. Lying immediately behind this is the old billiard room and the principal staircase, with on either side two balancing wings organised with the eastern one containing an enfilade comprising a series of extremely elegant interiors, including the interlinked drawing room and morning room, and dining room beyond. The morning room in the centre, opening directly off the drawing room and sometimes now called the music room, is expanded outward into a dramatic segmental bow which once gave direct access to the garden at this side via the central window and a metal bridge over the basement sunken area. The general planning arrangement fully complies now with the more informal requirements of the day, while leaving the necessary feeling of tasteful grandeur still firmly in place. On the western side, a business room at the front preceded the master bedroom suite of two interrelated bedrooms and dressing closet, which also broke forward externally in the centre with a high chimneyed gable. Over the full first floor above, a very similar layout of further family and guest bedrooms proliferate with also the nursery, whilst below substantial kitchen and service accommodation is contained within a fully suppressed basement under the entire house, accessed by various skilfully integrated staff stairways deftly concealed within the main accommodation.

Crimonmogate today from the west, sporting its rather Germanic mansard roof addition.

In 1864, in response to the much larger families being produced at that time, a new mansard roof was placed above the old one in order to provide a further floor of additional bedrooms. Although quite cleverly done, and originally embellished with a heavily decorative wrought iron screen on top silhouetted against the sky, the result is extremely heavy and introduces an unlooked for, slightly Germanic, flavour to the exterior of the house. In addition the delicate balance of the east front was damaged as the wing was extended northwards with a single-storey extension,

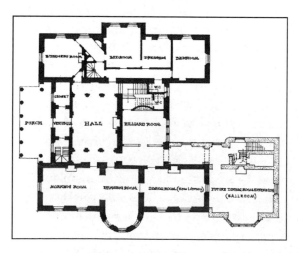

THE PRINCIPAL FLOOR PLAN:
CRIMONMOGATE

in order to create a new dining room, which was intended to double as the ballroom, complete with its own broad bay window overlooking the garden. At this point also the old dining room was refurbished as the library. A large glazed

104

The Obelisk at Crimonmogate commemorating Patrick Milne.

The south front of Crimonmogate dominating its grassed avenue.

The beamed ceiling
and glazed lantern in
the Entrance Hall.

The splendid full
height Entrance hall,
Crimonmogate.

conservatory also once extended out eastwards even behind this, which has now been entirely removed, and now partially replaced by a modern kitchen extension. The impressive and quite cavernous mid-Victorian kitchen tacked on to the basement also as part of the 1864 alterations, is consequently presently unused, awaiting some new and hopefully compatible function. Outside to the north the ground levels were considerably adjusted in order to slightly expand the rear service yard behind the house at basement level, which was successfully screened off by a high rubble wall.

In addition to the mansion house itself, like Park, the estate also boasts much other important contemporary work by Simpson executed within the next full decade. Immediately adjacent to the rear service yard is an extremely severe and simply built flat roofed rubble game larder of 1825 with cornices and brackets set over the openings. A fine laundry building of the same date now functions as the tractor store, and a little distance off a delightful octagonal ice-house nestles within the trees. This particularly handsome structure, also of rubble enlivened with margins and with openings on all of its eight facets, sits under a low pitched slated roof with broad overhanging eaves. Underneath within an

The Ice-house, Crimonmogate.

unexpected and very cool vaulted chamber, reached by a descending flight of external stone stairs, stone workbenches and an old cheese press still stand in attendance. Nearby a very substantial originally U-shaped rubble steading and stables block, built around an open-ended central courtyard also impresses, much of it built to a design by Simpson. The finally enclosing northern link range with its centrally placed matching gable and dramatic spired wooden tower is however of the mid-century. The doocot presently slightly lost within the woods some distance off seems also to be of this later date, as is a good deal of the much altered and extended largest lodge house situated at the north gate.

In addition to the essential estate facilities, Simpson also provided the design of the whitewashed dog kennels in 1834, with that of the polygonal walled fruit and vegetable garden a year later, which is now no longer unfortunately part of the estate. Most memorable however by far are the very remarkable designs he made for the two extremely fine little lodges he provided at the west and east gates.

The East Entrance drive Gate-house, Crimonmogate.

These very simple whitewashed rubble and gabled houses, both embellished with projecting low pitched overhanging roofs over walls punctured with squarish horizontal paned windows and also doors all contained within bold chamfered stone reveals, create an immediate statement of very considerable delight, originality, robustness and dignity. The east lodge in particular has also been further

The West Lodge, Crimonmogate, now a private house.

distinguished by the incorporation of a very simple four-columned proto-Doric portico placed at its entrance, seeming to anticipate its more sophisticated cousin up at the mansion house. Only a little distance off from the east lodge, Simpson was also responsible for the design of the mill-house, built there against the side of the little stream. An L-shaped structure, incorporating some interesting external Simpson flourishes, this presently unused building awaits its eventual conversion to some other useful purpose.

From Sir Charles Bannerman and his son Sir Alexander who planted the now mature woodland around the property, the estate passed through his daughter Ethel to her second son, Commander the Hon. Alexander Carnegie. From his son Major Raymond Carnegie the estate passed to the Hon. Jocelyn Carnegie before passing to his third cousin the Hon. Christopher Monckton. It was he who was responsible for initiating the programme of restoration still currently well underway, and also eventually selling the estate outside the immediate family for the first time since the house was built. At the present time the new owners of the property, the Honourable Mr and Mrs W. Stanhope, are happily and successfully completing their own very thorough programme of modernisation, restoration and refurbishment throughout the entire interior and exterior of the house. In addition they are also most anxious to recreate the immediate surrounding gardens and rescue the adjoining estate woodland, a task also now well underway. With only a little imaginative flair, Simpson's very fine estate buildings will doubtless also be rescued as well. The Stanhopes are most certainly fully intent on revealing yet again the superb quality of this, one of Simpson's finest and most complete domestic achievements.

If all this were not enough, this same year found Simpson engaged also on the design and erection of St Giles Church, Elgin, his undoubted ecclesiastical masterpiece, and at least the equal of any Greek Revival church in the country. The initial proposal was of course fraught with difficulties, the demolition of the ancient remains of the Muckle Kirk being understandably extremely unpopular with a large section of the Elgin townsfolk. The building however appears to have been in quite a sorry state latterly, and although probably capable of rescue, there seems to have been no question in Simpson's mind that it was going to be replaced with something new, 'modern' and thoroughly Greek into the bargain.

Simpson's superb homage to the Monument of Lysicrates, Elgin.

The design however owes a considerable debt to H. W. Inwood's St Pancras Church in London which introduced the concept of the classic tower based on the Tower of the Four Winds in Athens.

The earliest authenticated record of St Giles, Elgin was in 1224. The church then comprised a nave, side aisles and a chancel, probably thatched with heather, and with a central square tower. In due course it was burned, along with the adjacent Cathedral, by the Wolf of Badenoch, but its very stout walls survived sufficient for the church to be quickly restored. In 1679 the roof collapsed and the entire nave was destroyed in consequence. Restored again in 1684, the fabric survived until around 1740, when the side aisles were removed to widen the thoroughfares on both sides to ease the passage of traffic. The old chancel, which since 1621 had operated as the Little Kirk, was also removed in 1800, leaving a rather apologetic truncated nave. The Church Heritors eventually determined on completely rebuilding the church, with almost no thought to the final cost, demanding only that the very best design and materials should be employed. By 1826, Archibald Simpson was busily engaged on the design for a completely new church to accommodate a congregation of 1200, and by the 16th January 1827, the foundation stone had already been laid. The anticipated cost was £8700, a very considerable sum of money at that time.

Simpson's side elevations on his Elgin masterpiece ably illustrate his sense of severe restraint.

St Giles Church, Elgin from the rear revealing the full drama of Simpson's Lysicrates tower.

St Giles confronts the High Street in Elgin with a superb homage to the Temple of Zeus in Olympia.

The serene and very elegant interior of St Giles Church, Elgin demonstrates Simpson's concern with pure form and surface sophistication. Note the very handsome pulpit is in fact a much later addition.

In a building period of only three years, Simpson created within a slightly tapering island site embedded in the old High Street, a monumentally austere six-bay rectangular box church, magnificently dramatised with a noble portico on its west front, while reducing into a narrower projecting vestry at its eastern end over which a supremely elegant high Grecian tower rises. The front, recalling the ancient Greek Temple of Zeus at Olympia, with a hexastyle Greek Doric portico and fluted columns, plain architrave and frieze with carefully spaced laurel wreaths, and a plain pediment above, completely dominates the western end of the High Street, which it confronts. Within the portico itself, two smaller side doors flank the monumental central door, all etched by crisply executed architrave surrounds with a simple cornice over the higher door for additional emphasis. The side elevations are treated with typical Simpson severe restraint, incorporating a rhythm of long elegant windows broken only by a broad spandrel decorated with incised Greek-key ornament where the gallery crosses each opening. Unity is maintained by taking the front frieze, cornice and a block parapet all round the building. To the rear where the walls break back, this elevation, almost as important as the front, is given a very different treatment with paired pilasters either side of the central long end window providing a feeling of great strength. This is needed to support the high box-tower set on top, which is also provided with corner pilasters on all four faces together with long central louvred belfry panels with clock faces set above. Clearly inspired by the Monument of Lysicrates in Athens, this tower supports a pepper-pot section above, ringed with free standing fluted Corinthian columns, an entablature, frieze, cornice with antefixa, and a low dome tapering and then expanding into a trifoliate flourish on top. This, despite some later competition, is still by far the finest monument on the Elgin skyline.

GROUND FLOOR PLAN
St Giles Church,
Elgin.

 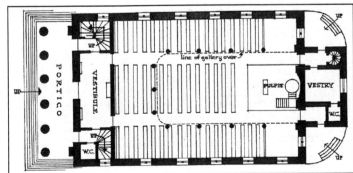

Within, a broad shallow vestibule terminates at both ends with staircases up to the gallery level whilst giving access to the church itself through a pair of arch-headed double doors, aligned on the twin interior aisles. An extremely austere note is maintained throughout in a very cool interior where ornament is used only very sparingly. The boldly axial arrangement unfolds with a rhythmic progression of five high windows, above and below the gallery, flooding the interior with light. The upper gallery, enlivened on its balcony front with a continuous bold Greek-key motif, lends a sense of scale and dignity with a succession of Doric columns also giving necessary support. The drama is terminated at the east end behind the communion table by the end wall, enlivened by a full height shallow central segmental recess, held by slightly paired giant wall pilasters for additional emphasis, recalling also something of the august exterior behind. The beautifully panelled and domed replacement pulpit, set into the central recess and supported on a single Doric column, might easily have been made for the church apart from its far too elaborate gilded balusters. It was in fact introduced only as recently as 1981, when it was removed from Newington Parish Church in Edinburgh during that church's

This general view of the interior of St Giles from the upper gallery again demonstrates Simpson's continuing sense of sophisticated elegance coupled with severe geometric restraint.

conversion into the Queen's Hall. At this time also some of the front pews were removed to allow the creation of a much larger area around the communion table, enabling the more flexible use of the space for various recitals, concerts etc, regularly held in the church.

The beamed and compartmented ceiling overhead is also particularly memorable for its sense of calm, order and extreme design simplicity. Another feature worthy of note is the cast iron framed windows, still equipped with their original glazing. The glass is embellished with a most delicate overall repeat pattern of yellowish stylised flowers surrounded by an arabesque design involving yellow flowers against a dark red background. These windows are very shortly to be fully restored. Interestingly also the church was originally illuminated at night by candles until 1831, when gas became generally available in Elgin. It was almost a hundred years later however before the lighting was provided by electricity. Originally also there was no heating until a boiler-house was created within the basement under the tower. In the early days too, only a harmonium was provided to accompany the congregation, until in 1883 a Willis organ was eventually installed. This has been enlarged and refurbished on a number of occasions before the organ was finally reconstructed and refurbished yet again in 1982 by Woods Wordsworth & Co of Leeds, when it was bravely relocated at the very rear of the church, involving also the quite unfortunate loss of the cock-loft at the back of the gallery in consequence.

Behind the pulpit at the east end, there is a vestry and a spiral stairway which affords access up to a further office and four more levels before terminating in the Lysicrates tower, in total all some 112 feet high. Within various ascending square chambers are the bells, the clock mechanism, and access to the roof. The main roof trusses themselves are remarkable for their massive timbers, which are strengthened by various cast iron rods and connections. Sadly the roof covering itself, which was originally in lead sheeting, has been totally replaced with bituminous felt some fifty years ago, when the condition of the lead began to present insuperable difficulties. Hopefully at some time in the not too distant future, this less than desirable finish may again be replaced in the originally specified lead. Further internal changes have also been carried out more recently, when like many other churches, the congregation were persuaded to remove the back rows of pews under the gallery and replace them with a partially glazed and screened off gathering area, complete with its own adjoining kitchen. This has certainly provided a useful anteroom to the church itself, no doubt necessary today when the church hall is not also accommodated on site. Despite these minor changes and even some of the more historic alterations, St Giles Elgin remains still very much as Archibald Simpson left it, a sublime and severely neoclassical masterpiece, a very fitting tribute to his unique and remarkable talent.

Back in Aberdeen in this same year, Simpson was also busy erecting Nos. 122–132 Union Street, on the eastern corner of Belmont Street. Reflecting his

122–132 UNION STREET, ABERDEEN. Scene of Simpson's office fire.

Aberdeen Hotel building on the opposite corner, this very typical four-storey frontage is given his obligatory unifying first floor string course, third floor sill stringer, and bold cornice and block parapet, all taken round into the five-window wide Belmont Street façade. Here also as usual, the chimney head is disguised as a broad panel placed on top of the parapet. As you would now expect the granite work is very good, and the detailing sharp and crisp. Unfortunately the commercial level arch-headed windows are largely no more, but this building is almost exceptional in still possessing its original fenestration above. The by now usual internal arrangement is grouped around a full height central stair serving the three upper floors and attics. When complete, Simpson moved his office into these premises. Despite now scant documentary evidence, Simpson's name has also always been associated with two further buildings on Union Street, further down on the opposite side at Nos. 95–99 and 101–105, and this attribution is most probably justified. Both these rather handsome buildings are extremely similar and occupy the full depth of the plot extending to the East Green behind. The design is typical, of three diminishing floors above a commercial ground floor, with central access doorway to a corridor and main staircase rising the full height of the building. Both five-window wide frontages have their unifying stringers, cornices, block parapets and wide central wall-head panels, but unfortunately the window astragals have all been at some time removed. Because of the differences in levels, both buildings have full basements and a sub basement below that. Indeed No. 95–99's sub basement is created in the finest ashlar tunnel vaulting, executed in a manner which would have impressed even the Romans. Both buildings display granite work to the highest standard, and an elegance of execution, which is to be expected. Internally however things are rather different, as over time both buildings have been very badly used. Nos. 95–99 in particular has had all its internal partitions completely removed while

a cast iron frame has been introduced to provide sufficient support for considerably increased commercial usage. The roof was also taken off and replaced by a slated mansard, and the entire ground floor frontage opened up and re-faced with polished granite slabs. The premises were long occupied by Grant's the National Furnishers. In the 1980s Edmondson Properties Ltd acquired the property and carried out a major refurbishment, and whilst restoring back the original slated roof, only a late Victorian street frontage was reintroduced, of dubious parentage, but happily much more appropriate than what had gone before. Nos. 101–105 had been treated only marginally better, with slightly more interesting period internal plaster and woodwork surviving, particularly at the upper levels. However, despite the retention of most of the old Princess Café interior at first basement level flanking Correction Wynd, much damage had been done with escape passageways and fire exit stairs most recently introduced between first floor and lower basement level. Acquired in the late 1990s by Scottish Life, the building has also been internally and externally refurbished, strengthened by the introduction of an internal steel frame, and given a more unified shop front treatment to Union Street. Truly, if these are indeed Simpson buildings, (which seems almost certainly the case), then only the external stonework, some of the flooring and the roof of Nos. 101–105 could now be described as his work.

The following year, 1826, found Simpson appointed architect for the Town and County Bank, and the design and erection of their premises at Nos. 91–93 Union Street. This location, centrally positioned on the building range between Correction Wynd and the projected new street down to the harbour (the future Market Street) called for something rather more magnificent, reflecting also the importance of the client and occupier. In a design owing a considerable debt to Burn's Castlegate Bank, Simpson articulated his arrangement in a five-bay façade of two diminishing upper floors, controlled by giant flat Tuscan pilasters supporting a plain architrave, frieze, bold cornice, and low plain parapet. All this was supported on a dramatically rusticated base arcade with deeply inset arch-headed windows and two doorways, outlined with plain ashlar surrounds. The inset windows at street level were boldly blocked by finely executed sculptural plinths. The bank itself fully utilised the ground floor where the impressive banking hall took up most of the available space, in addition to the first floor offices and necessary storage basements situated underneath. The side door at the eastern end of the building gave separate access up to the let out second floor accommodation and attics above. The bank premises subsequently became the offices of the Scottish Provincial Assurance Company.

Despite the efforts of the Planners, in 1971 the Town Council allowed this very accomplished façade to be demolished, the price they were apparently prepared

THE TOWN AND COUNTY BANK, 91–93 UNION STREET, ABERDEEN.

Despite very valiant efforts by the Planners and many others this important frontage was carelessly sacrificed in the 1970's to make way for the banal new façade of British Home Stores.

to pay to entice British Home Stores into the city. Given however the much greater loss of the New Market premises behind, this perhaps pales into relative insignificance. The fact that the new 'modern' frontage is banal, and quite noticeably 'faked up' to achieve the necessary scale suitable for its location, simply begs the question why the original infinitely superior frontage could not have been retained in the first place.

This year however disaster struck. Just as he had successfully settled into his new office in his newly completed building at 130 Union Street at its corner with Belmont Street, a fire starting in the grocery premises of a Mr Cooper on the ground floor, quickly engulfed the entire building along with Simpson's offices above. This calamity was in no small measure due to the incapacity of the local fireman's equipment to adequately douse the flames. Indeed at one point a considerable number of citizens volunteered to form a line all the way down to the Denburn in order to pass additional buckets of water up to the scene. All was to no avail however, his drawings, schemes, collections of books on architecture and various related subjects, all going up in flames. For a practice as busy as his, this was extremely inconvenient not to say problematic, and he was also forced to temporarily move his house and office into No. 8 Belmont Street, where he began to urgently pick up the pieces. He would however shortly remove to a slightly more fashionable address at No. 22 Crown Street, (on a site now occupied by the old Post Office), before finally settling for premises in his completed Bon Accord Square area. No. 130 Union Street meanwhile, languished as an empty ruin until 1830, before work commenced on its total internal restoration and refurbishment.

Meanwhile Simpson had embarked on yet another delightful house design: that of a cubic but also asymmetrical version of his earlier Boath House type, built at Tillery near Udny. Here also we have the very early appearance of an attached kitchen and service wing, in conjunction with a much reduced basement cellarage

TILLERY HOUSE TODAY.

The old service wing to the left, which survived the fire has been converted into the main house, leaving the still burnt out shell to be sometime restored.

area under the new house. This wing is also very largely responsible for lending the house its overall very agreeable note of informality, despite the retention of a still quite formal and symmetrical main block. The entire building is built of squared granite, rendered with margins and with its principal elements carried out in granite ashlar.

The estate had been acquired from the Udnys of Udny in 1788 by a certain John Chambers who was a successfully retired planter from the southern States of North America. The rather plain mansion house he erected on the site was however to be substantially absorbed within the service wing of the new house by his grandson's architect Archibald Simpson, leaving him absolutely free to create his fine new Grecian ensemble alongside. The interior consisted of a well-integrated suite of elegantly restrained reception rooms, developed around a cupola and a circular main stairway. The basically finely balanced main block was also given considerable emphasis externally by the inclusion of a single-storey tetrastyle Doric portico proudly proclaiming the front doorway. Above, a floor of bedrooms was introduced, crowned by a continuous cornice and low blocking parapet broken by his usual broad panels, placed centrally as required. On the return south elevation, the almost repeated three-bay design is boldly

TILLERY HOUSE IN ITS HEYDAY.

This design introduced a more informal massing with a service wing extending out to the left in preference to the previously all-embracing basement of some of his earlier houses.

punctuated in the centre by Simpson's now favourite half round, three-windowed full height two-storey projecting bow, effectively expressing the principal drawing room, with the lesser drawing room and dining room placed on either side. As usual also his low, piended slated roof nicely capped the overall design. Unfortunately for Tillery however, in 1936 a careless servant consigned the main block to the flames, a long drought ensuring that the local fire brigade had insufficient water to extinguish the fire. Only the service wing was left intact and still habitable. Currently lived in by Mr and Mrs L. Moffat, the saveable, but hauntingly gaunt shell of the old mansion house still awaits hopefully its sometime rehabilitation, when it will successfully again complement its well restored service wing.

At the same time, a good deal further to the north at Fochabers, we find Simpson engaged in work for the old Duke of Gordon at Gordon Castle, maintaining what would develop into a long and fruitful connection with the Gordon Family and their Estate. His immediate task would be the commission to erect the East Lodge, terminating an important axis created by East Street within the town, and supervising the rear entry into the estate and the proposed

THE EAST GATE LODGE, CASTLE GORDON, FOCHABERS.
This delightful octagonal tower terminating the axis of East Street in the town, owes a great deal in its design to the Tower of the Winds in Athens.

future Home Farm complex, then under active consideration. On this occasion something necessarily grand and immediately striking was required at this important access point from the town side, striking also an appropriately distinguished note. His compact and original design, possibly owing something to Playfair and probably a good deal more to the Tower of the Winds in Athens, revolves around a two-storey eight-sided tower equipped with a low slated octagonal roof overhead with its broad overhanging eaves adding considerable extra drama. The very long elegant ground floor windows are enlivened with crisply executed cornices with end brackets, and all the windows are glazed horizontally throughout, in a manner which would continue to enjoy a considerable vogue with Simpson. The boldly projecting porch to the main front is punctuated with a dramatic, deeply recessed arched opening about the main door, with a typical Simpson little Grecian pediment placed overhead. Meanwhile a further single-storey subservient wing also with over-sailing eaves, extends outwards to the rear, successfully completing an extremely distinguished asymmetrical ensemble.

The year 1827 commenced with Simpson also receiving two outstanding and extremely important commissions for mansion houses in Angus, one near Brechin and the other just north of Arbroath. Stracathro House, a late but spectacular classical exercise near Brechin, and one of his largest house commissions, was designed for Alexander Cruickshank, who had recently acquired the estate on the death of his father who had amassed a considerable fortune in Jamaica. Built to a compact but deep centralised plan, as a basically two-storey expanded rectangular box in sandstone, Simpson organised his now typical two-window wide ends, to contain a broad recessed in antis Graeco-Roman Corinthian porch, punctuated in the centre by a magnificent advancing tetrastyle portico as porte cochere. The design, including the five-bay side elevations and the plain but matching rear, is unified by a continuous plain frieze, bold cornice and balustrade, which effectively hides the roof, lending the mansion the air almost of a public building. This is the first instance of Simpson using this device, as he usually liked to make a feature of his roof, however little, above the parapet. The rear facade, plain but still distinguished, sits above a fully exposed but only half deep service basement brought out to form a terrace across the state room frontage, supported on rusticated arches. The staff bedroom accommodation in the roof far above this centre block is contained within a much later added slated mansard.

Internally the long august vestibule between the library and the business room leads directly from the carriage porch into the magnificent central Roman tribune,

The imposing entrance front of Stracathro, having acquired its single storeyed wings.

The splendid segmentally curved principal drawing room ceiling, Stracathro.

The august Tribune hall at Stracathro, an interior of Roman gravity.

Stracathro's sandstone allowed Simpson greater design freedom than
his more usual granite.

The Stable-Block at Stracathro, incorporating one of Simpson's favourite
doocot towers.

Letham Grange,
with only the
barest bones of
Simpson's centre-
block surviving

a high noble rectangular space in yellow scagiola, reduced to a square by flanking screens of Corinthian columns. A glazed central oculus in a vaulted ceiling allows vertical light to illuminate the dramatically patterned black and white marble floor. This gives on to a magnificent enfilade of state rooms with drawing room, saloon and dining room all arranged en suite. These rooms continue the imperial tone with remarkable plasterwork compartmented ceilings, the one in the saloon being a segmental arch allied to a screen of Corinthian columns across the terrace front. The quality of the woodwork with its guilloche enrichment and the marble chimneypieces throughout is also equally superb. Terracotta, black, muted green, gold, stencilling and gilded leather vie with one another within exquisitely detailed Graeco-Roman classicism. On either side of the vestibule towards the front, a beautiful library balances the parlour, while beyond that, fine suites of bedrooms and family rooms predominate. The principal stair is also extremely fine in a full height top lit chamber with delightful wall paintings set against Pompeian red and muted green. Balusters garlanded in gilded ivy enliven the stair flights. Upstairs, although the scale as always diminishes, a marvellous spinal corridor of receding arches and shallow domes in a manner clearly inspired by Dance and Soane, introduces restrained but elegantly designed family and guest bedrooms. Above this level predominately female staff accommodation is located within the mansard roof already mentioned, while below in the extensive basement mostly male staff, kitchen and service facilities are found.

Beautifully integrated but slightly later matching wings of 1840 complete with tetrastyle anta order attached porticoes and pediments, extend the magnificence of

The somewhat altered and considerably extended rear elevation of Stracathro reveals the significant fall in levels between the front and the back of the mansion. Note the terrace formed over the lower service basement creates a superb viewing platform for the main state room enfilade immediately behind it.

the state rooms into a beautiful cast iron glazed roof conservatory to the south balanced by a billiard room, smoking room and pantry to the north. To the rear, both these wings sit up upon rusticated arched basements, matching that of the main house itself. In addition to the Mansion House, Simpson was also responsible for the very fine quadrangular stables built slightly to the west within the estate, complete with central doocot tower and a noble pedimented arched entry. The two-storey block, with a typically low first floor loft in the now usual Simpson manner, is faced with sandstone ashlar enlivened with a finely channelled, coupled antae triglyph frieze. A half-moon walled garden, a gardener's cottage, various gateways and a separate laundry building all within the magnificent grounds, complete a very remarkable architectural ensemble. The property was eventually acquired by Sir James Campbell in 1874, and it was his eldest son the Rt. Hon. James Alexander Campbell who further enlarged the estate and provided much of the very fine furnishings of the house. His great grandson, Lt. Col. W. J. Campbell Adamson of nearby Careston Castle, inherited the property in 1934, but unfortunately both the house and 203 acres of the grounds were taken over under threat of requisition to the Government in 1949, in order to further accommodate expanding Stracathro Hospital at the end of the Second World War. The beginnings of the hospital itself initially commenced its own rather separate existence in 1939. The Mansion house, still surviving today in remarkably good condition, served as the home of the resident hospital doctors until comparatively recently. The property is however at the time of writing up for sale, with the tantalising prospect that this very remarkable and considerable Archibald Simpson achievement may yet be fully restored to something of its former magnificence.

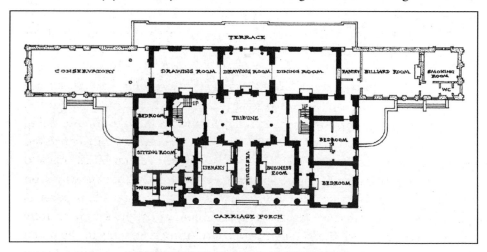

THE PRINCIPAL FLOOR PLAN: STRACATHRO

Meanwhile not very many miles to the east, at Chapelton just north of Arbroath, Simpson was also busy with the design and erection of yet another of his very restrained boxes, that of Letham Grange. The property had just been acquired by John Hay, an ex-Provost of Arbroath, who had successfully combined both the estate of Letham with that of Grange next door. Letham went back into the mists of time when it was the property of Arbroath Abbey and was first mentioned in a grant of 1284 to Hugo Heem. By the middle of the sixteenth century it had reverted back to the Abbey and there it stayed until the middle of the eighteenth century. At about the same time the adjoining Lands of New Grange were acquired by John Demster and eventually passed to

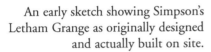
An early sketch showing Simpson's Letham Grange as originally designed and actually built on site.

his son 'Honest' George who was forced to relinquish them rather suddenly in order to raise the necessary money for him to pay a £30,000 fine for bribery at the General Election, where he had intended to become Member for Perth Burghs. Bought by William Moir of Lonmay, after only two generations, the Lands were available for sale again. Once conjoined with Letham however, John Hay embarked on a tremendous programme of improvements: drainage, establishing the lake and planting thousands of trees around and throughout the grounds. In the centre, on the edge of a commanding natural terrace overlooking the Vale of Brothock he elected to replace a much earlier edifice, asking Archibald Simpson to design and erect a modern mansion house. Being a bachelor, the initial house was not terribly grand, the design being conceived in purely geometric terms as a bold five-bay two-storey central block, flanked on the entrance front by low three-bay square apparently roofless wings on either side, framing a rather original façade ennobled by giant plain pilasters supporting a broad Grecian pediment. The accommodation sat on a fully suppressed service and kitchen basement, incorporating fragments of the much earlier house on the site. The fine sandstone ashlar was finely wrought around all Simpson's very elegant, elongated ground floor windows, with exquisite architrave surrounds, cornices and brackets. To the rear the garden façade was dominated in the centre by a magnificently bowed giant Ionic portico, rising the full height of the house up to the parapet, above which was placed a lovely hemispherical dome. Internally around an elongated central hall, the principal en suite reception rooms comprised a quite small saloon in the centre flanked by the rather elegant rectangular drawing room and dining room on either side on the garden front. The wings contained the parlour and library to one side and the master bedroom suite and estate offices on the other.

Simpson's typically restrained and pedimented centrepiece with single storey flanking wings are still just discernable underneath a wealth of neo-Baroque extravagance which later overloaded the house.

Unfortunately this very restrained and chaste exercise, now only really existing in prints, lies somewhat buried beneath slightly later accumulations after the property was acquired by James Fletcher in 1877. A man of very considerable enterprise and wealth, having gained a fortune allegedly by marrying one of the daughters of a schooner skipper named Fletcher, he was actually born the son of William Jack in Avoch. Multiplying his wealth dramatically in 'marine insurance' and some other grey areas, he returned to Scotland in due course and bought the estates of Letham Grange and Rosehaugh in the Black Isle. Obviously totally unimpressed by elegant Grecian restraint and finding a bachelor pad far too small for his family-sized requirements, he immediately set about the almost complete transformation of the mansion, employing John Robertson assisted also by John Rhind (an architect from Inverness), for the purpose. By a stroke of good or bad fortune, over time the new work has weathered to a noticeably greyer hue than Simpson's original beige sandstone, making the 'additions' quite easily discernable. The main rooms to the garden front were both considerably enlarged and provided with central bow windows, the original portico and dome were reconstructed supporting now a high box-tower, and on each side the enlarged wings were also heightened by the addition of a floor of bedrooms. An entrance porch and quarter quadrants were introduced at the front while a large conservatory was also moored alongside the newly enlarged withdrawing room. Perhaps the most obvious design departure on the house was however the introduction of very heavy stone balustrades and parapets taken all around both the older and newer work, in an attempt to achieve some unity. The roofline, now pierced with many urns and finials on top of this, bristles in vigorous, almost Baroque agitation, presided over by its great square tower, suggesting from a distance anything but a work by Archibald Simpson. However all was not entirely lost. Internally a completely new galleried stair was created, while on the ground floor especially, everything that might have been restrained was swept away in favour of high-Victorian considerable excess. The much more spacious circulation and rooms were re-plastered, many pitch pine ceilings introduced, while heavily gilded leather ceiling and wall coverings enriched the reception rooms, all finished beautifully with carved timber dadoes, folding doors and chimney pieces. The additional family rooms were equally grand, if slightly more intimate, while on the bedroom floor above many new rooms at both ends greatly increased the level of sleeping accommodation. Also within the magnificently maturing grounds a walled garden and stables were erected as well as a vast greenhouse built to supply the family with all the flowering and fruiting exotica they could possibly wish for. In 1977, the house and estate was bought from the Fletcher Trust and was converted successfully into a Hotel and Conference Centre. This is arranged around two beautiful golf courses created out of the grounds, as well as a Curling Centre, and areas of discretely distributed but tastefully designed modern residential villas.

It was also in 1827 that we first hear mention of a scheme for a central city improvement to create a new thoroughfare between the gate of Old Marischal College and the spire of St Nicholas Church, through the area of slums existing at the back of Broad Street, Guestrow and Flourmill Brae. In his report to the Commissioners regarding the possible rebuilding of the college itself, Simpson mentions this proposal also as a desirable civic improvement worthy of consideration. Despite being mooted subsequently twice again, this particular initiative failed to attract any interest.

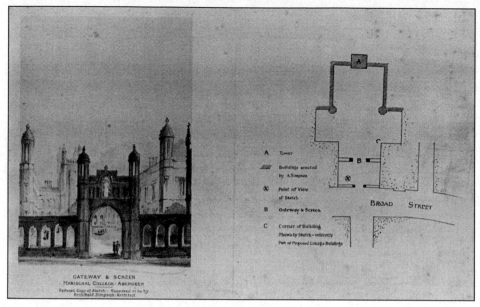

SIMPSON'S ULTIMATE BROAD STREET, PROPOSALS IN ABERDEEN.

Despite more than one attempt to symbolically link the main Gateway of Marischal College with the spire of the Church of St Nicholas, neither the gate or the necessary thoroughfare materialised.

In this same year Simpson was persuaded to become a member of the Aberdeen Artists Society, an organisation established primarily by his great friend James Giles. Dedicated to "the mutual improvement of painting and the furtherance of the arts generally in Aberdeen", apparently the only requirement for membership was that you had to be "of fair moral character". The most onerous condition of membership however was that work had to be submitted on an annual basis for a major exhibition held in the city. In fact there is no actual record of Archibald Simpson ever having submitted any architectural drawing or even a perspective for the show, although latterly he did send along the occasional model of some scheme he was currently working on. Of course at this particular date it is extremely unlikely that anyone would have considered an architect's drawing to be a work of art in itself.

The following year 1828, Simpson was working on a much more modest mansion of quite a different character, this time executed in a completely astylar no-nonsense, rather more Italianate manner at Pitlurg, just north of Ellon in

Aberdeenshire. Now more usually known as the House of Leask, the ordered rhythm of extremely elegant windows around its two-storey main block is held under a low pitched roof again provided with bold broad eaves. As more usual also now, a lower scaled two-storey service wing (but still built in this instance set over a basement) was incorporated, provided also with its own low pitched roof and

THE HOUSE OF LEASK (PITLURG).
Originally entirely rendered, this very understated house has recently been completely and imaginatively restored following its total consignment to the flames as long ago as 1928.

terminating gable, successfully completing an overall asymmetrical composition. In the external treatment of the three principal facades, here Simpson exercised very considerable restraint, the whole enterprise relying entirely on order, rhythm and beautiful proportions, enlivening a basically quite plain mansion. The only very slightly wider opening accommodating the door on the main front, provided the merest hint of a central emphasis. The unusually very long ground floor windows, here taken almost right down to the floor of the principal reception rooms, also lent an airy feel to the very elegantly restrained suite of interiors. The south front was additionally enlivened also by the incorporation of one of Simpson's now almost obligatory central bows swelling out in the centre. The exterior was also for very many years completely rendered throughout, and remained so indeed until the completion of the recent restoration.

The house was initially designed and built for General Gordon Cumming, but was tragically completely burnt out in 1928 following a disastrous fire. The stark ruin was acquired in 1987 by Mr and Mrs D. Gaucci, who very courageously embarked on an extremely ambitious programme of reconstruction and restoration within the basic existing shell of the house, recreating in the process much of its original interior. At present the main block, which for its modern manifestation has not been re-rendered, is now virtually completed and inhabited except for the still ruinous adjacent service wing, which awaits its eventual salvation. Presently further restoration work is continuing on an adjacent outbuilding, which is being made into a garage block.

In the recreation of the interior, the rear entrance has acquired a rather greater prominence than before with the modern kitchen and en suite dining arrangement established on either side of the back door. The principal bow room to the south has however been extended well back into the house through an internal screen of Tuscan columns to create an extremely impressive apartment, while the east range has been virtually recreated basically as before as two elegant rooms on either side of the old main doorway which now functions principally as an entry from the garden. A modern staircase gives access to bedrooms above. The surrounding enclosed policies, a mere shadow of their former condition, are still there to be brought back to something of their original glory. Unfortunately much of the vegetation which once framed the mansion itself has been entirely lost save for a few mature trees, and the main entrance driveway from the east is no more. The outstanding restoration work here however remains a considerable testament to the vision, commitment and courage of the owners, and hopefully also a very pertinent inspiration to others.

This year also found Simpson rather urgently back at Gordon Castle however, on this occasion engaged in the complete restoration of the East Wing, which had been very badly damaged in a fire. This particular catastrophe, following on as it did very swiftly after the unfortunate death of the old Duke himself, required immediate reconstruction work to be put in hand. At this time of course the Castle was still a great Renaissance Palace complete with huge classical wings originally designed by John Baxter in the mid-eighteenth century. These extended out on both sides to present a very remarkable frontage 538ft long. Not then for nothing was this great pile described as the most magnificent edifice north of the Forth. While refurbishing much of the wing in a rather more up-to-date revamped version of the old arrangement, all for the not inconsiderable sum of £3,260, he took the opportunity of comprehensively rearranging the original centre to create a dramatic domed and top-lit first floor rotunda, originally intended to serve as the chapel. This fine space was however only the climax of a spatial sequence beginning on the ground floor below, with an octagon created as prelude to the stairway, climbing up the periphery. Despite being wholly internal, the old chapel is now used as a drawing room, giving direct access into the adjoining sequence of Simpson reception rooms.

The East Wing of Gordon Castle as restored after a fire by Archibald Simpson.

Gordon Castle itself however has fared rather badly since Simpson's time, the Dukedom itself dying out with the Fifth Duke in 1836. The Estate was then inherited by the Duke of Richmond and Lennox, who unfortunately considered the castle to be only his secondary seat, much to its eventual detriment. In due course the castle was sold to the Government in 1938 to pay off death duties, and by great misfortune found itself used by the British Army during the Second World War. Like many another house in a similar position, by the time that the Gordon Lennox family bought it back in 1953, its condition was such that most of the Renaissance centre block was riddled with dry rot and had to be demolished, save for the most historic squarish high tower. In consequence almost the whole of the east wing and only part of the west wing, found themselves suddenly left very much in glorious isolation. The East wing continues to be lived in however and is embraced by beautiful lawns and gardens, surrounded by a still magnificent estate.

1828 commenced with Simpson setting his mind again to the problem of creating a suitable layout for the Skene lands at the Damlands to the west of Aberdeen. Rejecting the complexity of Elliott's original proposals, he envisaged a much simpler basic arrangement. Confronting the new Alford Road (Albyn Place) with a long, well set back terrace, this was broken at two points with north-south streets, connected just south of the old Skene Road by an imposing crescent. After only mild interest, and no actual take up, these proposals were destined to gather dust in Simpson's office for a few years more. Meanwhile as Crown Street continued its southward way down to the old Dee Village at the bottom, Simpson's name has been associated in the past with the design of at least some of this street, as well as a set back cottage-style block at Nos. 134–138. The frontage of this particular exercise is raised high above a slightly suppressed basement but with three entrance doors, the centre one provided with a segmental arch, holding the interest, and with recessed panels set into the granite ashlar above both the flanking doors. This centrepiece is balanced on either side with one-bay arrangements with windows, at basement, and ground floor, with at first floor further windows as small dormers set within the slated pitched roof. The fine balance here however has been more recently badly marred by the very unfortunate introduction of a selection of 'modern' designed windows and doors.

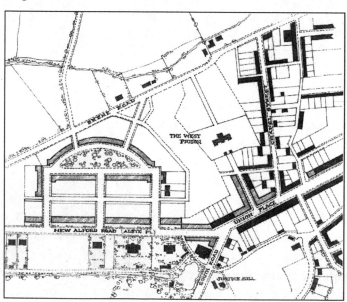

Simpson's modified layout plan for the Damlands of Rubislaw in the West End of Aberdeen. In the event only a tentative start was made on this proposal before it was eventually abandoned.

1828 is also notable for the advancement of an idea in Aberdeen that Archibald Simpson and John Smith should combine their remarkable talents in order to achieve an appropriate architectural climax to the western end of Union Place, at Holburn Junction. The scheme envisaged the design of a very noble church, capable of accommodating a congregation of 1,400, placed axially on the triangular site bounded by Alford Place, Wellington Place (Holburn St) and Alford Lane, and dramatically punctuated by a commanding tower, some 150 ft high. In the event nothing seems to have become of this bold initiative, the Union Street terminating tower in question, having to wait until Christ College was erected by Thomas Mackenzie on the rear part of the site in 1850. The anticipated church, (replacing the old Free Church in Huntly St.), also materialised eventually as Gilcomston South Church, the last building actually to be built on Union Street itself in 1868, but at the corner of Summer Street.

In 1829, Simpson was again in the north, where he was occupied with the design and construction of the very extensive new Home Farm complex for the Trustees of Castle Gordon Estate at Boghead, just to the east of Fochabers. These

An august Triumphal archway creates the entry into the courtyard of the impressive Home Farm complex at Castle Gordon, Fochabers.

buildings, among the most ambitious and sophisticated farm buildings he ever built, but which are no longer required by this great estate, are currently occupied by G. A. Duncan & Sons, operating their grain business, farming interests, and an engineering firm as well from the premises. Boghead is a most impressive farming ensemble, which although carried out in the typically economical Simpson

In a design successfully unified with many overhanging eaves and gables, arch-headed windows, lunettes and various granite margins and stringers are thrown into relief today by the coating of terracotta coloured paint, subsequently liberally applied to Archibald Simpson's rendering.

manner, successfully combines low-pitched slated roofs, harled walls, stone margins and dressings within a composition embracing a bold stone triumphal arched entry, held between long symmetrically designed wings on either side, punctuated with an advanced pair of gables. Unusually but understandably also in this quality of estate, rather more expensive stone architraved round arch-headed windows have been employed on the long flanking elevations, unifying the ground floor windows with their smaller relatives directly above illuminating the upper loft space. Through the central stone archway, an extremely spacious courtyard is entirely surrounded with an assorted array of originally farm related buildings. All this is achieved of course within his normal and basically symmetrical plan arrangement. The rendered finish to the walls has of late also been given a new coating in a quite strong terracotta colour, which while not in itself unattractive, might have amused Archibald Simpson.

Adjoining this complex, another much more modest U-shaped cowshed building was executed in a broadly similar manner, the cross fall over the site rather spoiling any pretensions it might have had originally to symmetry, on paper at any rate. Over the road, a semi-detached cottage also designed by Simpson still survives, complete with rendering, margins, cornices with brackets over windows, and dormers breaking up into the slated roof above. The pair has been successfully extended out to the rear more recently in order to successfully embrace modernity, including the provision of bathroom and kitchen extensions.

A little further west at Forres in this same year, he also embarked upon some alterations to the old Freemasons' premises when they were elevated to the status of the Town Hall. Creating a very august double cube, echoing something of his Crimonmogate vestibule, pillastered walls, a compartmented ceiling and a central

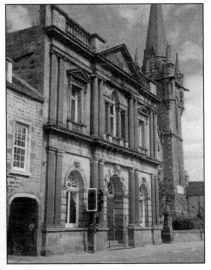

THE FORMER TOWN HALL BUILDING, FORRES.

This Simpson design was subsequently very heavily overloaded when the building eventually became the Mechanic's Institute.

Simpson's surviving hall ceiling, now seen through a plethora of heating panels and light fittings.

glazed roof lantern complete a quite distinguished chamber. The preceding entrance hall and stair also serve a small upper gallery, set above a low Ionic screen introduced into the side wall. By 1855 however, the building had become the Mechanic's Institute, introducing a programme of extensions built on to the rear and by 1901 a major external makeover rather swamped the original frontage in any event with a rather showy kind of heightened classicism. Internally however the hall survived intact and it has now happily returned to fulfil its originally intended local function.

Meanwhile in August of this same year in a dreadful storm, a deluge etched in the local memory forever as the Muckle Spate, proceeded to descend upon this region. In its wake, in addition to widespread surrounding devastation, two arches of the 1804 Spey Bridge over the river at Fochabers were completely swept away, forcing the immediate reintroduction of the old ferry as a temporary expedient.

Back in Aberdeen, the perceived need to facilitate an improved crossing of the River Dee much farther to the east than that provided by the old bridge, and also improving at a stroke the access to both the Torry and Nigg areas, eventually persuaded the Council to put the resolution of the matter out to competition. Although no record of the drawings now exist, papers found in Simpson's office at his death clearly indicated that he and John Smith had been in competition over the design of the new bridge, which was intended to be built at the point of the narrowing of the river at Craiglug. In the event of course Smith won the competition with his noble suspension bridge, which still manages to span the river despite its fast deteriorating present condition. In addition to the pylons and the approaches however, Smith was also responsible for almost three miles of very difficult access road construction on both sides. Samuel Brown was appointed the engineer in charge of the engineering aspects for the suspension span, while the metalwork was designed and manufactured at the nearby Abernethy Iron Foundry on the banks of the river just to the east. Hopefully this structure is not destined to eventually join Simpson's Triple Kirks as yet another unfortunate ruin, monument to the apparent current indifference towards the work of this city's greatest architects.

At this time also to the north of the city at Woodside, the considerably developing Mill-Town there in the shadow of Barron's Mills, Grandholm Mills and Gordon's Mills, felt itself increasingly in need of a Chapel of Ease to more conveniently serve the growing community. Up to this time the poor villagers

WOODSIDE CHAPEL OF EASE

An exercise both in extreme economy and architectural restraint, this very simple and august building regrettably has now been converted into flats internally.

had to walk all the way to St Machar's Cathedral in the Aulton, a distance of almost two miles, twice every Sunday and in all weathers. As early as 1828, a committee of the most notable parishioners got together to investigate the matter and by early 1829, Simpson's design for the building had been accepted and the work immediately instructed to commence. The site selected was at the top of Queen Street directly off the new Great North Road. The shortage of funds being paramount, the extremely simple but august design very ably illustrates yet again Simpson's natural ability to create a very great deal out of very little. The walls of the imposing rectangular box are of squared rubble, with dressed margins provided around the arch-headed windows, which progressively march down both sides. The principal façade is similarly treated with identical single arch-headed windows placed on either side of a wider central arched doorway, complete with a transom and very elegant inset quarter Tuscan columns. Above, a continuous all round ashlar stringer is placed directly under the gutters, the gables on the front and rear ends thereby treated almost as giant pediments with their dressed moulded surrounds, defined also by the pitch of the low slated roof. At the back, a single-storey extension in the centre swells out as an external expression of the pulpit and presbytery behind. Again we have a very real piece of simple architecture, full of elegance and grace, exploring sophistication, colour, texture and basic form, in the most economical of manners and using the cheapest possible building materials, with the exception only of the most minimalist ashlar details.

WOODSIDE CHAPEL
OF EASE

An exercise both in extreme economy and architectural restraint, this very simple and august building regrettably has now been converted into flats internally.

Internally the church was also particularly successful with its width exaggerated by a U-shaped upper gallery supported upon beautifully wrought Doric columns. The spacious interior was flooded with light by tall arch-headed windows, highlighting the low relief decorative panels on the ceiling. Additional unity was provided by the insistent large scale Greek key ornament taken all around the face of the gallery front, aping its successful introduction earlier at Elgin. The pews, executed along with the rather grand axial pulpit in dark stained mahogany, were set out on either side of a centralised section, determining two side aisles running down immediately in front of the gallery columns. The entire Chapel complex, provided with certainly one of Simpson's finest church interiors, was completed and opened on the 9th May 1830.

However misfortune was never very far away, and following the Disruption, the congregation eventually split, necessitating the building of yet another church in Woodside, and a resultant almost continual squabble over who was to be liable to pay the outstanding costs of building the initial Chapel in the first place. The building survived successfully for almost one hundred and fifty years with only the repositioning of the organ cases to both ends of the upper gallery, disturbing its interior in the early 1930s. Very unfortunately however dwindling congregations forced the eventual closure of this very fine church, which has found itself reinvented at least internally, as residential apartments, necessitating of course the complete destruction of the noble interior. More happily, apart from the imposition of new inset windows, the original extremely restrained exterior remains virtually untouched.

It should also be noted that around 1830, a small Roman Catholic Chapel made its appearance in Woodside, at the bottom of Tanfield Walk. Although much altered, the distinct bones of a broad eaved building with arch-headed windows down both sides, executed in squared rubble with granite margins, suggests at least the style of Archibald Simpson. Certain coarseness, however, in its general handling would imply that he himself was not involved, the design being much more likely to be the work of a local architectural admirer.

Back again however in Elgin in 1830 Simpson, having just completed his work on St Giles, was appointed the architect to design an Institution dedicated to General Anderson's mother's memory, for "the support of old age and the education of youth", the motto he had emblazoned above its entrance. The story of Andrew Anderson and his mother is worthy of retelling, responsible as it is for the construction of this fine building. About the year 1746, Marjorie Gilzean (or perhaps Gillian) of Drainie near Elgin became enamoured of Andrew Anderson, a youth from Llanbryde, who had just joined the Hanoverian

The east façade of the Anderson's Institution in Elgin.

Regiment which was then billeted around Elgin. Shortly of course the regiment moved on, and Marjorie and Andrew with it, to service abroad. Unfortunately Andrew died rather quickly in unknown circumstances, leaving Marjorie a widow with an infant son. By 1748 apparently she was back in Drainie to find that both her parents were dead, and that their croft was overgrown and completely neglected. Despondent, she managed to create a home for herself and her child in the sacristy of Elgin Cathedral, then about the only part of that building in a habitable condition. The room itself was only five feet square with windows and a fireplace. Some of the town's people took pity on the pair, providing them with food and clothing. When it eventually became obvious that young Andrew had some intelligence, he was even provided with a place at the local Grammar School as a 'pauper loon'. In return for this particular privilege, the boy was required to sweep out the classrooms, set the fires every morning, and to carry out any other necessary odd jobs. When he eventually left school, he succeeded in securing employment with an uncle in Llanbryde for a short period, before his probably inherited roving streak eventually found him setting off to seek his fortune and see the wider world.

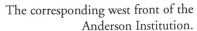

The corresponding west front of the Anderson Institution.

His talents and initiative soon bore fruit, and he quickly prospered, rising in time to become a General and also amassing a considerable fortune with the East India Company in that subcontinent. Always conscious of his humble beginnings however and the sacrifices his mother had made, by 1815 he had arranged in his Will for a Deed of Trust for the sum of £70,000 to be used to endow an Institution to be built in Elgin. The premises were intended to house fifty impoverished or orphaned children as well as giving them minimal education sufficient to secure them adult employment. In addition accommodation was to be provided for ten aged persons, who had to be over the age of fifty-five and be decent, respectable and godly. It was also a requirement of the endowment that in addition, the School should also provide free education for three hundred day pupils from the town of Elgin itself.

Unfortunately General Anderson died in London in 1824 at the age of seventy-seven, and it was only by 1830 that Elgin Town Council was ready to commence the construction of Archibald Simpson's design for the complex to be built in his memory. The site selected was on the lands of Maisondieu, then slightly to the east of Elgin, and the total allocated cost was in the order of £15,000.

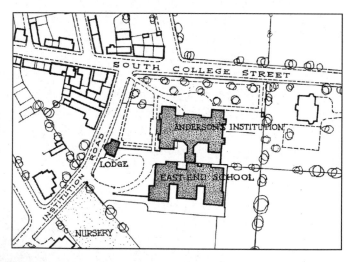

Simpson's Layout of the Institution and the East School, Elgin.

Balancing Gillespie Graham's Gray's Hospital at the other end of Burgh, Simpson obviously felt that something at least as powerful was required at the eastern entry into the town. Conceived within a basically compact H-shaped plan with an additional central leg to the rear, and constructed entirely in sandstone, the design is controlled by an all round plain frieze and heavy cornice directly under the shallow pitched slated roof. The boldly articulated two-storey elevations are also dramatically pierced with many window openings etched

The splendid central dome over the communal hall interior.

Certainly one of Simpson's most accomplished designs, the Anderson Institution in Elgin presents a most imposing front to the street, presided over by a domed pepper-pot tower for added emphasis.

The East End School, Elgin, abutting the back of the Anderson Institution behind.

The severely understated frontage of the East School, expressed as three related blocks.

The delightful little shared entrance Gate-house, on Institution Road, Elgin with architrave surrounds and brought down to the base-course on the more elongated ground floor windows. Also plain and double inset versions of the same window are used for contrast as well as for further emphasis. The window frames are also designed in his more horizontal manner, in keeping with his most usual practice at this time. In this instance too, his advancing end wings, crowned by his favourite low Greek pediments, are unusually provided within a three-window wide gable treatment. These wings successfully contain between them an extremely august entrance front, which is composed of a very bold centrepiece, set between two bay plainer ends. Paired pilasters with windows in between and with decorative panels inset over, support a recessed entrance porch with giant Ionic columns held in antis, emphasising a monumental entrance doorway, surrounded by a crisp entablature, cornice and long elegantly carved brackets. The windows at either side of this, illuminating the internal vestibule, were carefully inset into the masonry only a matter of fifty years ago. Above this and the very bold cornice, the low parapet is contained in the centre by higher blocked ends positioned only above the pilasters, and also supporting a fine central sculptural group behind which rises a high pepper-pot tower with a circuit of pilasters holding aloft a frieze, cornice and low dome. This feature however appears curiously unfinished. The basic design treatment is successfully taken virtually all around the building to the seven-bay west front and eight-bay east front, both given even further prominence by boldly projecting out the second last bays at either end. On the west these projections restrain a centrally placed single-storey five-bay Doric porch. The east elevation virtually repeats this arrangement minus the porch, and with four window bays set between the advancing second last bays instead of three.

THE ANDERSON INSTITUTION:
GROUND FLOOR PLAN

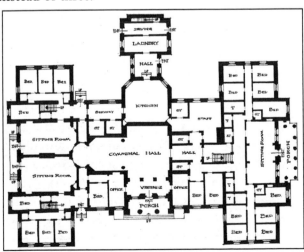

At the entrance of the building, the broad shallow vestibule accesses at either end various offices, the reception and the stairways and corridors serving the institution. Directly in front however, an arch-headed door immediately opens into an unexpectedly full height high-domed central hall, created within a very august interior space extending out to the east where the noble arch supporting the dome is held on freestanding eight-sided stone Doric-styled columns. This very impressive space is top lit by Diocletian windows, inset under the radiating flat-ribbed dome. Beyond, the central wing also extends back to embrace the kitchen, laundry and service areas, and is at least physically joined at any rate to the East End School Simpson built subsequently beyond, although it appears that there was never any connecting door between the two complexes. This very carefully considered building opened in 1832, has been successfully adapted over the intervening period by the creation of individual en suite rooms and up-to-date general facilities to create a modern residential home for the accommodation of some fifty-six people. The Institution is still also managed by a Private Trust, which now accepts also Local Authority placed residents.

In addition to the main building complex, Simpson was of course also responsible for the very charming little gate lodge constructed at the entrance and shared by both the Institution and the slightly later adjoining school. In a chaste but now slightly modified design, the lodge terminates with a chamfered end all under broad overhanging eaves and a low pitched slated roof. Its most notable feature is the twisted, spiral ribbed chimney set on top of a notional blocked pediment, emerging out of the faceted roof facing on to the street. Sadly however time has decreed that this element is now only a concrete facsimile of the original.

Also, as he was building the Anderson Institution itself, Simpson also embarked on the design and erection of the East End School, which was located on the site immediately next door, and accessed separately directly off the adjoining Institution Road. Constructed for the education of over three hundred and fifty local children, including the children from the Institution as well, the design, which took over three years to build, developed basically stylistically as a single-storey version of his adjoining Anderson's complex. The School, opening in 1833, unfolds in a very restrained symmetrical composition, built within a basic E-plan arrangement, attached to the end of the centre wing of the Institution immediately to the north. The main spine of classroom accommodation allows the projection of three further classroom wings to the south, the various resulting gabled ends being crowned by Simpson's favourite Grecian pediments set over a plain frieze, acknowledging those of the Institution itself. The central block only is also furnished with a block parapet, taken slightly to a central peak, creating the most minimal central emphasis possible. The extremely understated drama is as always, completely underscored by fine proportions, elegantly glazed windows with narrow side slips, (those on the main façade being double inset), and sharp but minimal classical details utilised throughout. Despite the fact that like most old schools, many modifications have been made over time, the integrity of these buildings is still fundamentally intact. When an increasing school roll necessitated the considerable enlargement of the premises, a completely new modern school block was built a little distance off, happily sufficiently far away not to compete with Simpson's original august statement.

Meanwhile back again in Aberdeen, Simpson commenced the building of two very distinguished houses at No. 18 and No. 20 Albyn Place. Possibly seen as something of a flanking pair even from the outset, this might suggest that the very wide site left between them may have already been earmarked for some hoped for quite prestigious later building. Both mansions are extremely similar in style and scale, and most especially in their two-storey over basement cubic ashlar mass. Their centres are similarly boldly expressed by projecting single-storey flat-topped granite porticos, that of No. 18 provided with fluted Doric

NO. 18 ALBYN PLACE, ABERDEEN.
One of the (almost) pair of fine out-riding pavilions framing the principal site left vacant on the south side of the street, awaiting a suitably important development.

granite columns, quite a novelty in the Aberdeen of the time. Following the future amalgamation of both these houses into the old Girl's High School in the early twentieth century (now Harlaw Academy), their interiors were of necessity very substantially reconstructed in the process. In the event also it was necessary for many of the windows to be fairly radically altered to comply with new internal floor levels, most especially evident on the return side elevations. This presumably was also required to meet high standards of day-lighting, at that time considered necessary for the provision of modern classrooms. Notwithstanding, the eventual ensemble was still quite sensitively handled and successfully combines together with the slightly later Mrs Emslie's Institution at its centre, to present a faintly rambling but none the less impressive frontage to the street. This has been further enhanced also by the creation of considerable front garden areas, perfectly reflecting the slightly later ones laid out subsequently on the other side of the street.

Simpson's name has also always been associated with the designs of No. 25 Albyn Place and even more especially No. 26 as well, both lying just to the west of Albyn Grove. No documentary evidence now appears to survive verifying this one way or the other, but in terms of overall design, handling of space, workmanship and fine internal treatment and detailing, these houses could certainly both be by his hand, displaying all of his most usual design characteristics of this particular period.

No. 25 has an original two-storey three-bay plain ashlar centre above a fully suppressed basement to the front, which could very easily be his, despite the imposition of a slightly heavy and later distyle single-storey pedimented portico implanted in the middle. Further advancing end wings at either side provided with very Simpsonian style pediments were carefully attached by Russell Mackenzie in 1865 and are relieved also by Simpson-style windows complete

NO. 26 ALBYN PLACE, ABERDEEN.

A very delightful villa almost certainly by Simpson carelessly damaged by the imposition of a dormer window behind the pediment.

with architrave surrounds, brought down to the base-course in the case of the ground floor openings. Some in addition are even highlighted with stylistically compatible cornices and console brackets, placed over their heads. The interior, which has long been converted for office use, is still reasonably well preserved, if somewhat altered.

No. 26 next door is even more delightful, and carried out in a square compact design reminiscent of the villa manner more usually associated with John Smith. The main rooms are however set up upon a semi-suppressed basement, under an all embracing slated pavilion roof which also accommodates the less important bedrooms. The three-bay front is dominated by a projecting distyle timber fluted Doric portico, established centrally at the head of a broad flight of granite steps. The design is very well controlled, with under the eaves, a plain frieze carried right across the smooth ashlar walls, contained by elegant flat corner pilasters provided to terminate the composition at either end. Unfortunately over time, some subsequent owner, anxious to create perhaps some additional bedrooms, has seen fit to irrevocably damage the original exquisitely simple frontage, by imposing a broad box-dormer immediately above the apex of the portico, much to the overall detriment of the house. Notwithstanding, the entire arrangement simply reeks of Archibald Simpson, an impression even further heightened, if that were possible, on entering. The particularly well preserved and quite recently restored interior rooms and circulation, simply underline all the reasons for its architectural attribution to Simpson in the first place. Here elegantly cool spaces, exquisitely restrained plasterwork, and very fine timberwork, effortlessly combine with extremely delicate neoclassical detailing to create a most memorable neoclassical architectural ensemble.

Further to the west over the Tyrebagger Hill at Kinellar, Simpson found himself employed also almost continuously between 1830 and 1835, carrying out a number of essential but fairly mundane commissions, for necessary and additional modern farm related buildings around the existing Caskieben House. These included designs for its Home Farm complex and various new residential buildings and cottages for staff, to be erected upon its then much more extensive surrounding estate, for Alexander Henderson. The property was of course once part of the vast Lands of Cordyce, centred on Caskieben, which at that time was a substantial fortified house located at Keithhall near Inverurie. Granted to the Johnstones in 1316 by a Charter from King Robert the Bruce, over time the Keiths acquired much of the land until the remaining but still large estate comprised only the Tyrebagger hill and all the territory between Blackburn, Dyce and the River Don. At this time also the ancient name of Caskieben was transferred to the site outside

The Home Farm
Stable-block at
Caskieben,
Blackburn.

Blackburn. Latterly the property was in the hands of the Burnett family until in 1792 it was sold to Dr John Henderson. He had only recently returned from Jamaica where he had made his fortune in sugar. By 1814, the house and estate had passed to his son Alexander, and it was he who commissioned Archibald Simpson to advise and design the various new buildings.

It seems almost inconceivable that an architect of Simpson's standing at that time, and one who was also extremely busy in this period, would have been particularly interested in accepting a relatively small commission involving only the design and building of a modest complex of farm buildings and three variously sized estate houses. The distinct possibility certainly remains that he might well have been asked initially to extend Caskieben House itself, the original structure being only an extremely plain, smallish, mid-eighteenth century affair. Of two and a half storeys, three bays wide and with a pedimented and pilastered door as its only redeeming feature, the roof was crowned with a central attic and gablet placed high overhead. This very simple original core most certainly eventually boasted a later pair of single-storey balancing wings, tantalisingly complete with very Grecian pediments, which might just suggest Simpson's own personal contribution, long before the entire edifice was tragically consigned to the flames around 1910. The present very stylish replacement house, which apparently still incorporates a very small portion of the original, dates from the subsequent rebuilding. In consequence now with any degree of certainty, only the estate buildings and cottages bear testament to Simpson's considerable talents in that area, as now evidenced at Caskieben Estate.

The former Laundry and Staff accommodation wing for the Home Farm complex at Caskieben Estate.

Executed in his usual reduced Classical style and generally under an all embracing over-sailing slated roof, he created most of the Home Farm Stable block building and designed and built the Factor's House, along with a small unrelated cottage, and a distant farmhouse. The Home Farm building itself as built by Simpson, originally comprised a U-shaped single-storey squared granite main block slightly west of the pre-existing earlier farmhouse, and extending down the hill where it developed into a two-storey returning wing. This latter element contained behind a segmentally arched door, the harness room, and behind two further arched door openings, additional spacious storage for two coaches, placed immediately next door. A substantial grain store was positioned overhead, servicing both by gravity and water power a threshing mill also situated below, and accessed from both the higher ground to the rear and the lower courtyard to the west. This also necessitated digging the building well into the slope, resulting in the creation of at the same time, a higher and lower open yard on either flanking side. To the east of this at the far end of the original stables range, he also built a balancing storey and a half cottage cum laundry building. Both these particular structures were provided with oversailing low pitched roofs, horizontal stringers and feature gable windows, blocked or otherwise, crowned with cornices with brackets. The first floor cottage accommodation was also given half dormers breaking into the roof. Because of the considerable slope, the new complex conspires to create a degree of charming informality, impressively building up into a notable composition. A slightly later lower two-storey western extension with a single-storey return wing provided further accommodation in due course adding also to the picturesque nature of the scene. The buildings were subsequently adapted over time for use basically as a cowshed, until the present owner, Mr Charles Marshall, acquired the property in 1986 from the Davidson family of local paper making fame. Much restored along with the adjacent Home Farmhouse itself, this fine complex of buildings is now primarily used as stabling for horses.

Some distance off to the north, on a magnificent tree encircled site overlooking the valley of the River Don, astylar Bendauch was built originally as the Factor's House for the estate in a beautifully controlled storey and a half, T-shaped arrangement ending in three terminating gables under an all embracing

THE FACTOR'S HOUSE, CASKIEBEN.
A delightful house of very considerable charm, a later doorway and a flat roofed kitchen extension to the rear damages its perfectly judged sense of assurance.

overhanging low pitched slated roof. The suppressed partial basement supports basically rendered walls with stone stringers and margin surrounds, cornices and brackets about the doors and most of the windows, with neat little arch-headed windows tucked high up on the gables under the projecting roofs. Containing a drawing room, dining room, parlour and work room on the main floor, with bedrooms above and kitchen with storage below, the house has survived almost intact, save for the slightly unfortunate addition of a flat roofed modern kitchen extension, tacked on to the rear. Even further round the estate, facing towards the far off village of Dyce, Simpson also designed Standing Stones, an extremely simple but still charming little two-storey three-bay cottage with an original single-storey wing extending out to the rear. Although the front has been very

The Mains of Dyce Farmhouse, Dyce.

slightly diminished by the inclusion of a not altogether insensitive modern porch, the end gabled and heavily eaved rendered design is still very noticeably his.

Even further off, just short of the Don Bridge to the north of Dyce itself, the farmhouse at Mains of Dyce also makes an interesting appearance in a design frequently attributed to Archibald Simpson. Designed in a somewhat neo-Jacobean style with high slated roof, and with his usual diagonally set high stone chimneys, and three typically sharp and spiky dormer heads breaking into the eaves-line, the two-storey three-bay balanced arrangement about the central hooded doorway is successfully carried out in rubble with a rendered finish and stone margins. These very interesting, varied but modest little domestic designs had all developed stylistically from his previous design experiments carried out variously at Park, Crimonmogate and at Castle Gordon Estates. Interestingly also, it seems very possible that another version of Mains of Dyce may well have found itself being built in far-off Lerwick in the Shetland Isles as late as 1846, probably as the intended residence of the local bank manager.

It is quite disturbing to note however that in 1839, his old client Dr

A very simple exercise at Standing Stones, Caskieben, rather too enthusiastically modernised in recent times.

Alexander Henderson, in his capacity as one of the managers of the Aberdeen Royal Infirmary, publicly denounced Simpson for his apparent mishandling of the affairs of the hospital contract, quite unjustifiably as it turned out. The matter revolved around the late demolition and clearing away of remnants of the old infirmary building which the contractor Rainnie apparently was very dilatory in carrying out. Simpson of course very stoutly defended himself, and Henderson was forced to make a public apology by his fellow managers at the end of the day. One wonders however what might have come to pass between Simpson and his former client for this unpleasantness to develop in the first place. Perhaps he had just sent him a note of his fee.

Archibald Simpson's name has also long been associated with the possible design of a rather handsome and distinguished mansion in the newly expanding Cuparston area of Aberdeen, built also around 1830. Named Granton Lodge it is very certainly in the 'style of Simpson' although unfortunately no evidence is now available to prove exactly who the architect actually might have been. The mansion is executed very sharply and quite unusually for Aberdeen in sandstone, in a diminishing but two storeyed rather cubic box-style, set up over a semi-suppressed basement and under a low slated roof with heavily expressed broad eaves taken all round. The three principal facades are carried out in sandstone ashlar with the back, (east elevation) in squared granite rubble with a pedimented gable in the centre. The main entrance front faced south with a broad central doorway and steps, with the western principal room façade boldly broken by a projecting half octagonal canted bay in the centre. This provided the now almost mandatory main central drawing room with a second drawing room and dining room balanced on either side of it. All the ground storey windows are also very typically long, extremely elegant and provided with cornices with finely detailed consoles all crisply executed. Sadly the central cornice to the front of the main bay has been sacrificed to accommodate a later canopy (now itself no more), and the original cast iron balconette and garden access stairway below has also been removed unfortunately along with the entire garden itself. The blanked off principal south-most main window is also unfortunate but could still be reversed. Internally, although some sacrifices have been made in the subsequent splitting up of the property into apartments, much fine plasterwork and woodwork remains in a series of still very good rooms. The house of course used

GRANTON LODGE, NOW EMBEDDED INTO GREAT WESTERN PLACE, ABERDEEN.

In a design demonstrating all of Archibald Simpson's usual refinement and attention to detail the loss of its grounds, its outlook and wrought-iron balcony has been particularly unfortunate.

to stand centrally within a delightful small garden estate, its entrance facing directly on to Cuparston Road (now Great Western Road). It was very severely hemmed in however only slightly later in the nineteenth century when the surrounding area fell victim to the relentlessly expanding mid-Victorian city. In common with a number of rather charming out-of-town villa properties, which had already begun to develop sporadically along the new Deeside Turnpike leading out of the city, the surrounding grounds were largely abandoned to the development of substantial rows of granite tenements in what would become Great Western Place and Great Western Road in due course.

Meanwhile Archibald Simpson was approached by yet another of the Aberdeen Incorporated Trades, this time the Shoemakers, to fully investigate the development potential of their considerable land holdings at Ferryhill, lying just south of the city, between it and the River Dee. Ferryhill had become something of a favoured location for quite substantial villa development even in the late eighteenth and early nineteenth centuries, as it occupied a very fine position not far from the town, enjoying at that time extremely pleasant uninterrupted views, east over the expansive River Dee estuary, and south over the distant slopes of Kincardineshire.

With houses in Crown Street now reaching almost as far down as the old Dee Village at the bottom of the hill where the Howburn breaks through to join the Dee, the Shoemakers were confident that the time was now right for them to exploit their land assets near the city in a similar manner to their Hammermen and Tailor brethren. They, as we have already seen, succeeded in pioneering a totally new concept of planned residential living in Aberdeen, at both Golden Square, and in the Bon Accord area further west. The Shoemakers' lands, lying as they did on either side of the ancient country road extending all the way up the hill to the north gate of Devanha House, had of course very great residential development potential, but like the even more distant Damlands area in the west end, still seemed to be too remote from the existing town centre at least as far as the better off citizens were concerned.

For the more observant also, the almost inevitable and inexorable encroachment of the considerably expanding harbour and all its associated industrial activities up the estuary and along the valley of the River Dee itself within this period, would also have been of very great concern, leading as it would to future problems for the successful overall residential development of the area, most particularly on its eastern and southern fringes. A major iron foundry, distillery and brewery had already made an unfortunate appearance along the northern riverbank, taking full advantage of the plentiful water supply and the easy access provided by John Smith's new roads. At this time also of course, even the remotest possibility of future railways overwhelming the area further with additional noise, tracks, marshalling yards and engine sheds, would not even have been conceivably imaginable.

For the moment however, Simpson's architectural involvement would prove to be for him only the beginning of a long association with the Ferryhill area, which he rightly foresaw would eventually become a very desirable residential suburb at the end of the day. Industry and railways would ensure that the balance would swing very firmly in favour of the west end of Aberdeen for first class residential expansion, certainly as far as the most affluent citizens were concerned at any rate. Even in the year immediately prior to his untimely death, Simpson was again recommending further planned expansion in both the Ferryhill and west end directions, as only two necessary elements in an extremely ambitious programme of civic developments and improvements he envisaged would be carried out across the whole city.

On a final note in this year, Simpson was also invited to join the exclusive Mill of Maryculter Friendly Society, which had just then formed. The society consisted of a group of most distinguished local gentlemen, intent on holding

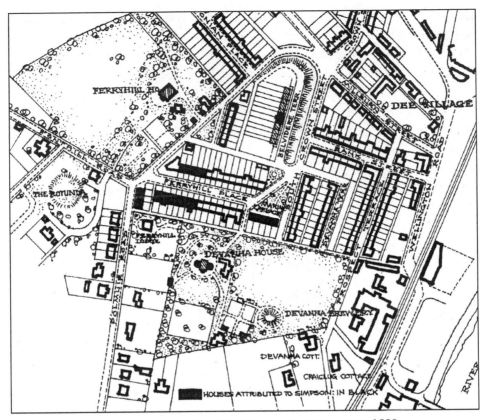

PLAN OF THE FERRYHILL DISTRICT OF ABERDEEN, CIRCA 1880.

Illustrating the various stages of development between the original suburban villas and the later arrival of the railway accompanied by associated industrial enterprises, Simpson's contribution to the area with the commencement of Ferryhill Place, Belvidere Terrace (now Marine Terrace), Marine Place and probably also the start of Devanha Terrace, certainly represents the high point in the expansion of the suburb, initially carried out for the Shoemaker's Incorporated Trade.

an annual meeting and dinner at the Mill Inn roadhouse immediately adjacent to the River Dee Bridge at Maryculter. Although the Society was conceived primarily as a club, doubtless it was also brought into being with the additional intention of greatly facilitating very private discussions on various matters of mutual interest and local importance. At this period of continuing economic buoyancy there was certainly a good deal to interest as well as concern them. In any event, the maximum number of members at any one time was restricted to twenty-one. The Society finally disbanded in the changed world of 1860.

A Fair Body of Work

Simpson's third decade commenced in the period when the City of Aberdeen had already transformed itself from a medieval Burgh into the dramatically expanding neoclassical town, which still forms the basis of the present day city centre. Most of the major new central streets and radiating turnpikes were now all in place and this allowed for the development of a scattering of small villas and mini estates around the fringes of the town, as well as a number of more industrial centres and some rather refined residential suburbs too. In addition many new streets, some of increasingly integrated house and tenement designs, were beginning to appear especially to the north and west of the city in the old Lochlands area, Rosemount, and Gilcomston. As the more well-to-do people began to invade Ferryhill and the west end to seize for themselves a more modern, orderly and gentile environment, the possibility also again arose for the development of the fully planned and integrated street, attempting to emulate similar recent achievements in both Edinburgh and Glasgow.

During this time, the growth of the granite industry was also to be of profound importance. From a position at the end of the eighteenth century when granite was considered fit only for rough walling, the material had now proved itself to be superior in both durability and strength to any other stone, and was now also workable to a remarkable smoothness, sharpness and even delicacy of appearance. In this period of change in almost every aspect of life, the industry had not been idle either, opening up new deposits, quarrying now actually much deeper into the ground, and in consequence tapping into richer, much better quality subterranean deposits. The parallel development of steam driven power also enabled the deeper quarries to pump themselves dry, while allowing cutting and polishing tools to very quickly improve. Huge quantities of granite blocks, pavement slabs and road cassies were being regularly exported to cities in the south and even as far as America, as the industry enjoyed a considerable boom. This decade would in consequence witness the erection of some of the finest granite ashlar buildings ever built in this region, with the successful attainment of the smoothest of smooth walls. There was also a noticeable increase in the use of restrained decorative elements such as moulded architrave surrounds, cornices, brackets and crisper detailing generally, as all these flourishes became more commonplace. Simpson's temperament however would still make the severely spare neoclassical terraced town house all his own, even though he would always oscillate between that and the slightly richer textural effects made possible in his equally successful but cheaper, mix and match classic rubble style.

However by this time, despite the popularity of the classical small villa introduced by John Smith, it was becoming increasingly clear that the stylistic ascendancy of the Greek Revival, was seriously on the wane. This was not yet quite the case in Scotland where, despite the early pioneering efforts of William Burn attempting to introduce full-blooded Gothic and Scotch Baronial, neoclassicism would still have room for further development well into the century in the very gifted hands of practitioners like Alexander 'Greek' Thomson and others. Increasingly during the 1830s however, the appropriateness of Greece for domestic work was being seriously questioned, the style eventually being relegated for use only in buildings of a more public or 'serious' nature. In the equally important ecclesiastic field, as well as classicism, Perpendicular or Tudor Gothic with its attraction of insistent verticals, flattened arches and fan vaulted ceilings, was shortly also to be almost completely eclipsed by a return to full Gothic. As historical romanticism as an idea increasingly seized the nation's imagination, Tudor and Collegiate Gothic also made a marked impact on the vastly expanded University and Educational Institutions now being built throughout the land, where classicism itself suddenly seemed to be out of date. These new stylistic trends of course spilled effortlessly into the domestic field, to inspire potential clients stirred by the romance of some distant past, and anxious also to be at the cutting edge of the latest fashion. The perceived need for greater informality generally was increasingly expressed in asymmetrical massing, while greater standards of relaxation and comfort dictated the emergence of less formal styles of interior decoration. Paradoxically, houses if anything became even more hierarchical in their layouts, and generally grander in terms of size and scale, in direct consequence of the increasing wealth generated by the Industrial Revolution and the expanding British Empire. Whilst desirous of achieving a suitably showy arrangement of reception rooms and bedrooms mainly to impress visitors, increasingly the family retreated to a more private suite centred round the parlour or library. The staff and service requirements were now relegated to a subservient attached wing, even if the house still retained a partial basement, increasingly used only for cellarage and storage. Even the far north-east of Scotland was no longer oblivious to these trends, and in the hands of both Simpson and Smith, important incursions would be made into all these design areas.

Simpson's middle period got underway with the redesign and rebuilding of the severely damaged bridge over the River Spey in Fochabers, a commission actually commenced in 1831. The Duke of Gordon most generously provided the necessary funds of £6,000 for the replacement of the fallen structure, and Simpson was appointed architect. As the river bed had moved to the western side over time, this condition had been largely responsible for the undermining of the central pier and the collapse of the two western arches in the first place. Simpson boldly took the extraordinary step of erecting a large single span archway clear of all obstacles complete with verticals and cross bracing all carried out in massive timber beams. The effect, although completely unexpected, is still very impressive, despite half the remaining structure surviving in stonework. However efficient and quick this solution was given the ready local supply of available timber, the structure only survived until 1853, when it was noticed that rot had set in. Restoration work was carried out but the respite proved only

THE SPEY BRIDGE, FOCHABERS

The metallic more modern version of Archibald Simpson's original wide timber span, replacing the two former stone arches which were swept away in the Muckle Spate, still spans the River Spey at Fochabers although the old bridge has now been effectively bypassed by a modern concrete version.

THE TOLL HOUSE, SPEY BRIDGE, FOCHABERS

This charming and very characteristic Simpson design has quite recently been sensitively
doubled in size by the addition of a rear wing extension, replicating the most salient
features of the original.

temporary. Eventually the entire structure was replaced in a matching design
built in cast iron, successfully still spanning the river today.

At the same time, Simpson was also employed to design and erect the
delightful little Toll House, (now rather effectively extended), which commands
the western end of the bridge. This charming, originally asymmetrical little
cottage, terminated at one end with a broad canted bay, is all embraced under a
typically low-pitched slated roof with overhanging eaves and decorative wall
brackets. The horizontal glazing, also typical of this period and emulating that
of the nearby East Lodge at the Castle, is set in window openings which, along
with the adjacent doorway, are embellished with extremely crisp cornices
supported by decorative brackets in his usual manner.

In Ferryhill in 1831, Ferryhill Place at last began to be laid out, the new
street connecting the road to Devanha House (built in 1813), with the new
thoroughfare down the hill, eventually to be named Polmuir Road. The houses
at its western end, which really must be to designs by Archibald Simpson,
anticipate those of both Marine Place and Victoria Street by many years.
However no actual physical evidence now remains verifying the authorship of
Nos. 20–30 and 17–27, except for the undoubted quality of the work itself.
These horizontally arranged linked classic cottage terraces at either side of the
gently descending thoroughfare were given exceptionally long front gardens for

FERRYHILL PLACE, ABERDEEN

Ferryhill Place introduced Simpson's classic linked Aberdeen cottages for the first time within
this terrace built of granite rubble enlivened with ashlar stringers and dressings.

the period, reflecting perhaps their perceived still rustic environs. The houses
also increasingly emerge out of the ground, resulting in the initially semi-
suppressed basements being almost fully exposed at the eastern ends of both
blocks. Stringers at ground floor, dressed margins, nicely recessed ashlar panels
under the principal windows, plain architrave surrounds around the doorways
with cornices supported by console brackets on either side, and smooth ashlar
flights of steps, contrast beautifully with the basically squared, plain rubble walls.
The effect is a charming but relatively inexpensive interplay of colour, surface
and texture, presided over by a high pitched slated roof containing bedrooms,
expressed by the now normal canted dormer windows centred on the main
window rhythm below. Despite however this promising start, Ferryhill Place
would languish for a little while, perhaps because it was still seen to be just too
far out of town. When interest revived, fully two-storey terraces of a diminished
character and design were abutted directly on to the originals by some later
hand, still however completing a handsome street.

Along the way, still on the Shoemakers' lands, Simpson also designed in this
year, an extremely noble domestic introduction into the area with Belvidere Terrace

(now Marine Terrace), built on top of a flattened summit, which necessitated considerable preparatory works in the form of impressive retaining walls against South Crown Street as it made its way up the hill. The design, envisaging a two-storey semi-detached centre block over full basements with single-storey link terraces ending with further two-storey terminal pavilions, attempted to reintroduce the domestic palace block solution into Aberdeen again. Work on the row itself did not actually get underway until 1837, when unfortunately only two houses commenced. Perhaps the more far-sighted could already envisage the increasingly industrialising estuary of the Dee, changing for ever the still charming view. Certainly various establishments were already lining the banks of the river in the form of distilleries, breweries, foundries and a brick and tile works. The bulk of the scheme was to be successfully revived after 1880 however by J. Russell Mackenzie and Duncan MacMillan, regrettably even then still minus the terminal ends. These unfortunately had to wait until the 1970s when they were eventually realised in an altogether different style, material and scale. Notwithstanding, the terrace still makes a very brave show indeed, with its bold unifying cornices, successions of exquisitely modelled architrave surrounds around windows and doors, rhythms of broad entrance steps with wrought iron railings, and the paired

MARINE TERRACE, ABERDEEN

Formerly Belvidere Terrace, Simpson's sophisticated integrated street design failed to attract the necessary interest, having to wait until the early 1880s to achieve even partial completion. The unfortunate modern end wings were realised in the 1970s.

two-storey houses in the centre. Sadly Simpson would never be so ambitious in the field of domestic street architecture again, doubtless as a direct result of the apparent early failure of this, one of his finest architectural creations.

Meanwhile on Donside, just below Strathdon itself, Simpson embarked on one of his most audaciously grand and imposing commissions. Created for Sir Charles Forbes Bt., the vast extension at Castle Newe was built with money bequeathed to him by his father, who had made a fortune as a merchant in Bombay. The work incorporated and completely absorbed the earlier T-plan freestone house on the site built in 1604, and which in itself may have prompted the excursion into his own very personal version of the Jacobean style. Perhaps it was just the historical connection or the drama of the mountain scenery all around, but whatever, Simpson responded to the riverside setting and the magnificent backdrop of Ben Newe, by creating a truly memorable ensemble in an extremely cool, smooth, and crisply executed display in the local Kildrummy freestone. Certainly incorporating a

CASTLE NEWE, STRATHDON

Elegant and serene against the dark wooded background of Ben Newe, Simpson's neo-Jacobean masterpiece confronts the River Don with this very fine design, incorporating also a hint of India. Demolished 1927, the stones were to be reused in the building of the Elphinstone Hall, Aberdeen.

The river frontage of Castle Newe. Note that the leaded ogee-caps on the end tourelles were subsequently replaced with lower and slated versions, before the end of the century.

distinctly Indian flavour, acknowledging at the same time the main source of the family wealth, the boldly horizontal still basically symmetrical main front was very firmly anchored at both its corners by high circular towers brought up into lead covered ogee-shaped domed tourelles, which were subsequently slated. This façade was further enlivened with broadly projecting straight gables at either end, contrasting with the two more delicately expressed box-bay windows (set either side of the garden entrance) and both terminating in ogee-shaped gable caps. The wilfully asymmetrical west facing entrance elevation was dominated by a grandly arched and projecting carriage porch, again anchored with its own smaller versions of the circular, domed and ogee-capped towers. At first floor window head level, a continuous stringer lent unity all around, stepping up and down over the window heads on its way. On the ground storey Simpson also introduced something of a personal novelty that he would repeat again elsewhere, with the appearance of three long closely spaced round-headed windows inset into both of the end gables illuminating the major apartments immediately behind. All this and the similarly designed but lower scale service wing extending off to the east was outlined against the dark treed slopes of Ben Newe behind, exaggerating also the diagonally set serried rows of tall chimneys overhead and the climax of the high box-tower which reared up dramatically over it all. Remarkably now however only Simpson's original

A very remarkable early coloured photograph of the entrance front of Castle Newe.
The earlier house survived on the left, embellished also with dramatic new chimneys.

I am greatly indebted to George and Elspeth Hardie for the use of these remarkable
photographs of Newe from their very considerable family archive on the mansion.
Elspeth's grandfather, Sir Charles Forbes, was a pioneer of early photography and was
responsible for taking many fine studies of the great house itself and its very beautiful
surrounding Donside estate, before its destruction in 1927.

Simpson's rather splendid wooden model still remarkably survives today at House of Newe.
Note the original T-plan 1604 Jacobean house remained just to the left of the carriage porch.

This remarkable coloured photograph of Castle Newe in the early morning was taken by Sir Charles Forbes in the early 1920's.

A surviving original drawing illustrating the east elevation of Castle Newe.

model of his proposals still survives intact at present day House of Newe, once the castle's dower house and now its successor.

Even in this refreshing new direction for Simpson however, recalling perhaps even something of his very earliest exercise at nearby Druminnor, as has already been noted there was still a lingering symmetry, along with an all embracing smoothness of surface coupled with sharply cut openings and very delicately wrought but minimal mouldings, which were indeed the hallmarks of all his previous neoclassical work up to this time. It is certainly the case that his very obvious natural affinity with this new approach, was its quite close stylistic association with the very classicism which had originally historically superseded it in the first place.

Internally however an extremely refined, basically classical arrangement still held sway but charged with crisp Jacobean inspired plasterwork, mostly carried out in his very much reduced and rectilinear strap-work manner. The rather splendid suite of very opulent, impressive interlinked reception rooms unfolded, served by an elongated Jacobean hall, dramatically beamed all along its length, together with a grand staircase directly off it. The principal apartments were all placed along the south façade, set to one side of the main entrance and bedrooms proliferated on the floor above, reflecting the basic arrangement below. All this is however now unfortunately just a photographic memory, as financial difficulties experienced by the family in the early 1920s forced the sale of the house and much of the estate as well resulting in the complete demolition of the castle itself in 1927. As some sort of compensation, at least the fine quality local freestone masonry was set aside for reuse by A. Marshall Mackenzie and

The Gallery Corridor serving the principal apartments.

The main staircase – note the use of the ivy balustrade originally introduced at Stracathro. These balusters have subsequently found themselves reused again at the House of Newe along with many other very interesting artefacts and treasures, saved from Castle Newe.

Simpson's model of Castle Newe sits on its late Regency table within the splendid Classical-Indian entrance hall in the castle.

The interlinked principal drawing rooms of Castle Newe illustrate the general air of opulence within the Donside mansion, photographed just prior to its demise.

his son, for the building of their splendid Elphinstone Hall and Cloister extension to Aberdeen's King's College which commenced building in 1929. Apart from a former stable block and laundry building, which was subsequently refurbished incorporating elements of the castle into a modern residence, all that now survives of this once proud mansion is residual stonework and some still magnificent trees which once dramatically framed its serene walls.

At this same time at the far end of Union Street in Aberdeen, at Nos. 381–389, instead of the more usual two storeys above basement type, an unusual double town house block of three full storeys over basement made its appearance, attributed to Simpson and illustrating most of his design signatures. With first floor and second floor stringers and a typical cornice and low

381–389 UNION STREET, ABERDEEN

parapet in an elegant seven-bay design, the western return gable remains remarkable for its very Simpson-like treatment with a broad chimney head and inset blocking pieces on either side. It also boasts a fine phalanx of square granite chimney pots above in an ashlar design, executed almost as if Smith's building at 393–399 next door did not actually already exist to obscure it. Long deprived of its domestic ground floor and basement, the now commercial part of this building was long occupied by Chivas Brothers who operated a first class grocery business there for very many years, augmented by an excellent restaurant, which took up the first floor. The property is now occupied by Michie's the Chemist with the Careers Scotland offices situated immediately next door.

Just slightly to the west of this at the junction of the South Road with Justice Mill Lane, Simpson completed a villa for Mrs Yeats of Auquharney, one of the first houses to be built along that thoroughfare. The resulting design, somewhat akin to his slightly earlier version at 26 Albyn Place but devoid of the porch and the corner pilasters, had a plain but beautifully proportioned ashlar three-bay front centred on a broad entrance doorway and a flight of granite steps. The principal floor, made up of drawing room, dining room, parlour and two family bedrooms, sat over a full basement containing further bedrooms and a kitchen with service quarters. Above, a slated pavilion roof presided over all, with all-round broad eaves. A high walled service yard was built immediately behind the house, while in front Simpson formed a paved forecourt hard on to the corner itself, enclosed by railings of a most unusual wavy design. Dr William Kelly and G. M. Fraser considered this house to be a superb example of Simpson's capacity to create a delightful design out of very

MRS YEATS OF AUQUHARNEYS HOUSE (demolished).

little, and lamented its loss when, towards the end of the century, it was replaced by Victorian tenements.

The following year, as his work on Castle Newe continued, Simpson was also appointed to alter and extend nearby Craig Castle, an ancient structure situated only slightly beyond Lumsden. Dating mostly from the mid-sixteenth century and occupying a most beautiful, almost secret position within the valley, the original great rendered L-plan castellated mansion survived relatively unchanged beside John Adam's more classical later masonry wing of 1767, together with its free standing rusticated gateway. Simpson was asked to add to this by providing a new but very limited single-storey central wing, comprising an entrance hall, a drawing room and dining room, connecting the two parts of the house more effectively

CASTLE CRAIG, LUMSDEN
Simpson's compact garden front extension.
The two storeyed box-bay window is later.

together. Built very close to the edge of the ravine in front of the castle, the extension is relatively plain except for a great canted bay window to the drawing room, which commands dramatic views of the wooded valley. Unfortunately Simpson's wing was destined to be badly damaged in a fire, but the interior was subsequently quite faithfully restored.

From the august entrance hall, which has been very well recreated, but minus its original wood panelled walls, a beautifully proportioned drawing room and dining room lead off which have also been again refurbished following extensive recent repairs to the roof. The drawing room and hall ceilings in particular were recreated in Simpson's extremely rectilinear manner in an arrangement of flat strap-work enclosing elongated plain ceiling panels with delicately decorated little bosses placed at the intersections. In the absence now of Castle Newe's splendid interiors, the plasterwork here in both these rooms, demonstrating a mature Simpson neo-Jacobean character, is now the only remaining work of a similar quality to remind us of that once proud but long demolished mansion house.

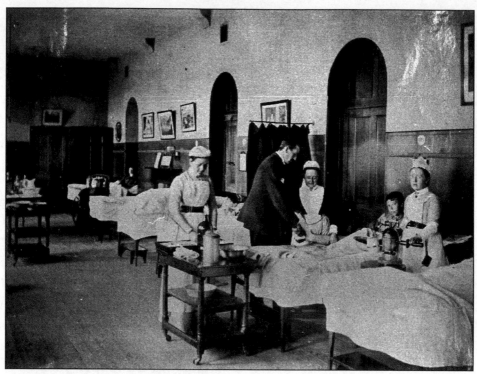

These early photographs taken within Simpson's wards at Woolmanhill illustrate
the very considerable advance that had just taken place in the standard of medical
care which was provided within the City of Aberdeen at around this time.

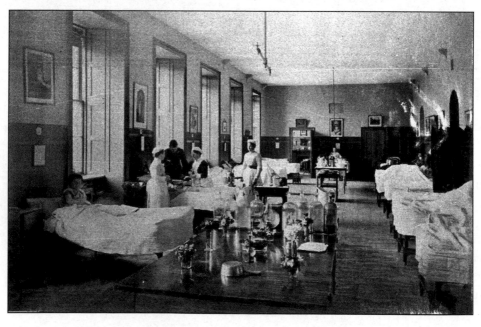

Simpson completed 1832 by securing one of his most important commissions to date, which was destined to heavily occupy him for the next six years. Some time previously in his capacity as City Architect, John Smith had indicated to the Infirmary Managers that the existing 1739 "factory like" premises of the hospital could be made good and in 1819 actually went as far as building on a new extension wing to the rear. However within the matter of only eleven years the decision was made at a meeting held in March 1830 to completely rebuild the premises. Both John Smith and Archibald Simpson were asked to submit plans but as both architects were extremely busy at the time, their proposals were not forthcoming until 1832, which was somewhat brave of them in the circumstances of this considerable project. Fortuitously for Simpson, his old client Bailie Galen, one of the Institution's managers, was so over-committed himself that he felt he could not continue in his post. In consequence he recommended his brother-in-law for the position who was none other than Simpson's elder brother Sandy. Duly appointed, this may well in itself have been all that was necessary to ensure that Simpson's scheme was selected. Sadly in any event Smith's proposals no longer survive for comparison but they could hardly have bettered Simpson's. In compensation, Smith would soon be extremely busy himself, however, extending William Adam's Gordon's Hospital, where his design apparently outdid Simpson's, and William Burn's much more magnificent solution was vastly over budget.

The Managers of the Infirmary had asked for proposals to completely replace the old premises with the new building being capable of being constructed in phases to allow the smooth transference from one part to the other. Reverting to his generally preferred H-plan layout for buildings of this type, the economy of plan, the obvious day-lighting advantages of such a shape, and the excellent natural cross-ventilation possible with this arrangement, produced a most impressive solution effortlessly capable of the phased building requirement. The winning design proposals described a slightly more ambitious complex than the one actually built, for Simpson suggested an elaborately planned ground floor extending further back to the rear, enclosing a semicircular-shaped entrance court. Beyond this he had also laid out a large formal garden area, surrounded by an impressive continuous northern colonnade.

One of Archibald Simpson's most serene and accomplished neoclassical statements, his distinguished three-storey thirteen-bay wide block, has the two-bay wide end wings advanced by one bay forming effective end pavilions to the front and rear. The principal façade contains in the centre a noble five-bay attached giant portico carrying through both the upper floors, and sitting on top of a rusticated base inset with double recessed windows. The plain frieze and cornice is taken all round the building, with a parapet and a broad Greek pediment placed in the centre. The surviving drawings also clearly illustrate that, as in many of his more prestigious commissions, Simpson originally anticipated placing a sculptural group in this extremely important position. It would seem however, judging from the almost total lack of executed sculpture on most of his work, that this element of the design was usually the first to go, presumably in the interests of economy. The two side elevations to the east and west of this frontage are treated in a broadly similar manner with only nine bays, the middle three being advanced with a four-pilastered attached portico crowned also with a plain Greek pediment. Over the parapet, the roofs are just visible and in the centre floating majestically over it all is a most splendid dome, so positioned that it appears centrally on all four elevations. Once in lead, these elements are now copper. On the two upper floors, all the windows have architrave surrounds, except those situated between the columns within the porticoes. The first floor architraves are also actually taken right down to the first floor stringer. For additional, emphasis, the two first floor windows in the front advanced wings are given their own elegant cornices and brackets. The north front, which over time has become the entrance elevation, was much more modestly treated with an additional plain infill ground storey of offices and hospital administration accommodation. The new Infirmary also introduced revolutionary new standards of medical provision into the city for the first time, complete with extremely spacious, well lit and ventilated, airy wards In true neoclassical fashion also, the state-of-the-art operating theatre was situated as you would expect, absolutely symbolically in the most appropriate manner possible, directly under the beautifully presiding copper hemispherical dome.

The building phase did not however advance as smoothly as its eventual end success might suggest, the enormous sums expended being a considerable

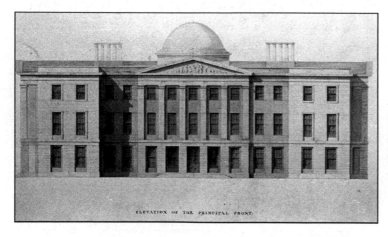

ELEVATION OF THE PRINCIPAL FRONT

Simpson's original elevation of the south front of Woolmanhill. Note the incorporation of sculpture within the central pediment.

SIMPSON'S
COMPLETED
INFIRMARY,
WOOLMANHILL.

Simpson's layout
plan – in the event
the colonnaded
garden did not
materialise.

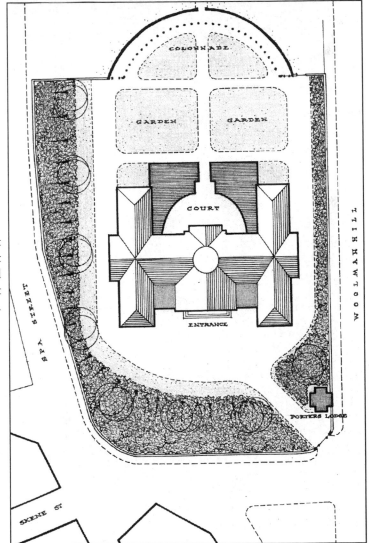

The first phase western wing of the Infirmary, Woolmanhill,
on top of its high retaining wall.

The east front of the Infirmary, Woolmanhill, with later medical blocks
just visible on the right.

concern to the Managers. After the completion of the west wing (the first phase of the work in 1834), it actually took the casting vote of the Chairman for the rest of the work to proceed to completion. At the end of the day the cost amounted to £16,700, a very considerable sum for the time, and the contractor selected to build it was Alexander Rainnie. His firm was destined to execute very many of Simpson's finest and most prestigious later buildings. Fully complete in 1839 to its slightly diminished plan, the Infirmary was designed to accommodate two hundred and thirty patients. However as early as 1844, Simpson was again engaged by the Managers to erect a new Fever House at the rear of the complex, together with a Porter's Lodge on the Woolmanhill frontage. This actually still exists, rebuilt subsequently in a new location slightly to the north, flanking the future main vehicular entry. Beyond this, later in the nineteenth century, Simpson's Fever House was removed to much enlarged premises at the City Hospital in Urquhart Road, while the site was reused for the erection of three large related hospital blocks round a central courtyard. Increasing pressure for additional bed accommodation forced the virtual departure of the Royal Infirmary to a virgin site at Foresterhill in the late 1930s, where now modern medical provision has almost completely filled all of the available land. Despite its present slightly forlorn state, the old complex awaits early reinvention as offices and possibly flats, heading a new planning initiative for the Woolmanhill area. Hopefully the success of this will ensure the survival of Simpson's august masterpiece in this important northern flank of Aberdeen city centre. One of his most profoundly neoclassical buildings, its combination of simple utility, within extremely elegant and restrained design, married to the bold external expression of the power and strength of its finely modelled granite ashlar walls, remains unmatched in his work. Indeed as David Chalmers of the *Aberdeen Journal*, and future Simpson client so eloquently observed at the time, "Mr Simpson has left a monument of himself which will last for ages".

Meanwhile Simpson was very actively involved in the design of a civic monument in competition with John Smith. A number of leading citizens had determined to erect a memorial to Dr Robert Hamilton, author of a celebrated book at the time on the National Debt during the Napoleonic Wars. To be erected in the City Kirkyard, Simpson's resolutely simpler and more angular design failed to sufficiently impress.

Hamilton Monument design

179

Simpson also successfully embarked on two rather far flung Church commissions for the Episcopal congregations, one in Banff and the other in Fochabers, both necessitating considerable travel. In a site on Banff High Street, he erected St Andrew's Episcopal Chapel, a small simple axial rectangular sandstone church, designed somewhat in his St Andrew's King Street manner, minus the side aisles. On the main front he also reworked a much reduced version of his Aberdeen building for the purpose. The four-bay long church again presents all its most noble drama to the street, with a great Tudor Gothic traceried window set over the main entrance door, held within a high gable between higher octagonal piers both diminishing upwards into crocketed pinnacles. From the entrance vestibule the restrained galleried interior remains largely as designed, described at the time as "of chaste simplicity, calculated to a solemn and sublime effect". The chancel was considerably extended like St Andrew's in Aberdeen in 1913, by the addition of a slightly narrower two-bay long extension on to its eastern end. A number of the elongated lancet windows have also been subsequently provided with stained glass, successfully introducing a most welcome internal note of colour. The situation of the church has also been considerably enhanced by the construction in 1853 of the Rectory building next door to the north, to a design provided by A. & W. Reid. With gabled front and mullioned windows, crisp stringers and high-chimneyed end gables, it is a neo-Jacobean design of which Archibald Simpson himself might very easily have approved.

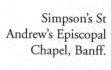

Simpson's St Andrew's Episcopal Chapel, Banff.

At the same time further west again at Fochabers, Simpson also commenced the erection of the delightful little Episcopal Chapel there for the Duchess of Gordon, built against the enclosure wall of Castle Gordon Estate itself, where it terminates the axis of Duke Street opposite in the town. The sandstone church, axial and also somewhat smaller even than Banff, to which it has more than a passing resemblance externally, the design was allegedly based on a French precedent in any event. The symmetrical gabled end is held between high square piers, carrying up to octagonal turrets and capped by tapering pinnacles. The gable itself is dominated with three elongated, elegantly hooded lancet

The Episcopal Chapel in Fochabers, with its later side stair extension.

The now very considerably modified interior of the Simpson chapel
with its series of superb Burne Jones designed stained glass windows.

Simpson's Episcopal Chapel terminates the axis of Duke Street in Fochabers

windows, with the central one higher (and also now blank), with a single round arch-headed entrance doorway below. Within, there is unexpectedly a ground storey now taken up with the Rectory, which was originally conceived as the original classrooms of the Episcopalian School. Above this, by virtue of a centrally positioned staircase, access was gained directly into the chapel proper, which was a very restrained interior, complete with originally a flat plastered ceiling. Built of six bays, the interior was in the first instance fitted out with box-pews and reading desks at the front, with also a private vestibule and stair entry provided for the Duke and his party on the left, in addition to a balancing vestry and robing room. The chapel is well lit by three high pointed lancet windows opposite each other on both sides, together with two similar windows flanking now the central organ on the entrance front (necessitating internally the blanking out of the main window still visible on the exterior), and three further windows at the altar end, surmounted by a later circular rose window, placed centrally high up on the now fully exposed gable.

The chapel was built on the instigation of Elizabeth, the last Duchess of Gordon, who wished to provide for the spiritual and educational well-being of those living in the neighbourhood of Gordon Castle. The completed work eventually cost £1,100, actually one hundred pounds more than originally anticipated, and the good Duchess sold some of her jewels to meet the additional amount. The schoolrooms were opened on June 1834, with the Chapel following on the 12th August, the same year.

In 1875, the Duke of Richmond and Gordon was responsible for the almost total refurbishment of the chapel at a cost of over £2,000. During this work, Simpson's flat plasterwork ceiling and box-pews were removed, and a fine dark stained high pointed ceiling was introduced along with hammer-beam trusses and a new arrangement of bench pews. Simpson's stair was also completely removed, in order to gain even more space for the congregation, and a new stairway was attached to the side of the main building at the front, in the event sadly compromising Simpson's subtle symmetry. Interestingly on the new stair, two lancet windows boast stained glass armorial panels dedicated to the Cornwallis and Bedford Families. I am very much indebted to Peter Reid of Robert Gordon University, for his totally plausible theory that these windows are now in fact all that remain of Simpson's originally installed chapel glazing. On the basis that all the six side-lancets of the chapel were reserved for family based armorial windows, the other four would have been undoubtedly dedicated to the Gordons, the Richmonds, the Palmers and the Manchesters.

However new stained glass windows, made by William Morris & Co to a design provided by Sir Edward Burne Jones, have subsequently been introduced. These are all carried out with a basically green overall foliate background design, and a figure dominating each long inset top panel, with a scene from their life infilling the square panel just below. In this manner, windows celebrating St Michael, St Raphael, and St Ursula on the left hand side confront St Caecilia, the Good Shepherd and St Andrew on the right hand. The three lancets to the north contain, in the centre, Christ on the Cross and the Virgin Mary, Mater Dolorosa with the Good Samaritan below on the left, and St John with Disciplus Delectus and Dorcas below on the right. The new rose window introduced immediately above when the flat ceiling had been removed, represents a scene with a central angel and scroll, surrounded by five minstrel angels. As well as their exquisite artistry, these windows also considerably complement this delightful little architectural jewel. The ground floor schoolrooms were actually converted into the Rectory early in the twentieth century and a new small extension wing was completed in 1975. The font was gifted by the Diocese of Norwich in 1981, and the altar was replaced in 1999, when it was moved slightly further forward.

Despite on the face of it an extremely lean year in 1834, with only competitions and no record of any new commissions coming in at all, a look at Simpson's work in progress clearly demonstrates that his office was very busy indeed at this time with a considerable amount of work in hand. Indeed the workload had reached such proportions that by 1835 additional staff were required. It is now that we learn that Archibald Simpson took on Thomas Mackenzie as an assistant, who also incidentally made the acquaintance of James Matthews at this juncture, who was already working in Simpson's office at this same time. Matthews was actually a grandson of the builder of the Union Bridge and had worked previously in the London office of George Gilbert Scott for some years before moving back to Aberdeen. Mackenzie on the other hand, always appearing to have been a gifted intuitive designer, came from a family of architects in Perthshire. Indeed before moving this far north, he had already worked in his father's office in Perth after it had been taken over by his elder brother, as well as in his other brother's office in Dundee. He even managed a short stint in Smith's Aberdeen office in addition to working with Simpson, before moving much further north to Elgin where, after completing two years with William Robertson, he took over the practice himself in 1841. In 1844, he and his old friend James Matthews entered partnership together and opened up their own Aberdeen practice. By 1850, they had already introduced Historical Romanticism into the City with St John's Church, Crown Terrace, and Christ's

College, Alford Place, signalling the imminent demise of neoclassicism at the same time. Dying of a brain fever in 1854, Matthews soldiered on alone until he was joined by Thomas's son, A. Marshall Mackenzie.

1835 however found Simpson again involved in an attempt to resurrect his old Damlands of Rubislaw Scheme for the Skene Lands in the west end of Aberdeen. At the same time as reworking his proposals he proceeded with the design and construction of Nos. 1–6 Rubislaw Place in his most severe but sophisticated town house ashlar style, introducing this type into the west end for the first time. Along the way he also commenced design work on Nos. 21 and 23 Waverley Place, both of which however were finally to be built only after 1849 at the end of the day.

RUBISLAW PLACE, ABERDEEN

Simpson at his most severe, introduces his Bon-Accord type house into the west-end. The imposition of later dormers and window fenestration well illustrates how damaging these various elements can be, especially when done with as little sensitivity as here.

At the other end of town, on the north side of Frederick Street almost at its junction with Park Street, he was also busily engaged in the design and construction of the famous Doctor Bell's School. The Reverend Andrew Bell

DD, a one-time chaplain to the East India Company, had left the vast sum of £120,000 for the establishment of schools giving elementary instruction in the Madras System which was very highly regarded at the time. The system, sometimes called the Monitory System, involved the most gifted student teaching the student immediately below him and so on all the way down the line. The money was intended to establish institutions in Edinburgh, Leith, Glasgow, Aberdeen, Old Aberdeen, Inverness, Coupar and St Andrews, the latter being his old home town. £9,791 was allotted to Aberdeen of which £2,791 was to be spent on a similar school in Old Aberdeen. Simpson was asked to prepare plans by the Council in 1834, and given the civic nature of the request, it would seem likely that John Smith the City Architect, would also have presented proposals as well. Simpson in fact received the commission and advanced his design, which commenced immediately and was opened late in 1835. The premises, designed to accommodate upwards of four hundred boys and two hundred girls in a building of two floors, was built for the lowest possible building rates, its total lack of extravagance and any pretension being noted even at the time. What this suggests the building looked like is now quite impossible to determine, as no print or photograph of it now survives. Sufficient to say that the school duly opened to 236 boys and 143 girls, all paying the sum of a penny ha'penny for the privilege. The smaller, even cheaper school actually built in the Aulton in School Road was obviously even less architecturally successful, attracting the unfortunate description that "it was a sufficiently repellent example of what was provided when cheapness was the only object... etc. etc."

The Frederick Street premises occupied the entire site, there being apparently no surrounding playground, with the building extending all the way back to Princes Street. Latterly coming under the auspices of the Aberdeen School's Board, at the turn of the twentieth century the adjacent houses to the west were acquired, the school demolished, and an entirely new building erected called Frederick Street Public School. This rather dramatic and imposing double-domed edifice with rooftop playground and spacious all round schoolyard, has itself now been abandoned, and converted very successfully into a modern Business Centre for the area.

Meanwhile at Sauchen, many miles west of Aberdeen in the heart of Gordon country, Simpson embarked on a quite delightful mansion at Linton House. Simple, severely classical but completely astylar, with rubble walls at one time harled with stone margins, the main three-bay two-storey front is enlivened with a boldly projecting entrance porch, pierced by a deep arch-

Linton House in its heyday – note the rendered finish

THE PRINCIPAL FLOOR PLAN OF
LINTON HOUSE.

Linton House today, fully restored but minus its external rendering.

The drawing room looking into the sitting room at Linton House.

The entrance front, Linton House.

The principal drawing room, Linton House.

The gallery hall staircase, Linton House

headed doorway and crowned with a low pedimented broad-eaved roof, which is taken all around. The flanking ground floor room windows are adorned with cornices and brackets, and the design is further sharpened with dressed margins and stringers placed at the basecourse and immediately under the soffit of the eaves. The garden façade is also boldly centralised with a projecting gable, embracing a canted bay, enlivening the principal drawing room. Off to the left of the entrance a delightful asymmetry is achieved by the extensive U-shaped lower scaled four-bay service wing, which completes a very charming ensemble. Following a very thorough programme of restoration a few years ago, the roof was re-slated and fully made good while the rough granite walls were exposed and repointed, sadly now minus their original all-embracing rendering.

A gem by any standard however, inside the air of very elegant restraint continues with beautifully understated interiors arranged compactly around a spacious vestibule and stair-hall beyond. The kind of house which simply invites you to sit down, the plan unfolds on either side of the cubic vestibule, with the study on the left and the sitting room and en suite drawing room to the right, with the dining room and parlour straight ahead across the hall. The galleried stair-hall itself with its high glazed lantern overhead, dominates the centre of the house, the gilded ivy-clad stair balusters bringing alive a very elegant space indeed. The beautifully restored reception rooms with their understated plasterwork and honeyed pine woodwork delight in their quite lavish refurbishment, even though some of the gilding and ceiling painting employed might well have raised Simpson's more spartan eyebrow. Beyond the reception suite is the modernised service wing, which still contains the original kitchen, laundry, stores, pantry and old staff quarters. Below the main block, a full basement contains extensive wine cellars, coal cellars and various storerooms. On the first floor, extending also right across the slightly lower service wing, a full compliment of bedrooms is accommodated, all refurbished and equipped with modern bathrooms.

Within the surrounding naturally beautiful fifty-acre wooded estate, Simpson was also responsible for the walled garden and the design of two charming little staff cottages. Nearby is also a very typical Simpson Home Farm grouping (now unfortunately no longer part of the estate), and laid out in a courtyard arrangement complete with an integral farmhouse wing. A barn, fronted and relieved with blind arches, is flanked on either side by two elliptical entrance archways, leading into the spacious courtyard behind, enclosed on three sides by typical storey and a half farm buildings. There is also on site a very interesting pyramidal-roofed doocot building, which together with the most southerly range of the complex was completed slightly later in the nineteenth century by the architect J. Russell Mackenzie.

At the same time a little distance off at Cluny Parish Church (North Church, Sauchen), Simpson must also have designed there for the family the eminently simple but very elegant Linton Burial Enclosure. An extremely Grecian understated granite ashlar-walled drama, it is equipped with four broad gables open to the sky and an entrance opening complete with architrave surround and fine wrought iron gate.

Back in Aberdeen, the continuing survival of the East Church of St Nicholas was apparently causing some concern, to the minister at least at any rate. This

St Nicholas Church, Aberdeen circa 1800.

very venerable building, the ancient choir of the originally conjoined church, had long been in separate occupation from the neighbouring West Church along side. This church, having become unstable in the 18th century, had been replaced to a classical Basilican design supplied by James Gibbs. It would also appear that the minister of the time, Dr Foote, was actually beside himself simply because his colleague Dr Murray had just succeeded in occupying Smith's magnificent new North Church in King Street, much to the former's annoyance. Galvanised, he sought Archibald Simpson's report on the fabric of the building, which although certainly requiring some repair was definitely saveable. Almost a rerun of his Elgin experience, the demolishers, named in the press as the "Destructives", vigorously presented their case that the building was beyond saving, making much of Simpson's report that "the church is quite unfit for the purpose of an auditory". It should be noted however that John Smith, who was also involved initially and unsuccessfully in the design competition with Simpson in 1834, reported rather differently. Deciding eventually to retain only the outline of its foundations and its lower St Mary's Chapel underneath, the Town Council proceeded to select Simpson's replacement design which commenced in 1835. Although by the standards of his time Archibald Simpson's attitude is completely understandable, the great advance in building technology since the Middle Ages having made wide clear spans eminently practicable, his general architectural feeling for the distant past must again be severely questioned. Notwithstanding the quite vocal opposition, down the ancient fabric eventually came, and up went Simpson's modern Gothic design. Perhaps it was this ill feeling from the very start, perhaps it was the fact that a classicist was playing with Gothic, perhaps it was even the implicit constraints of a building built directly on the ancient foundations of an earlier building, but in any event the new church has always been criticised for the dryness of its Gothic, even from the outset. From the outside, the drama of the eastern end embracing the old basement Chapel on to Correction Wynd is quite successful with its angles, crocketed pinnacles and tripartite hooded Gothic windows making quite a fine show. It is on the flanking elevations however that Simpson's rather feeble buttresses particularly fail to convince, in an overall fairly stiff design. Maybe it was the august presence next door of Gibb's great Basilica which cautioned overwhelming restraint, for even a classicist might have seen that more insistent Gothic pinnacles here could have been considerably more effective. Certainly when the work was initially finished, within a churchyard at that time devoid of its trees, the disparity of scale, material and design between the West and East Churches was particularly marked. As it is however the high pointed and hooded traceried windows above the lower squared tripartite

Simpson's initial design for East St Nicholas Church. The new spire however did not materialise at the time.

193

versions set under the internal three-sided gallery, are all well enough executed in inset sandstone. Perhaps the main difficulty is the fact that the architecture seems to have been very sparsely carved out of the smoothest and sharpest of granite, again in complete contrast to the West's bolder, more cosmopolitan sandstone, underlining a certain coldness of execution which seems inimitable with the true spirit of Gothic. Paradoxically however, in this particular instance, the redoubtable Lord Cockburn recorded in his diary that he at any rate was for once quite impressed with the rebuilding, stating "the Churches have been excellently repaired and including its burial ground and handsome Façade of a railing along a street, it is a great honour to the place." As well as the new church however, Simpson's drawings clearly indicate that he had also hoped to remove the last vestige of the old church altogether, by replacing the medieval leaded spire with a soaring pinnacle of his own, owing more than a little to the majestic spire of Norwich Cathedral. At the end of the day this particular additional extravagance did not happen, a possible sop perhaps to history, although more probably there were insufficient funds available.

Inside however things substantially improved, although it should always be remembered that the church was fairly faithfully restored by William Smith, after a disastrous outbreak of fire in 1874. The strongly axial arrangement terminates on a severely plain wall, set back in the centre between the flanking side galleries, and pierced with a tall arched opening, which gives on to a broad chamfered bay containing the altar up a broad flight of steps. The decorated flat-ceilinged interior with its boldly curved wall brackets is flooded by the light of five great windows on either side, augmented by a similar number of squared windows under the galleries. The carved balcony with insistent Gothic arched arcading executed in pine, complete with serried rows of pews and the repositioned off-centre pulpit, combine to create a feeling of satisfying and very notable drama. Indeed it is impossible to disagree with Dr Cooper, a subsequent minister of the church, that the interior "had a dignity, simplicity and even grace, by no means common in the Gothic of that time."

Originally, the church was illuminated at night by an ultra modern gassolier complete with an elaborate reflector, the whole thing being cooled with water, which apparently circulated for that very purpose. The failure of this mechanism and the resultant catastrophic fire which ensued, quickly reduced the church to a granite shell, taking with it also the adjacent ancient medieval leaded spire, which crashed in through the roof, much to the consternation of the citizens who looked on incredulously. The restoration of the building commenced in the following year, together with the erection of William Smith's

THE EAST CHURCH OF ST NICHOLAS, ABERDEEN.

A difficult design exercise immediately next to a medieval spire and a Basilican Church designed by James Gibbs, Simpson's modern Gothic replacement just fails to convince.

The broad, spacious and completely uninterrupted interior however is an entirely different matter.

E & W St Nicholas
Churches, immediately
prior to the fire.

much more magnificent granite spire which now dominates both churches in a
manner never dreamt of by its ancient predecessor.

At the same date, Simpson is also credited with the completion of the
extremely effective design of the old North of Scotland Bank premises in
Fraserburgh, where in a bold and very accomplished Ionic design the corner of
Frithside Street is most beautifully turned into Broad Street. No actual evidence
now seems to exist to verify the perpetrator of this delightful composition, but
its quality and real sense of elegant classical drama very strongly suggests the
hand of Simpson as the only practitioner at the time capable of such a jewel. As
Simpson was also destined to carry out a number of the North of Scotland
Bank's work throughout the north-east, this could perfectly well have been the
first of many such future commissions. Designed as a basic two-storey above
basement L-plan block, a quarter corner drum was introduced filling the re-
entrant, preceded by a beautifully paired Ionic colonnade in front, supporting a
balcony, frieze and cornice with an extremely delicate cast iron balustrade on
top. The low pitched slated roof is given quite pronounced eaves, set
immediately over a slightly projecting frieze stringer, with a central chimney set
at forty-five degrees disguised as an urn completing this particularly delightful
ensemble. Unfortunately someone has seen fit to irrevocably damage the
originally designed elegant corner-stepped arrangement with the introduction
of a curved retaining wall, which now rather conceals the entrance. Internally
after the stylish oval vestibule, much that is original survives although the

THE NORTH OF SCOTLAND BANK, FRASERBURGH.

former banking hall in the north wing has been sadly reinvented in a late-Victorian manner by the introduction of a much too heavy dentilled cornice accompanied by unnecessarily squat Corinthian columns set at either end of the centrally introduced ceiling beam. The western wing however happily still contains its original elegantly simple ancillary banking rooms at ground and first floor levels around an extremely distinguished centrally placed split circular staircase set within a noble cylindrical top-lit domed interior, worthy even of Robert Adam. Happily, abandoned by the Clydesdale Bank in due course, the property, still in good condition, now functions as the premises of a modern Property Showroom.

Meanwhile in Lower Deeside at Drumoak, the local congregation finally determined to abandon their auld Kirk in favour of a new, modern and much larger church to be built to a Gothic design supplied by Archibald Simpson. There had been as we saw at Park, a church at Drumoak since 1157, when Pope Adrian 1V issued a confirmation to the See of Aberdeen. The glebe was considerably enlarged in the nineteenth century and in 1835, this precipitated a desire for more commodious premises. A completely new site was found on a rise about a mile from the old building and the new church was duly erected, minus in the first instance the proposed adjoining manse. The church is a quite typical Simpson design, being a slightly enlarged reworking of his original Kintore, within a simple rectangular five-bay box, intended to accommodate a

The august interior of Simpson's Drumoak Church looking north.

congregation of six hundred and thirty. The front is enlivened with a narrower single-bay entrance projecting out to the south, punctuated with square granite corner buttresses, crocketed pinnacles and a central bellcote perched on the apex of the gable. Five pointed Gothic lancet windows line the walls on either side, (the final ones being blank), with a more dominant tripartite traceried window implanted centrally on the main gable. All the windows are hooded with granite mouldings and are expressed also within chamfered granite reveals, successfully contrasting against the basically rendered external walls. Clear diamond glazing, outlined with a plain amber coloured band for internal dramatic effect, is leaded directly into the window surround stonework. Larger red diamonds with

DRUMOAK PARISH CHURCH

One of Simpson's more modest Gothic designs recalling his Kintore Church of 1819.

The interior of the church looking south towards the upper gallery.

centrally placed stylised flowers, incorporated near the heads of the side windows, subtly underscore their even internal rhythm.

The extremely restrained, distinguished and much admired airy interior with its plain plaster ceiling, its pine-lined dado, panelled gallery front, pulpit and pews, has a noble simplicity, terminating at the north end on the centrally placed pulpit and a gable dominated by three high lancet windows. The stained glass panel in the central window was installed in 1959. Behind the pulpit against the same wall, a small single-storey vestry extension projects externally with chamfered corners. As at Kintore however, there is also the quite surprising appearance of rather Doric-looking columns supporting the internal gallery, the paired central ones suggesting that the church probably had a central aisle prior to the refurbishment carried out in 1880. The area under the gallery has also been recently curtained off, in the now almost obligatory manner, to create a milling area for the congregation, resulting in the loss of a number of rows of pews. At the end of the day however, Simpson's intended new manse to accompany the church did not unfortunately materialise, the design being given in 1836 to his great rival John Smith. Given the architectural success of the church, this decision might suggest that Simpson's commission did not end perhaps very happily, at least as far as the minister and the congregation were concerned at any rate.

On the other side of the River Dee at Durris opposite, the house and estate there had just been acquired by one Antony Mactier, another successful merchant home from Madras, who immediately determined to further extend the earlier mansion. Simpson was immediately called in again and between 1835 and 1838 he created a classical squared granite three-bay three-storey box, two bays deep and with a central north-facing pedimented gable with Venetian window, over a single-storey segmental bow window below. The slated, piended roof with two centralised granite chimneys rose above the low parapet taken all round, underlined with a bold cornice. This new work was abutted directly on to his earlier extension wing, with a single-storey blank arcaded corridor wall and a projecting two-storey very spartan looking three-arched port cochere attempting to affect some sort of transition. Later accumulations of wall ivy helped assimilate all this with its earlier harled tower to the south, but the ensemble could not be described as a notable success. This could not be said however about the very magnificent adjacent stable block, which is situated some distance off up the hill. Although there seem to be no records or plans now existing which would definitely settle the matter, the stables (which were built at the same time as the latest extension) must surely be to a Simpson design. The basically symmetrical layout of broad H-shape squared granite built block, with

The very handsome Stable Block at Durris House – now very well converted into apartments.

storey and a half buildings culminating in a central pedimented gable delineated by paired pilasters on either side of a tall arch-headed entry, rises up in the middle over a low pitched, slated and broad-eaved roof, to terminate in a tall octagonal tower. This seems obviously developed from Stracathro and surely anticipates some other towers including that of the much later Woodside Parish Church. Originally built as a doocot, it is enlivened with a high cornice and broadly projecting eaves terminating in a flattish leaded roof, finial and weathervane. To the rear of the stables, two matching little staff cottages are very firmly attached to the ends of both wings, thereby completing an extremely delightful grouping indeed. Some distance off at the entrance gate, Simpson also provided one of his most delightful little gate-houses, complete with over-sailing roof, now considerably and very sensitively extended.

The stables were totally restored in the 1990s when they were imaginatively very successfully refurbished as a superb residential complex. Perhaps less fortunately, Durris House itself was relieved of much of Simpson's second phase, even before the house was acquired for the Control Centre for Aberdeen's Civil Defence organisation. Even more recently in the 1980s the remainder of its Simpson work was removed and replaced by new, rather more Georgian-like work, all unified and snow-cemmed brilliant white along with the adjoining older tower. The end result, forming a rather unconvincing architectural ensemble, is also now divided up into apartments.

In 1835 Archibald Simpson was also invited by the Town Council to submit a report and scheme for the widening of the Bridge of Dee, in direct competition with his old rival, the City Architect John Smith. Demonstrating again apparently his complete lack of any affinity with the past, although he found the old structural piers and foundations to be sufficiently sound, his

Simpson's final extension to Durris House created a new range to the north of his previous wing. Most of Archibald Simpson's work at the House however has been subsequently demolished.

scheme envisaged totally encasing the old freestone bridge with extensions built of granite ashlar on both sides. New pavements were also proposed to be cantilevered out even further, creating additional extra width. However ingenious this solution, one thing was absolutely certain, the old Bridge of Dee was clearly intended to vanish, completely buried under a brand new skin. With the usual lack of Civic urgency in such matters, both Simpson's and Smith's proposals were submitted to James Walker of Westminster who just happened to be in Aberdeen in 1839 on business connected with major harbour works. Happily for posterity he proposed a much more sensitive treatment, which simply matched the existing and doubled it in width. The work was entrusted to Smith and commencing in 1841, mercifully still exists undisturbed, despite various unsuccessful attempts more recently to widen the structure yet again. Long may this continue to be the case, despite undoubtedly modern traffic greatly increasing.

This same year, the Aberdeen advocates who up until now, largely used various rooms at the Courts to meet and conveniently discuss professional matters, determined to build a suitably grand new meeting place for themselves, sufficient also to house their extensive library which was presently kept above the old Records Office building at the corner of the Castlegate at the old Justice Port. After some difficulty, they selected the most prestigious site remaining at the bottom end of town, at the corner of Union Street and Back Wynd, immediately next to the Churchyard and Smith's recently completed very elegant Ionic Screen. Doubtless most anxious to obtain the best possible design for this important site, they approached both Archibald Simpson and John Smith and invited them to prepare proposals. At the end of the day Simpson, very probably due to pressure of work, gracefully declined the offer and withdrew from the competition, thereby handing Smith the commission and enabling him to realise one of his most elegant and dramatic central Aberdeen designs.

1836 found Simpson unexpectedly again on the move, as he left his house in Crown Street temporarily for a rather more humble address at No. 3 Little Belmont Street. By the end of the year however he had removed again into his extremely fashionable new home at 15 Bon Accord Square, a house of course that he had designed himself. He had also designed and built the house immediately next door, to be conveniently occupied by his brother Sandy and his young family. Simpson subsequently located his office premises nearby at No. 1 Bon Accord Square.

Almost immediately afterwards Simpson became involved again with the development of Albyn Place, where at last there seemed to be at least some interest. He had embarked upon the design of Nos. 2–16 the previous year, but only two of these houses were actually commenced and built to completion at this time, the remainder of the terrace being finished and slightly altered in execution by Mackenzie and Matthews after 1847. However the much longer than usual front gardens provided, clearly indicated that Simpson's early layout was still basically the intended overall plan, the more spacious gardens accurately still reflecting his initial intentions for the prominence of his Albyn Place terraces within the development. The rest of this particular planning initiative however would be finally abandoned as a scheme in the early 1840s,

ALBYN PLACE, ABERDEEN

Simpson's initial houses immediately on the right were subsequently extended into this
distinguished but still severely understated west end of Aberdeen terrace, a typical
neo-classical residential street.

when a much less ambitious layout was initially adopted. The revised
arrangement did however make the future realisation of Rubislaw Terrace and
gardens a possibility, for which all Aberdonians should now be eternally grateful.

Some twenty miles to the north, just out of Old Meldrum, Simpson also
became involved in the massive modernisation and recasting of Meldrum
House, the ancient seat of the Meldrums, Setons and then the Urquharts since
the thirteenth century. Centred on a huge estate, the old house had developed
over time in a rather piecemeal rambling fashion, so that in 1836–39, Simpson
was employed to rectify matters. Removing a two-storey wing which once
formed one side of the ancient courtyard, he virtually recreated the house in his
appropriately Jacobean style, by raising a broad three-storey front, terminated
with advanced crow-stepped gables and enlivened by ogee-shaped lesser gables
and gablets, over windows etched against a high slated roof. His new eastern
return wing was anchored by a balancing two-storey pavilion end, complete
with corner towers with conical slated roofs, which he replicated to match the
original 13th-century arrangement still existing at the other side. With the

MELDRUM HOUSE

One of Simpson's largest domestic commissions, he virtually doubled the original house in size with this spirited neo-Jacobean exercise. Unfortunately in the 1930's the house was considerably reduced.

judicious use of harling, leaving exposed various margins, stringers and copings, he successfully completed an overall unity and basically balanced architectural ensemble. Various more prominent windows were singled out for further elaboration with hooded mouldings, and in the centre a boldly projecting carriage porch proclaimed the entrance with a powerful three-faced arch-headed stone structure. Internally a rather magnificent new first floor suite of reception rooms was created along with upper floors of bedrooms, arranged over a ground storey now mainly devoted to kitchens and service accommodation. This quite impressively extravagant pile, boasting some eighty-six rooms and some very grandly furnished interiors, was however very considerably reduced in the 1930s, losing into the bargain much of Simpson's architectural contribution, when further major alterations were also carried out. The third floor was completely removed along with the projecting east wing, the entrance porch was demolished and an entirely new entrance formed at first floor, utilising a redundant stairway acquired apparently from distant Castle Fraser. Much of Simpson's stonework was in the event however reused, lending the house still a noticeable Simpson air, despite also the complete loss of its external harling. Notwithstanding its truncation and the quite rambling nature of the interior, this is still an impressive mansion house, well maintained and completely refurbished as a Country House Hotel, shortly to be considerably extended again. The surrounding estate is now very largely given over to an extremely fine golf course and centre.

Much further north meanwhile and just east of Keith at Inverkeithny, and about a mile up a long driveway through dense woodland, a truly lovely and very striking extension to Haddo House there (which surely must be to a design by Simpson), made its appearance joined to the rather plain original three-storey mansion behind. The new work, seemingly anticipating elements of much later Thainstone, was contained within a T-plan two-storey classical block of great distinction, finished in rendering with stone dressed margins and stringers. To the new asymmetrical front, the heavily projecting eaves of the slated pitched roof, forms above the continuous all round under eaves stringer, a broad pedimented

Haddo House, Inverkeithney in its heyday

gable over the three-bay end. Long elegant windows at ground floor dictate smaller squarer versions on the bedroom floor above. On the return elevation a swelling bow advances while on the other end is placed one of his boldest portes cochere, complete with three high arch-headed openings and a stringer above, which further supports a square tower sporting his favourite triple arch-headed window arrangement on all external faces. Above this a low-pitched broad-eaved pyramidal roof terminates the design. Within the re-entrant just formed, a glazed porch rather successfully fills the space. Unfortunately all this and a range of offices built slightly to the north, is in a perilous state of increasing dilapidation as the now long abandoned mansion house continues to seriously deteriorate. With the building probably in a condition hovering on the point of no return, the current owner is apparently quite unperturbed, content presumably to see this wonderful design creation crumble completely and unnecessarily away. Tantalising fragments of the original paintwork are still just discernable within the extremely sad interior of this ghost of a house, almost lost now within the advancing surrounding woodland.

Haddo House today, a sad and crumbling ruin, almost completely overgrown.

In Aberdeen at this time in Ferryhill, an extremely severe and understated granite ashlar block of town houses made its appearance at the top of the hill in a terrace named Rotunda Place. The five houses, all executed in the smoothest, crispest granite, with long elegant windows and door openings set up upon a semi-suppressed basement, have no recorded architect, although the whole

Rotunda Place, now 1–6 Polmuir Road, Aberdeen.

thing strongly suggests Simpson's hand and seems to anticipate his later accredited designs for Albert Street in the west end by some years. The rotunda in question of course refers to a round, probably man-made feature of ancient and long forgotten origin, which is now rather successfully hidden within the grounds of the old Cowdray Club in Fonthill Road opposite. Rotunda Place itself of course has long been renamed Polmuir Road.

This same year witnessed Simpson very busily engaged at last on what would prove to be his largest and also one of his most important commissions. As far back as July 1824, both Simpson and Smith had been approached by the Principal of Marischal College to examine the ancient fabric of the existing college buildings with a view to submitting a joint report on the matter. Finding the fabric to be in quite a sorry state, and the accommodation to be completely inadequate for modern purposes, both men were asked to submit proposals for a completely new complex. The fact that this initiative may have been encouraged by the refurbishment and new extensions being carried out at King's College in the Aulton at this very time by John Smith may be completely immaterial. Whatever, Smith at the time being too busy, the commission was handed to Simpson virtually de facto. He immediately cast around looking for alternative city sites for initially an entirely new building. At first by far the most favoured location was the Barracks site on the Castlehill, but unfavourable responses from both the Government and the Council swiftly put paid to that. The final selection was settled on an old factory building at the north end of Belmont Street overlooking the valley of the Denburn. His very dramatic initial design envisaged a resolutely Grecian, classical block conceived fully in accordance with the Principal's stated wishes, raised up high with a grandly magnificent broad portico, surmounted by a high central dome which would have dominated the north of the city centre. The scheme was eventually generally approved and sent off to the Treasury in London for their consideration. Very unfortunately however Simpson's only other office copy went up in flames with his offices in 1826. The following year a Commission visited the city to examine the problem but it was 1834 before the King's Architect, Robert Reid was sent north with the intention of producing his own proposals for a new University Complex. In the event his scheme was heavily indebted to Simpson's earlier scheme. Even at this time however local opinion was very divided, with a faction persuaded that the best course of action would be for King's and Marischal to unite, preferably on a site in the Aulton in the immediate vicinity of King's College. As could be imagined this wasn't exactly music to everyone's ears as our old friend Lord Cockburn noted even as late as 1842

Old Marischal College, Aberdeen. Unfortunately this building failed to meet the requirements of the day.

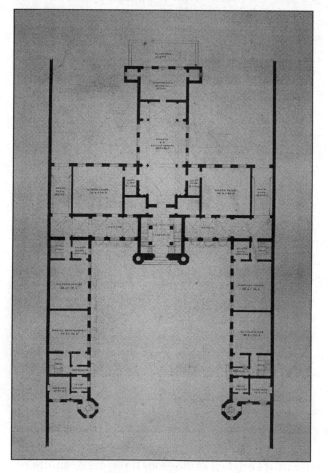

NEW MARISCHAL COLLEGE

Simpson required all his ingenuity to squeeze his accommodation into the very restricted site of the old college. This complex, much altered and extended, still exists at the heart of the present buildings.

with the New Marischal College actually finished: "The attempt to maintain two Universities in such a place is absurd. They should have given up the one in the town and made the old venerable well placed academic-looking King's College the single seat of their science. It is vain to speak about a thing so reasonable to either of these two parties each of whom would rather see its favourite establishment in science besides extinguished, rather than yield to the other".

In the middle of 1835, Alexander Bannerman MP actually went so far as to submit a Bill to Parliament in order to gain the necessary authorisation for the unification of the two universities to proceed but in the event this was all that was required to galvanise the Council into total and complete opposition. Events now moved swiftly and a new design by Archibald Simpson was approved, this time allowing the replacement of the existing buildings, but built on the same site and allowing for the new to be built, while the old college functioned until the completion of the new building. The design, which is curiously slightly smaller looking than it actually is in fact, was created around three sides of a quadrangle, in a two-storey over full basement rather stiff and formal perpendicular Gothic style. Embracing a central four-pinnacled tower within a three-bay cloistered range established on either side, these return in nine-bay wings facing one another across the quadrangle, to terminate in octagonal towers rising up through an open arcade to ogee-capped granite domes. Behind the central tower, another shorter wing extended out to the rear containing principally the main Hall with further accommodation on two floors below including the Public School and the Anatomical Museum. Overlooking the quad on either side, various departments devoted to Greek, Divinity, Oriental Languages, Medicine, Logic and a Medical Museum, were arranged with most of the spacious lecture rooms provided with tiered raked seating The complex also contained sixteen classrooms, departments of Philosophy, Chemistry, and Anatomy along with a Museum and a Library. The impressive Public Hall on the upper floor was reached by a very grand divided staircase underneath the central tower coming up to an open gallery accessing both the spacious Museum and the Library, from which it climbs again in a broad straight section to the Hall itself. All these principal spaces and rooms, boasting fine and important early-Gothic inspired ribbed plasterwork and details, still survive within the subsequent late-Victorian extensions added at the end of the nineteenth century. The building was finished externally in granite ashlar with moulded granite hoods over all the windows to the quadrangle. Interestingly, and probably for reasons of economy, the inset mullioned and traceried windows are all executed in more easily worked sandstone, now just beginning

Simpson's earlier University proposal intended for the site subsequently occupied by his Cathedral of the Disruption at the end of Belmont Street.

MARISCHAL COLLEGE, 1840-93.

An early photograph of Simpson's College complex as he originally completed it.

At the turn of the nineteenth century, A Marshall Mackenzie would more than double this quadrangle, treble the height of Simpson's tower and build the splendid neo-Perpendicular Broad Street front range.

Simpson's original core buildings at the centre of Marischal College today.

Simpson's
former Natural
History
Museum
interior, still
survives in
another guise.

The splendid main staircase of Marischal College, situated immediately under the high central Tower, is notable for its powerful drama and the quality of its Perpendicular Gothic detailing.

to prove that its wearing qualities are not a match for granite. All this was built behind the existing old college building, necessitating in due course considerable under-building, and when the old structure was eventually demolished a great deal of up-making in levels was necessary to create the finished quadrangle itself. As well as the constraints imposed by the old college, the presence of the even more ancient Greyfriar's Church also considerably influenced the overall layout. The new building, described by its admirers even at its inception as "having a striking attention to economy but combining elegance with convenience of arrangement", commenced detailed design and erection following the successful acceptance in August 1836 of an estimate of £21,420 from Alexander Rainnie, builder. This made the construction of the new University College by far the largest single building contract to be undertaken in Aberdeen up to that time.

The foundation stone was laid in 1837 and the complex finished by 1841. When almost completed however, the ensemble, despite apparently exhibiting some considerable charm (if the evidence of prints and paintings of it executed at the time can be believed), did not altogether win general approval. Lord Cockburn characteristically let it be known, "They boast much of their new Marischal College, confined amidst paltry buildings, its position is bad, it has no architecture, and its construction implies the destruction of the old buildings, which sets all they will do utterly at defiance". Again it would appear that Lord Cockburn was not one of Archibald Simpson's natural admirers. It is certainly true that in this instance, Simpson's perpendicular Gothic, while unquestionably exhibiting considerable dignity, also displays a certain coldness, again possibly exaggerated by the use of granite ashlar, which is somewhat reminiscent of his East St Nicholas Church Gothic. Notwithstanding, as the project reached completion, Simpson proceeded to attempt to rectify at least one of His Lordship's criticisms by resurrecting his bold scheme for the creation of a new symbolically axial street between his New College and his St Nicholas Church to the west. He contemplated also considerably widening the access from Broad Street into the quadrangle itself to allow for the erection of a delicate arcaded screen of Gothic arches as an appropriate prelude to his design which would as a result achieve far greater prominence in the city centre. The broad new thoroughfare envisaged the demolition of much of the Guestrow and Flourmill Brae opposite, an area of quite insalubrious slums, and represented a considerable civic improvement at a time when both the adjacent Kirkgates were still extremely narrow and tortuous. Nothing at all came of this proposal however until at the end of the century when in a very different adventure the whole of Broad Street between Queen Street and Littlejohn Street was removed (including old Greyfriar's Church itself), to make way for A. Marshall Mackenzie's extremely splendid perpendicular Gothic extravaganza, successfully overwhelming even Simpson's original complex. The considerable heightening also of Simpson's little central pinnacled box, into the dramatically vertical Mitchell Tower we know today, provided the city with still its symbolically tallest structure, in an overall complex which boasts to be the second largest granite building in the world, after the Escorial Palace outside Madrid.

The year 1837 commenced with the construction of the first two houses of Simpson's residential palace block in Belvidere terrace (now Marine Terrace).

MARINE PLACE, FERRYHILL.

More of Simpson's simple classic linked cottages.

Sadly these houses were all that would appear of this scheme, the bulk of the remaining design having to wait a further forty years to materialise and even then in a truncated form. At the same time however, in a logical eastern extension of the start made at the western end of Ferryhill Place, Marine Place commenced in an attempt to frame the entrance into Devanha House. The design of this simple but quite charming terrace of five linked single-storey classic cottages above semi-suppressed basements, has also always been attributed to Archibald Simpson, despite a lack of any evidence. The principal reason for this, in addition to the obvious merit and quality of the design, is the close attention to texture and detailing which was already displayed in Ferryhill Place itself, which of course has also been attributed to Simpson. The only really noticeable change in this design is his use of horizontal glazing, a pattern increasingly associated with him at this time. Unfortunately today even this window style is no longer completely consistent throughout. The terrace is set at the back of a triangular green with a sweeping driveway and surround of trees.

Although these have thinned out, the original gate piers still exist, complete with restored cast iron railings. To the immediate east, South Crown Street which aligns itself at right angles, continues with its namesake further north, to compose an interesting grouping. The rather similar classic cottages stepping down the hill on the eastern side of this street were built slightly later in a similar but debased style by another hand. In recent years there has been a tendency to attempt to "spot" further Simpson terraces in the Ferryhill District, but the repetition of some of his trademark features is not in itself an indication of his personal involvement however, especially when other practitioners and developers were perfectly capable of grafting on a few borrowed details here and there. Apart from the possible introduction to Devanha Terrace, very little in the surrounding streets illustrates much of the unity, restraint, rhythm, surface treatment and careful balance of solid over void always associated with Archibald Simpson's work.

Meanwhile Simpson completed this busy year with the extension of Lessendrum House in one of his most accomplished essays in his Jacobean style. The estate belonged to the ancient Bisset Family who had owned it since 1252 and the mansion Simpson inherited on site had been originally built in the seventeenth century. The design involved a major remodelling and extension of the dwelling, which explains the quite dramatic sense of asymmetry and informality achieved, especially on the main fronts. The principal reception rooms were established immediately above a low ground storey of kitchen and

LESSENDRUM HOUSE

service accommodation, with a great gable containing a broad canted bay window set between two high octagonal domed pinnacles. Balanced at the other end of a run of three high dining room windows is a high corner tower and surmounted by an ogee-leaded dome. To the north and west the asymmetry was reinforced by a short lower scale family wing incorporating some of the older house with a balancing gable, completing an exceptional design, further enlivened by diagonally placed chimneys breaking the horizontality of the slated roof. The result was certainly one of Simpson's most compellingly successful asymmetrical designs in his personal neo-Jacobean manner. Tragically however the mansion house went up in flames on the 12th January 1928, the Huntly Fire Brigade's lack of pumping equipment ensuring its total destruction even after they had arrived on site. Happily many of the priceless contents were saved, including two paintings by Van Dyke. The resultant ruins however have very slowly crumbled and deteriorated over time until today they are completely enveloped in a jungle of weeds and ivy.

The splendid garden front of Lessendrum, immediately
prior to the fire.

1837 also witnessed Simpson absorbed in the design of another masterwork in the form of Mrs Emslie's Institution, to be built on the remaining wide central site on the south side of Albyn Place, midway between Simpson's earlier houses at Nos. 18 and 20. The previous year Mrs Emslie, the daughter of a rich Aberdeen Wine Merchant and now a widow residing in London, determined to gift the very considerable sum of £40,000 in order to erect an appropriate institution in the city of Aberdeen for the accommodation of orphaned or destitute young girls.

Simpson's initial perspective of Mrs Emslie's Institution in Albyn Place, Aberdeen.
Note the charming little pair of gate-lodges flanking the central entry from the street.

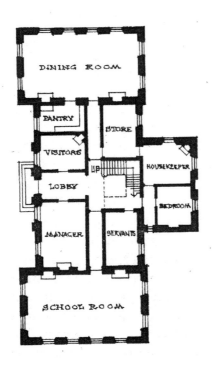

GROUND FLOOR PLAN

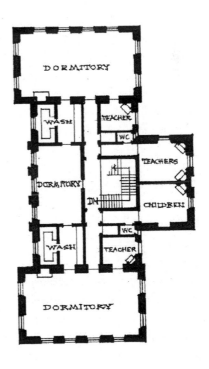

FIRST FLOOR PLAN

The building, designed as a truncated H-block, extending out at the back into a T-shape, was designed on two principal floors over a basement to accommodate schoolrooms and a dining room on the ground floor augmented with managerial offices and kitchen, with on the first floor a broadly similar arrangement devoted to dormitories, washing facilities and toilets. Externally as was his norm in this scale of building, Simpson advanced his end wings, which in this instance were two windows wide and were crowned by his favourite plain frieze and low Greek pediments. The recessed five-bay centre is dominated by a flat, four-pilaster anta order centrepiece, supporting a bold horizontal entablature which is only the second time such a feature made an appearance in his work. Above the unifying all-round cornice, a low parapet steps up to the centre, topped by a blocking course. It is clear from an initial perspective study for the building that Simpson had hoped to place a sculpture group on top of this, which unfortunately was omitted even from the final version of the sketch. The main entrance immediately below, up a short flight of steps, is distinguished with an arch and an architrave surround. All the windows openings are apparently simply carved out of the granite with only the jambs of the longer ground floor windows taken down to the basecourse, allowing for a recessed spandrel panel underneath. Down both sides, which were very obvious before the building became the centrepiece of the Girl's High School, four similarly treated windows continued the design all the way round to the rear. The building has always been particularly admired as the high point of Simpson's work in granite ashlar, in a contract where Alexander Rainnie again could be said to have surpassed himself in terms of granite workmanship. It should be noted that the building initially sat in the centre of an extensive garden setting, with two exquisite little gate-houses built on either side of the entrance established axially on the front door archway. The complex was completed and formally opened by Provost Sir Thomas Blaikie in November 1840.

Although much of the interior still survives relatively untouched, including the entrance hall, circulation, stair and some offices etc., the alterations necessary to form modern classrooms within the much expanded complex took their toll of much of the rest. Similar damage was inflicted on Nos. 18 and 20 Albyn Place as well when they were also absorbed into the overall scheme. Indeed given their quite extensive external changes, both these former houses fared slightly worse. New ranges of classrooms balanced by a large assembly hall successfully linked the ensemble together, in what was a difficult architectural problem, producing a charming if slightly rambling end result. The considerable set back however allows a finely landscaped frontage to address the elongated gardens of Rubislaw Terrace opposite.

THE CENTREPIECE OF MRS EMSLIE'S INSTITUTION

The builder Rainnie's fine standard of granite ashlar on this particular contract was never surpassed in Aberdeen. This centrepiece however failed to acquire its sculptural crown at the end of the day.

A considerably expanded Institution embracing link wings and absorbing also Simpson's two flanking houses at Nos. 18 and 20 Albyn Place, still just holds its own in the centre of the rather rambling complex.

Provost Leslie's of Nethermuir's apparently single storey classical villa at No. 28 Albyn Place, Aberdeen.

The following year found Archibald Simpson completing the design of one of his finest small villas built on the edge of the town. Commissioned by Provost Leslie of Nethermuir, to erect a residence for himself upon a broad plot at No. 28 Albyn Place Aberdeen, the design developed the illusion of an apparently single-storey mansion. A slightly paired Tuscan entrance portico is held in a three-bay centre between advanced single-bay wings projecting out on either side, and extended further westwards towards the rear, with a wing reinforcing an almost rambling asymmetry. Sadly all the original front windows have been replaced to a later design. Behind, a noticeably higher piended slated roof floats overhead with the lower front roofs also piended and brought over the wall-head to broad, all

This rear view of Provost Leslie's, exposes the fiction of its single storey villa pretensions.

embracing eaves. The now exposed squared rubble walls were originally rendered, with only smooth granite margins, ashlar spandrel panels under windows and stringers relieving what would have been a much more sophisticated external effect. From the garden side the single-storey fiction is immediately exposed, as the fully revealed basement floor and the bedroom windows of the roof accommodation above come clearly into view. The garden front is also dominated by an off-centre broad segmental bow, carried up into an interesting dormer roof arrangement, expressing the principal bedroom overhead.

Internally although the plan form has only been marginally altered, much later plasterwork and detail has been subsequently introduced to the overall detriment of the whole. However the main reception enfilade is still happily in existence to the garden side and the central main drawing room in particular retains its freely described low relief plasterwork ceiling. The entrance hall and circulation are also original, although later plaster decoration here also intrudes. The first floor bedrooms and basement service accommodation have actually been more fortunate, despite the house operating as a Club for very many years. Even the garden setting and the fine coach and gardener's house on the bottom lane have failed to survive, having only very recently become the site for extensive new offices, and associated car parking.

In this year also, growing public dissatisfaction with John Smith's Obelisk in St Nicholas Churchyard reached a crescendo. The red granite Obelisk had been put up in concert with the Ionic Screen as a fitting memorial to Sir John Forbes

SIR JOHN FORBES OF NEWE'S OBELISK
This Smith obelisk, which in its position within St Nicholas Churchyard apparently caused such offence, was removed to its present site at Barkmill by Archibald Simpson in 1838.

224

of Newe, a greatly respected individual and considerable benefactor to the city. The Council was eventually persuaded to take action on the matter and perhaps quite diplomatically requested that Archibald Simpson organise the removal of the offending memorial. He and the managers however totally rejected completely out of hand the suggestion that it be placed immediately in front of his almost finished new Infirmary in Woolmanhill. At the end of the day the Obelisk was found a quite appropriate resting place immediately to the rear of the Lunatic Asylum, an institution which Sir John had done so much to support. Interestingly further dedications have also found their way on to the other three plaques round the base, extolling the virtues of Sir John's son, the architect and the eventual completion of the Lunatic Asylum itself.

All through this decade, the rather revolutionary idea of building a large

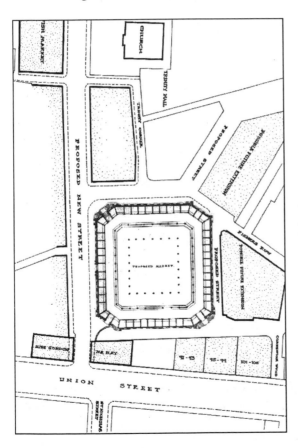

Simpson's initial aborted Aberdeen New Market proposals.

covered market in the city had been canvassed about, led by Alexander Anderson, a very prominent solicitor in the firm of Adam and Anderson,

Advocates, who was destined to become Provost in due course. In the absence of any real support from the Town Council, in 1838 a company was promoted to float the scheme and Archibald Simpson was engaged to carry out investigative designs. Of course at this time the area immediately to the south of Union Street was still occupied by an extremely insalubrious slum known as Putachieside. With John Smith's proposals for a new street down to the harbour having been put forward as early as 1810, combining his client's requirements with the civic ambition to see a new street formed, Simpson embarked on a plan envisaging the wholesale redevelopment of the area. His initial idea for the market itself was for a very large structure, 200ft square in plan with chamfered corners, and on two floors, enclosing a vast central columned space surrounded by individual small shop units, and with an upper gallery above. This bold proposal also allowed the formation of a new bridge street down to the harbour along with a site for a new fish market facing the new dock. In addition another cross street was suggested linking the new street with the ancient Green itself. However despite, or possibly because of the noble scale of these proposals, the scheme initially failed to find sufficient financial backing at this time. Pressing ahead however with obtaining the necessary Governmental approval for the new road, two years later a much altered proposal would be put forward, envisaging the new street built slightly further west, and the market building itself conceived in a much narrower and elongated form.

This same year, the Council settled on a site on the centre of the north side of Little Belmont Street in order to erect a new Town School. This initiative in fact first saw the light of day in 1835 when the site immediately to the west of the Schoolhill entry into Gordon's College was the hoped for location. Difficulties here forced a rethink, and eventually opinion favoured the Little Belmont Street position. Archibald Simpson and John Smith were both immediately invited to submit their proposals for the new school, and in the event Smith's dramatic little Doric jewel won the day. Long expanded into the Aberdeen Academy, and since converted into a public house within a shopping complex carved out of the late Victorian complex, the former school continues to adorn this charming backwater in the city centre to this day

1839 commenced with Simpson engaged in the design and erection of one of his most delightful cottage-orné style houses, this time on the eastern flank of the Murtle Estate on the south side of the North Deeside Road at Beildside. Murtle Cottage consists of a storey and a half squarish, traditionally gabled white rendered block, with a single-storey entrance porch extending out to the south. To the rear, a further single-storey wing has been allowed to develop in a not incompatible style, embracing further accommodation and a conservatory. However the main block is beautifully enlivened by first floor windows on the gables complete with exquisite little balconettes, and elongated narrow bay windows electrify the west front, placed on either side of the central window, which was probably also once the main door.

One of Simpson's other finest small villas also began construction in this year in the form of Westburn House, built on a large piece of ground on a knoll overlooking the North Burn of Gilcomston (now the Westburn), between the old Cornhill Road, the Low Stocket Road, (now Westburn Road) and next to a house long since gone called Loch-head. The client was David Chalmers, the Proprietor-Editor of the *Aberdeen Journal,* and a great admirer of Archibald Simpson's work. The apparently single-storey villa includes the usual kitchen and service basement, with some additional bedroom accommodation skilfully introduced into the first floor at the rear. The reception rooms were arranged in an enfilade facing south, served by an august hall preceded by a noble broad tetrastyle external Greek portico dominating the three-bay west front. Simpson's usual broad eaves and low piended and slated roof complete a most memorable design. The south front, with two-window wide ends balanced by a three-windowed segmental bow in the centre, has been rather heavily shaded by the later building of a not altogether inappropriate Victorian veranda, which is supported on delicate cast iron supports and has its own portico implanted in the centre where below, granite steps give access to the original garden grounds.

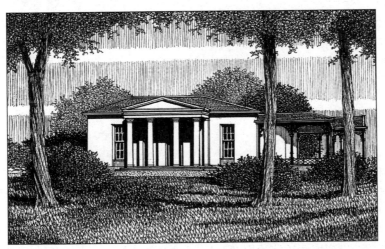

WESTBURN HOUSE, ABERDEEN
One of Simpson's finest classic villas for his friend David Chalmers.

Internally the house is beautifully understated with a succession of extremely elegant and spacious rooms, all provided with his usual discreet plasterwork, good woodwork and fine chimneypieces, still mostly *in situ*. Also as part of his commission Simpson designed a charming little related group of estate buildings, unfortunately now not in quite the condition perhaps they should be, flanking the old walled garden, which is now used as part of an enclosure for public bowling greens. These buildings have long been in the ownership of the Town Council; indeed the entire mini-estate was originally acquired in 1900 by the Municipality with the express intention of creating a public park to serve the fast developing northern fringe of the city. Having done service as a tearoom and latterly as a day nursery, the presently most unfortunate boarded up condition of the house itself is hopefully nearing a conclusion. Moves currently afoot should shortly see the mansion fully restored and used as the local Registrar's Office for the City of Aberdeen.

Around this time also, Simpson had become closely involved with the completion of the western side of King Street nearest its corner with Castle Street. A number of parties were interested in this prestigious location, particularly as it became known that the former New Inn could also be available for redevelopment as well. This building, now in the possession of Isaac Machray, would involve Simpson in the initial production of a sketch design for a completely new hotel scheme, intended to successfully turn the corner into King Street. However progress on this particular fantasy was slow and Simpson was appointed in the interim to design yet another building at Nos. 1–5 King Street for the Fire and Life Assurance Company. This handsome four-bay three-storey block proceeded apace but during its construction phase Simpson inadvertently became involved in a very unfortunate exchange with James Gillespie Graham of Edinburgh. Graham in his capacity as architect for the Commercial Bank of Scotland, had been instructed to produce a design for their intended new premises, to be built immediately next door to the north. This of course he had proceeded to do without having taken the trouble to venture the long distance north to even inspect the site. When the Council passed the plans to Archibald Simpson for his comments, he advised them that the proposed building was too high for its intended location and suggested that it should be lowered. After this criticism was passed back to Edinburgh, a further heated exchange of letters took place before Graham eventually resolved the difficulty by graciously lowering his building. Notwithstanding, his Edinburgh-inspired design clearly indebted to his Moray Place Development precedent, still makes very interesting comparison with the King Street architectural work of both local architects, Simpson and Smith.

Nos. 1–5
King Street,
Aberdeen

The Fire and Life Building meanwhile advanced, carefully set up upon a four-arched ground arcade (now unfortunately obliterated to form wide shop windows), within a rusticated ground storey. Above this the main first floor windows sit above low spandrel panels with architrave surrounds on the broad string course, each provided also with an individual cornice. Above this at second floor sill level, a further stringer supports squarer windows provided with architrave surrounds and cornices, in a noticeably busier arrangement than was usual for Simpson. Perhaps the southern competition next door had spurred him on to more elaborate things. Overhead, the design terminates in a bold cornice taken right across, with a low parapet and central Simpsonian-type panel above. The building made a fine statement at the time at the bottom of King Street, but any initial impact it may have had was about to be seriously eclipsed as Simpson finally embarked on the design of his superb Aberdeen masterpiece immediately next door, dominating the corner itself.

The scheme for Machray's Hotel having evaporated in the face of an approach from the North of Scotland Bank in October 1838, the most important site available in Aberdeen at this time was acquired by the bank, intended for its own headquarters building. The Banking Company had been established only as recently as 1836 in premises which Simpson had initially altered and refurbished at 41– 45 Broad Street. By 1838 however he was very busily engaged in the production of no less than six different schemes for the Castlegate site. He was not alone however, and by the end of January 1939, Simpson, John Smith and David Rhind of Edinburgh had all submitted proposals in a limited competition. Simpson's design ideas won the day, and as he had been previously employed and also useful in the acquisition of the site, this might be unsurprising. Initially setting up a two-storey block above the almost obligatory rusticated basecourse ground storey, he investigated various treatments all involving the principal entrance being placed centrally on the Castle Street façade. One such proposal involved a vigorous reworking of his Medical Hall portico balanced by chunky decorative window balconies with a Soanean-style roofline. However as his interest in the corner developed with the early appearance of a round domed temple penultimate scheme, this clearly anticipated his final very dramatic solution.

NORTH OF SCOTLAND BANK SCHEMES

Simpson's most profoundly Soanean design proposal, still however intended to directly confront the Castlegate in the heart of the City of Aberdeen.

One of Simpson's perhaps less inspired elevational proposals.

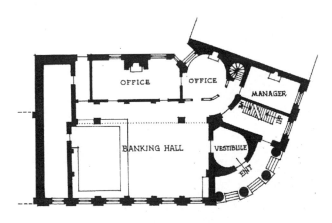

PRINCIPAL FLOOR PLAN
(as built)
NORTH OF SCOTLAND BANK

By placing the entrance resolutely on the corner Simpson was able to develop a six-bay front on to Castle Street with two corresponding bays on to King Street round the obtuse angled corner. Unfortunately for absolute perfection it would have been marginally better had he been able to provide a minimum of at least three bays on King Street, but this could not be. Selecting a far busier treatment than was his usual wont, the vertically disposed two-storey window arrangements were double inset into smooth walled ashlar surrounds allowing for the introduction of exquisitely modelled decorative spandrels at first floor, in a departure previously unheard of in his work. Between these features, the walls, treated as broad fully rusticated pilasters, support a modillion cornice at second floor over which a further storey of windows presides, also rusticated but with plain pilasters placed centrally supporting a further cornice and a blocked and balustraded parapet top. While this arrangement is established on both streets, on the corner Simpson pulled out all the stops with the introduction of a noble circular vestibule, preceded by a magnificent Corinthian giant tetrastyle quarter portico which, supporting its own frieze, entablature and modillion cornice, carries only a plain deep parapet above, a suitably august base for the terracotta group of Ceres, designed by his friend James Giles. To further emphasise this work, the third floor boldly breaks back to frame and further throw the statuary into relief. The sculpture shows Ceres sitting, supported by the British Lion on the right with a cornucopia on the left. The design was modelled by Nelson and manufactured by Routledge Lucas and Company of London. This fine group is now painted. Notwithstanding the fact that the Bank were anxious to make a very major statement on this corner and had even gone so far as to employ the most prestigious local architect of the day in order to achieve this aim, this work, frequently described as Simpson's Aberdeen masterpiece, illustrates in him a new, much richer train of thought. The design adopts a rather more Renaissance character, possibly even recalling something from his Italian journey of so long ago, but in any event this building is completely different in spirit from most of his earlier more spartan work. The foundation stone was laid with much ceremony in January 1840, with the whole complex completed by 1842. The contractor for the work was Alexander Rainnie.

Simpson's attention now begins to focus at last on the King Street corner

THE NORTH OF SCOTLAND BANK, ABERDEEN

Frequently described as Simpson's masterpiece, the design beautifully effects the turn of King Street into Castle Street and Union Street beyond. The design of the sculptural group was provided by Giles.

The equally splendid Banking Hall interior has been sensitively handled when converted into a bar.

The Archibald Simpson Bar today.

Internally the note of opulence continues, introduced by an august ovoid vestibule. This leads into a magnificent banking hall, itself introducing a new richness of finish into the city. Five tall windows flood the interior with light, throwing into relief a finely beamed and compartmented ceiling with panels centred on rosettes surrounded with bands of Greek key ornament. This is supported by marbled and gilded Corinthian pilasters on the walls, enriched also by a gilded copy of the Panathenaic Frieze borrowed from the Parthenon. The plain walls below are relieved with bands of parallel linear decoration terminating in corner squares, in a manner acknowledging Soane's Bank of England work in London. The heavy mahogany woodwork, the counters and the magnificently mosaiced floors in both the banking hall and vestibule, complete an interior of very considerable style and panache. The principal offices for the manager and interviews exit off to the north, while the principal staircase accesses the office floors above. The bank successfully operated on this site for a hundred and fifty years before planning policies, the requirements of business and the age of the motor car forced a move to perhaps the modern city's new principal corner at Queen's Cross. The now former bank headquarters, subsequently very tastefully restored and also much more colourfully and richly refurbished as yet another licensed premises, actually presently rejoices in the name "Archibald Simpson". He would be pleased!

Meanwhile in Huntly, the Duchess of Gordon, anxious to further commemorate the life of her late husband the Fifth Duke, engaged her architect again to design a group of initially four separate schools on a site just to the north of the town, previously occupied by two ancient towers, the fore-works of Strathbogie (Huntly) Castle. The design, developing across the major axis on either side of the principal avenue to Huntly Castle and Huntly Lodge beyond, was arranged within a parallel, mirrored pair of T-shaped buildings, carried out in a warm freestone ashlar, boldly terminating the long avenue north from the Town Square, quarter of a mile to the south. Each block contains two large classrooms on both floors, with toilets, cloaks and staffrooms being accommodated in the short projecting leg of the T-wing behind. These buildings are linked in the centre by a two-storey connecting range of offices boldly bridging the avenue to the castle by means of a triumphal archway. The crisp smooth two-storey walls, pierced by hooded long elegant mullioned windows, are all carried out with the serene elegance of Simpson's very own personal neo-Jacobean style. Above the eaves, plain octagonal corner chimneys as terminals between low pitched gables and ogee-shaped dormer caps, firmly break the line of the guttering and the slated pitched roofs. In the centre of this

The Gordon Schools terminates the northern axis from the town square.

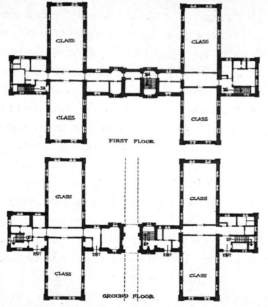

FIRST FLOOR

GROUND FLOOR

FLOOR PLANS: GORDON SCHOOLS, HUNTLY

Simpson's central tower recalls Wren's earlier Tom Tower in Oxford.

arrangement a boldly conceived arch forms a triumphal link between both wings flanked by tall very compressed two-storey ogee gables placed on either side of an elongated panel out of which soars a magical octagonal ogee-domed tower. This magnificently dramatic axial stop, clearly indebted to Sir Christopher Wren's rather earlier Tom Tower version in Oxford, contains the belfry and four clock faces on the principal facades.

The Good Duchess provided the £3,000 necessary for the building and the foundation stone was laid on the 27th February 1839 with great ceremony. The work was completed the following year and The Gordon Schools, including an Established and also a Free Church School for boys, an Infants' School and an Industrial School for girls, duly opened. Over time the schools have amalgamated and grown into a much larger complex, which has continued to develop mainly to the west. In the early 1970s the entire Simpson complex was very beautifully restored and now functions only as the departments of music and home economics within the much greater and extended modern complex. Nevertheless this beautiful building straddling the great tree-lined avenue through to the ancient ruined seat of the Earls of Huntly, certainly remains the symbolic and aesthetic centre of the establishment, presenting also a most appropriate prelude to the drama of the Castle and the Deveron valley beyond.

This year Simpson is also accredited with making the initial design for the laying out of Albert Terrace in the west end, a proposal initially forming only part of a much larger scheme. The fact that the earliest houses are single-storey linked classic cottages over semi-basements clearly emulating his original versions in Ferryhill Place and Marine Place, is explained by the fact that the

Albert Terrace, Aberdeen

original feu even went so far as to insist that the terrace "was to be set apart for cottages half or whole to be of similar style to those in Ferryhill". The work however may not have got underway on the houses until after 1848, when they were most probably erected under the supervision of Mackenzie and Matthews, Simpson's eventual west-end successors. The terrace was only completed however at its western end, as late as 1867.

By 1840 Archibald Simpson had completed his third decade as busy as ever and indeed this proved if anything to be one of his most prolific years. His interest in the west end continued, and of course his name has always been associated with the inspiration behind Albert Street, designed also in this year. Proposals for Nos. 1–23 and 2–18 were produced, to that rather individual Aberdeen manner which finds the western side built lower than the eastern side, presumably to minimise the shading effect on the higher side. All the houses are above basements, and the two-storey side clearly belongs to the Simpson tradition of minimal Spartan elegance, continuing the Rubislaw Place – Albyn Place type, already established along the way. The lower side is rather busier but the single-storey cottages here are in granite ashlar with cornices with brackets over the doors and windows, and with mostly railinged-off sunken forecourts in front. Built after 1849 however also by Mackenzie and Matthews, they were largely responsible for the increased sense of unity provided by the use of their standard flat pedimented dormers on both sides of the street.

Albert Street, Aberdeen

Simpson was also very fortunate this year to receive a number of important County commissions for large houses and substantial additions to existing ones. In the latter category, just north of Fordyce west of Portsoy, the Abercrombies of Glassaugh lived in some considerable style in a residence, which dated back to 1770, incorporating an even older tower. Complete with raised corner attic towers, the three-storey main block was nicely placed between two lower out-riding pavilions. Some later work of a rather Gibbs-style character continued the drama, until Simpson was asked to considerably extend the mansion by adding basically a south and west block on to the ensemble. Incorporating features from the original and using a rather Italianate style for the design, the two principal storeys above a basically kitchen and service ground floor, are contained within a rather severe seven-bay front, with the end bays brought very slightly forward. Not actually one of his most inspired efforts, his fully down to the floor windows on the first floor are enhanced in the middle and both ends by pediments over their possibly too restrained architrave surrounds. The remaining windows together with those of the second floor above, which are slightly squarer, make do with only the surrounds. The whole design is crowned

GLASSHAUGH HOUSE.
In its currently very dilapidated condition.

by a heavy cornice and parapet on which two groups of three squarish Soanean chimneys are rather improbably and precariously balanced. A very similar general treatment completes the slightly shorter west facing frontage also. A subservient bow, swelling out of the one storey lower eastern range completes the principal fronts, while the back still confronts the extensive enclosed walled garden to the rear. In the centre of the south front a slightly lacklustre broad flat-headed Doric entrance porch once completed the design, but this was subsequently demolished when the house was abandoned. Left to its own devices for many years as a shelter for various farm animals stratified apparently according to weight, rank and size, cows occupied the ground level, pigs were accommodated immediately above, and hens enjoyed the top floor.

Glasshaugh House in its heyday – not perhaps one of his finest efforts.

Originally a very fine top lit staircase behind the front hall gave immediate access directly up to the first floor where the elegant drawing room, small drawing room and dining room were grouped as usual en suite. Above this the stair continued up to the second floor to the nursery level where various secondary family and guest bedrooms could also be found. Although the roof still seems basically sound, all this is now open to the elements as the general fabric continues to deteriorate, window frames fall out and danger signs proliferate. More happily the adjacent rather handsome Simpson service and stable block building has been restored into a fine modern residence.

Not very far away, midway between Turriff and Aberchirder, Simpson was also appointed to design and build one of his largest mansion houses in the form of Carnousie New House. Conceived even from the outset perhaps on too grand a scale, the great axial Italianate extravaganza had to be diminished slightly even in execution in a less elaborate form. The mansion was built for Captain Alexander Grant, a very successful sea merchant and owner of a considerable fleet of ships. The tightly planned rectangle, which he commissioned, was set up high on a heavily rusticated basement containing the

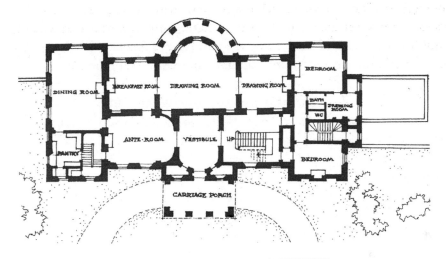

PRINCIPAL FLOOR PLAN: CARNOUSTIE

Carnousie New House, immediately prior to its unfortunate demolition.

Simpson's original front elevation for Carnousie was modified in execution.

entire kitchen and service accommodation, which also disguised the considerable cross fall over the site. By extending this lower floor apparently outwards at either end of the house, the dramatic horizontal terraced effect successfully created, concealed the additional staff accommodation in the western wing. Above, the squared rubble with dressed margins two-storey seven-bay centre of the house, was held between two slightly advancing two-bay wings, enlivened on the principal floor with Simpson's favourite arch-headed tripartite narrow windows. These were also exaggerated with ashlar surrounds, and underlined with a boldly projecting granite balcony at either end. In the centre the featured bow, designed originally to include a high arched external arcade, was eventually altered in favour of a simpler and cheaper more conventional half round porch held aloft by six slim Doric columns. A high broad panel intended for the centre immediately above the eaves was also omitted, complete with its flourish of four high classical urns, which had been intended to break the skyline. The low-pitched slated roof made a very considerable horizontal impact also with its broad all-round eaves, which reinforced by the long low chimneys also employed, completed a rather streamlined external appearance. The five-bay return end elevations continued the design on to the north entrance front where a basically very similar treatment, minus of course the basement, was dominated in the centre by a magnificently projecting Doric carriage porch.

This gave entry into an extremely impressive circuit of formal reception rooms, at least as spectacular as anything Simpson had attempted before, matching even the previous grandeur of Stracathro. The august vestibule was balanced on either side by an enormous staircase on the one hand and an apsidally ended anteroom on the other which led directly on into the reception room enfilade. In quick succession the great dining room, the breakfast room, the grand drawing room and the small drawing room completed a circuit, which returned back on itself into the grand staircase. Beyond this on the balancing western wing, a suite of master bedrooms, toilet and dressing rooms completed the principal floor. The first floor was totally taken up with family rooms, further bedrooms and the nursery. It still remains unclear however exactly how much of the interior was actually fully fitted up, and to what actual standard of finish.

The house appears to have been unlucky even from the very start. Certainly before completion Captain Grant had lost his fortune and was forced to sell, losing also his town house at No. 3 Belmont Street in Aberdeen, into the bargain. Whether this is the foundation of the local legend that the good captain committed suicide on hearing that his fleet had foundered, only for it to be discovered that the ships made port the very next day is difficult to tell. Notwithstanding, a further legend also has it that the stones from the eventual demolitions made their way into the fabric of Elphinstone Hall at Kings, in a manner very similar to the demolitions at Castle Newe. In any event, over time the great house certainly came tumbling down, still with a good deal of the formidable retaining walls of the service floor surviving half buried in the hillside.

Back on the southern outskirts of Aberdeen at Ferryhill, Simpson found himself also commissioned this year to remodel and extend Devanha House, at that time a rather modest two-storey little villa over a basement, with only a very excellent position and view to commend it. The plain basic house had been initially built by William Black, a local brewer who had originally also considerably embellished the delightful small estate round about. Following the acquisition of the property by John Blaikie, a local shipbuilder, Simpson was requested to considerably enlarge the house, and this he did, allegedly inspired by the prow of a ship, creating two superbly rounded ends, enlivened by giant Tuscan pilasters. On the garden front he extended the principal drawing room in the centre by creating a full height three-windowed segmental bow, where the central French doors give out on to a terrace protected by a charming leaded

The stylish rear central bow Simpson introduced into
Devanha House, Ferryhill.

roof, supported unusually by a delicate trellis. On the entrance front additional dignity was now required so a single-storey Doric portico was implanted in the centre, complete with fluted columns. Overhead above the eaves line, a pedimented little attic provided the necessary further degree of central emphasis. To achieve the required unity, the entire ensemble was stuccoed, lined with imitation stonework, and painted off-white. As well as further elaborating his grounds, a small stable building was built as well as a more distant conservatory cum greenhouse at the bottom of the extensive garden. Unfortunately although this fine house is still very well preserved, it has been subsequently divided up into apartments. The surrounding grounds fell victim to the inexorable advance of residential Ferryhill, and Devanha House has in the process long become just a delightful incident in an otherwise very pleasant street of variously styled houses.

Devanha House complete with its new rounded ends and central Doric portico.

This year was also particularly eventful for Archibald Simpson as his revised proposals for Market Street and the New Market itself were again presented to the public. A new alignment for the thoroughfare had been settled, immediately opposite St Nicholas Street, a revised and much more elongated Market Building was envisaged, and another new street to be called Hadden Street connected the ancient Green in the west with the new street. This initiative allowed also the formation of both Exchange Street and Stirling Street, running

Simpson's initial perspective sketch of his Market Street proposals for Aberdeen.

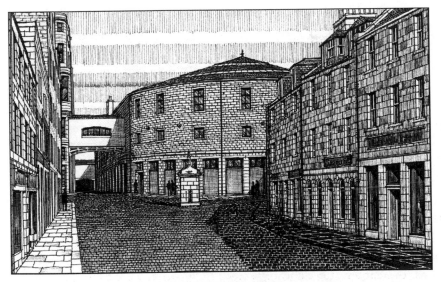

ABERDEEN NEW MARKET

The curved end of Simpson's great covered market building viewed from the historic ancient Green.

southwards to what would become Guild Street in due course. Generally welcomed by everyone as a new and important access, also removing at a stroke the dreadful slums, which disfigured Putachieside, approval was readily granted and work immediately got underway. The first task was to build the street itself, which for much of its early length comprises a very impressive tunnel vault placed over the ancient thoroughfare retained underneath, which connects Carnaigie's Brae with East Green. This accomplished, work got underway also on the erection of the flanking buildings at the Union Street ends of the street at Nos. 67 and Nos. 73–79. These buildings, conceived as terminal pavilions to both streets, represented Simpson's usual Union Street town house type, with three ashlar floors over a rusticated arch-headed window ground floor. In this instance however he carried the gable ends out at both sides forming a pavement arcade over the top of Market Street, rather dramatically framing the entry. His intention is still perfectly clear from the perspective view he had prepared, illustrating the new thoroughfare as seen from Union Street, including many of his own designs. Much of this however is now no more, the eastern pavilion being the first to disappear in the late nineteenth century, to make way for the erection of a new bank building on this important corner. The western version survived rather longer, being demolished as recently as 1929, to allow the erection of the handsome Burton's Building. In addition of course, the New Market building itself is now unfortunately long demolished, as is the new Post Office building at the opposite side of the street. This vanished along with his little single-storey arcaded link, reflecting its mirror image on the other side, still surviving but much damaged. In short however, this perspective only reminds us of the extent to which Simpson's fine original planning initiative in this particular area of the city has been regrettably and quite unnecessarily lost.

The commencement of the new thoroughfare however also allowed for a start to be made on the New Market building. The complex, certainly one of Simpson's greatest and most dramatically original achievements, was a pioneering moment in nineteenth century retailing in the city, creating a shopping environment the likes of which had never been seen before. The site now available for the development was much narrower than that originally envisaged, but the greater length achieved, fully compensated for that with the creation of a noble axial interior of a very powerful and impressive kind. The foundation stone was laid with due ceremony in 1840 by the Provost Sir Thomas Blaikie, amid some considerable civic excitement and the work very speedily got underway. The substantial fall in levels between all the principal streets surrounding the building, favoured the establishment of a basement level containing at the Green end the Fish Market, and along Hadden Street, various shop units. Above this an immense hall some 315ft long, 106ft wide and 45ft high was constructed on a vast scale seldom matched by the average cathedral or even the developing modern railway stations now appearing in many cities in the south. This extremely impressive space was held up by a circuit of external walls regularly punctured by windows and arcades of tall arch-headed piers with clearstorey windows, which as well as lending support for the roof also held up a first floor gallery of further commercial stalls. Most of the walling was executed in squared rubble to reduce costs, but the noble scale and the sweeping curve into the Green reinforced by the insistent rhythm of two levels of segmentally arched windows all round, created a sense of powerful dignity, floating on its base of wider windows designed specifically for the requirements of shops.

However it was to his Market Street elevation that Simpson reserved his most august inspiration, with the creation of a veritable tour de force. In a composition clearly emulating the pylons of some ancient Egyptian Temple, great almost unadorned planes of granite ashlar rose up retaining an anta order in the centre which itself supported a deep architrave, bold cornice and parapet which built up to a central decorative panel. Very tall windows dominated the centre, while two classical windows with architrave surrounds and cornices with

The very powerful, almost Egyptian influenced Market frontage to Market Street. This great building was needlessly sacrificed in the 1960's to modern development.

brackets, centred on the flanking walls to illuminate the front stairways up to the gallery level. Very unfortunately during the erection of the vast low-pitched iron and timber beamed roof trusses however, a noticeable sagging began to appear. In the event, and embarrassingly for Simpson, John Smith and the firm of Fairbairn of Manchester were approached in order to resolve the difficulty, which was eventually achieved by further strengthening the metalwork. The client however took the sensible precaution of retaining both Smith and Fairbairn as structural consultants for the remainder of the commission.

The New Market, a name it enjoyed all its days, finally opened in a glittering pageant on the 29th April 1842, in front of a vast crowd of the assembled citizens packing into the hall and filling the surrounding galleries. The interior was bedecked with decorations and the ceremony was duly performed with great dignity by the Lord Provost. A number of bands, the choir from Gordon's College, and pipers from the 42nd Regiment, provided the necessary musical entertainment as the crowds promenaded through the building on that first afternoon. Most of them could hardly have imagined such a large covered space before. The building established a new trend and was quickly popular with perhaps the southern side becoming the most fashionable, possibly because it was farthest away from the butchers. The butchers mainly occupied the eastern side nearest the Market Street entry, contributing greatly to a memorable odour of sawdust and blood, which was such a feature of entering the building from that side, even up to its eventual closure in 1970. Grocers proliferated, as well as fruiterers, poulterers, bakers and confectioners, while every kind of sea creature imaginable was for sale down the august granite stairway into the Fish Market below. As Hadden Street also very quickly became the haunt of Aberdeenshire farmers every Friday, when they thronged in force into that particular thoroughfare, various farm suppliers and seedsmen established themselves there in the low level shops along the market side of the street.

By as early as 1845, a brave attempt was made by a local consortium of businessmen to purchase the Market Building in order to convert it into the city's first main Railway Terminus. Mercifully possibly for the city, the asking price was too high, and for posterity's sake the site lying immediately to the south was subsequently fully investigated. Indeed Archibald Simpson himself became very actively involved with the early railway proposals, preparing various initial designs for the new terminus. For the purpose a very famous view from Torry was prepared, to illustrate to the Town Council the effect the proposed railway viaduct might have had on the overall appearance of the town. At the end of the day, problems with the building of the viaduct, the disastrous collapse of some of the work during construction, and national financial difficulties following the end of the Railway Mania, forced a fairly drastic rethink of the entire project within the city. In due course the terminus was temporarily established at Ferryhill while the viaduct into the town was realigned and raised slightly to suit a station situated higher up on Guild Street. Despite its resultant very dire visual effect within the natural Denburn valley defile, this decision certainly facilitated the eventual use of this alignment as a convenient linking route when the railway joining up with the north line was successfully pushed through and the Joint Station became a reality The New Market building itself however continued to flourish unabated, until exactly forty years after its official opening, when on the 29th April 1882, the entire building went up in flames from a small fire initially started in a basket maker's stall. Only one person was unfortunate enough to die in the resulting turmoil, but newspapers of the time relate many individuals jumping out of windows in order to escape the conflagration. After the end of the day, only the blackened stonework, including happily the Market Street, the Hadden Street and the Green frontages, complete with the Fish Market hall below, had survived.

An early photograph of Simpson's New Market interior before the fire which completely gutted it.

The premises were very quickly fully restored with the unfortunate introduction of a much cheaper lightweight metal angled roof truss supporting the new roof overhead. Indeed by common consent even at the time, the interior thus made good, never quite approached the drama of Simpson's original. However despite the reduced circumstances, the retailers and stallholders mostly continued to thrive, encouraging more modern outlets in due course to set up, such as toy shops, knitwear, buttons, wool shops, candy stalls and ice cream parlours, joining with the more traditional surviving outlets. Around the gallery much more rarefied pursuits were catered for such as philately, rare books and photography. However in the 1960s, increasing pressure to accommodate even larger department stores in the city, (on this occasion in the form of British Home Stores), effectively sealed the New Market's fate forever. Even the intervention of Sir John Betjeman could not save it, and in an act of wanton vandalism hardly matched in this city, down the great building came. To add insult to injury, in order to create an appropriately "modern" Union Street frontage for this development, the city also lost Simpson's Town and County Bank premises as well.

Simpson's splendid Market Building as immediately "restored" following the fire in 1882.
Note that his clearstorey was removed and a lightweight
metal-trussed roof was introduced.

Meanwhile to the north again, just south of Inverurie at Port Elphinstone, Simpson was also fully engaged enlarging what would turn out to be another great domestic masterpiece. A house had stood within the forty-four acres of rolling meadows at Thainstone for many years; indeed the Jacobites had put the earliest mansion to the torch in the eighteenth century, forcing the proprietor to flee to America. He went on to achieve a degree of considerable fame, and was one of the signatories of the American Declaration of Independence. Commissioned to modernise and extend the rather plain house initially rebuilt by Andrew Mitchell, the one-time British Ambassador to the Court of Prussia, he dying without issue, left his entire estate to Duncan Forbes, the younger son of the Baronet of Craigievar, Sir Arthur Forbes. Duncan subsequently took on the family name of Mitchell. Simpson arranged to add a substantial single-storey six-bay, Italianate and completely astylar new wing to the front of the

THAINSTONE HOUSE

One of Simpson's finest and most successful astylar designs, this accomplished new front extension, grafted on to the older house immediately behind, is now the centrepiece of a Country House Hotel.

existing house, all unified with rendering, granite margins and stringers, and set over a full slightly-suppressed basement. The result is made even more memorable by its bold high pedimented carriage porch with its three noble

A decorative plaster
panel within the house.

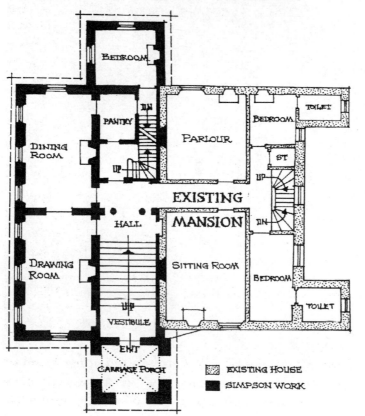

THE PRINCIPAL
FLOOR PLAN:
THAINSTONE
HOUSE

The splendid Entrance Hall stair, the introduction to Thainstone House.

The superb south front of Thainstone House today.

The former gate-lodge at Thainstone House, enlarged today into a residence of distinction.

The severely Grecian Moir Mausoleum in the St Peter's Cemetery, the Aulton, Aberdeen.

arches and internal dome placed at the junction between the old and the new on the entrance façade. Also notable are the high groupings of chimneys and the squat squarish tower floating above the roofline towards the rear with its over-sailing pyramidal roof. The roof of the extension wing and tower is also typically carried over to very broad eaves supported throughout on plain modillions all round, dramatically capping the design.

Internally, from an august vestibule which introduces a very imposing broad straight staircase, this climaxes on a screen of Ionic columns placed at the top, prelude to two very elegantly disposed reception rooms on the left, providing the house with a new drawing room and dining room. Complete with excellent woodwork and chimney pieces enlivening remarkably accomplished and beautifully conceived en suite interiors, the plasterwork throughout is also particularly fine. Three low relief antique panels were incorporated within the cool entrance stairway, a decorative oval and rich cornice was provided in the drawing room, and a simply panelled, but segmentally vaulted ceiling presides over the dining room. Adjacent, the old house was also reorganised internally so that at the same level, a sitting room, parlour and new linking circulation corridor was arranged around the old half-spiral staircase servicing all levels. Below in the only partially suppressed basement, new kitchen and service accommodation expanded the existing staff quarters of the original house, which also contained the nursery and playroom at this level. Two floors above this, the bedrooms were mainly disposed within the old house, with one new principal bedroom provided also within the low squat tower that Simpson had tacked on to the western end of his design, incorporated probably mainly for its external effect.

The house subsequently came into the possession of the Valentine family who lived there for many years before, like many others of its scale and type, it was turned into a Country House hotel. The mansion has more recently been very sensitively further enlarged to include a health spa and swimming pool, while much expanded public reception rooms have been added, very appropriately named the Simpson Restaurant and the Ambassador Suite. An additional new wing of forty-eight bedrooms, also very carefully emulating the basic style of the Simpson wing, projects out at the rear provided with its own over-sailing slated roof and matching little squat roofed tower. Designed happily in a completely complementary manner, the new range does not in any way detract from the integrity of the original, certainly one of Simpson's most satisfying and accomplished domestic designs.

Sadly however at the old gate entry to the original estate, now resolutely severed from its magnificently wooded driveway by the attentions of the Roads

Department's new dual carriageway, chance alone perhaps helped preserve another little Simpson jewel in the form of an absolutely delightful, almost minimalist little two-storey Gate Lodge. Acknowledging the big house, it too was given its own very striking little pyramidal roof together with a subservient and attached lower lean-to wing, providing extremely modest accommodation for the gate-keeper and his family. Following its separation from its parent, this now former little lodge was subsequently acquired and greatly enlarged into a delightful private house. With the addition of a new single-storey wing discreetly attached to the rear and set under a matching pavilion roof, the new range dramatically increased the size of the new dwelling without in any way diminishing the impact of Simpson's original fine statement.

Back again in the Aulton, in the Spital just to the north of the new city, his old clients the Moirs of Scotstown and Spital, exercising their historic rights over the Lands of Spital, asked Archibald Simpson to create for them a Family Mausoleum within the ancient confines of old St Peter's Cemetery. Built on the site of a former church building which apparently originally occupied the most prominent central position within the graveyard, he erected an extremely simple granite rubble box complete with a low-pitched roof, ennobled by low pediments placed at either end. It was additionally embellished also with several very Grecian details and a door set centrally on the principal end elevation. This successfully completed an appropriately simple, sober but none the less very effective design.

Finally in 1840, undoubtedly one of his most challenging years, Simpson was invited back again to his old Lunatic Asylum Building complex in Barkmill at Berryden, requested to add further kitchen and service accommodation on to his original design. The distant and problematic past now apparently long forgotten, the commission, although by its very nature quite pedestrian, was an extremely important public acknowledgement of Simpson's now considerable local public prestige. His re-employment again as Architect to the Managers must therefore have been extremely gratifying to him in the context of the difficulties of the past, further exacerbated by the vexed memory of the appointment of his great rival in the interim. From the existing evidence now currently visible on site however, it would be very difficult to be absolutely certain just how much of this particular building work still exists, given the very indifferent nature of many of the surviving buildings today. It is certainly undeniably the case that immediately behind the inner core of the present hospital complex, very little of any real architectural merit is now to be found.

The following year was extremely unusual at this period in his career, in that apart from work in hand, there were hardly any new commissions coming in. However one interesting task did emerge in the form of a Competition entry for a proposed Asylum for the Blind, to be built in Huntly Street, Aberdeen. The Trustees approached both Archibald Simpson and John Smith to prepare their own proposals for the new complex, following the failure of the earlier competition attempt in 1839. At that time a number of schemes had been submitted from all over the country, none however were deemed to have met the requirements of the trustees. Interestingly both Simpson and Smith had not deigned to join in this particular circus. Perhaps not surprisingly, the eventual schemes produced by both architects were quite similar, with their accommodation contained within an extended H-plan block, set well back from the street. Simpson's arrangement envisaged a nine-bay two-storey centre above a rusticated half basement, flanked by single-bay wings, returning by five bays on both the sides. Quoins emphasised all the leading corners while a projecting rusticated high archway proclaimed the entrance below a central scrolled panel supporting a raised sculptural group. Overhead and slightly behind this, an elegant tower with a low pyramidal roof made a powerful central statement. Smith's design was selected in preference to this however, "being most in

Simpson's unsuccessful Competition entry for the Blind Asylum in Huntly Street, Aberdeen.

accordance with the remit in point of expense which had been prescribed by the Trustees". Certainly Simpson's slightly more elaborate treatment and his central tower had the smack of additional expense. From his previous experience with the Managers of the Asylum and the local general disdain of architectural "excess", you would have thought that he might have known better. However Smith's also very fine building was eventually built, and continues still to grace the eastern side of Huntly Street to this day.

Simpson was also invited out to Pittodrie House at Chapel of Garioch, near Pitcaple in Aberdeenshire, to modernise and extend the old Scots house belonging to the Smith family dating back to 1480. Sheltering under the impressive lea of Bennachie, the old mansion dominated the centre of an expansive estate and heavily treed surrounding policies. Simpson largely ignored the old three-storey house, simply arranging a convenient straight stair link at the junction to effect a smooth join between his new ground floor reception rooms and the old principal accommodation on the first floor of the existing range beyond. The new work, all harled and composed inventively about a tall

PITTODRIE HOUSE

Reworking elements borrowed from Castle Newe, this spirited, but in this instance asymmetrical extension, blends effortlessly with the older mansion house behind it.

three-storey square entrance tower, is given a plain top balustrade inset between blocks disguising chimneys, dominating the southern end of the ensemble. A bold single-storey porch with an arched doorway and armorial panel embedded within the parapet above, projects forward as the entrance vestibule. A new adjoining west facing two-storey wing contains Simpson's fine drawing room and dining room suite with new good principal bedrooms placed overhead. This range is further enlivened on the main front with a full height splayed and projecting bay, with a gable to the west boasting a further single-storey canted bay of 1926, commanding the magnificent views over towards the Mither Tap. A further two-window wide range beyond terminates in one of Simpson's favourite round and lead ogee-capped little towers. Hood mouldings, stringers and simple stone margins also emphasise the plain geometry and basic simplicity of this asymmetric and delightfully informal grouping. Now converted and again sensitively extended into a very fine country house hotel, the mansion has become a popular and rather romantic venue for area weddings.

In 1842 Simpson went to work on a site at the top of Market Street, immediately opposite his New Market building, just then in the course of completion. The commission was to erect a new Post Office Building for the city, and this he did in an unusual design, reflecting something of the drama at the other side of the street. Exhibiting a distinctly Soanean influence also, the broad five-bay three-storey centre was flanked on either side by slightly advanced single-bay ends, held between paired giant pilasters supporting an architrave, plain frieze and cornice brought straight across the façade at second

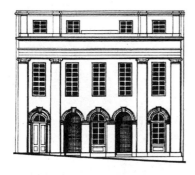

The Post Office, Market Street, Aberdeen

floor level. At first floor five very tall windows, horizontally glazed and elaborated with architrave surrounds, marched across the elevation while squarer but similarly treated windows on the second floor were contained within the raised attic. Below on the ground floor, an unusual recessed arcade with the main entry at its centre gave access to the spacious internal public office. The floors above were given over to the managers and staff offices. This very striking building, rather more effective in execution than on the drawings, survived for many years until the requirements of additional space forced a removal to the bottom of the street. The Simpson building in fact survived fairly intact until quite recently, minus of course its arcade which had been desecrated as usual to form modern shop fronts. The property was eventually destined to be entirely demolished however to facilitate the enlargement of Fraser's Department Store to the east. Now just a memory itself, these premises have been recently divided into two retail units.

In Huntly in this same year his old client the North of Scotland Bank, approached Simpson to design for them there new premises at No. 2 the Square. Built on an extremely prominent corner with Gordon Street, his treatment of the principal façade here, over a three-arch-headed architraved and pilastered window centred on the ground floor, is effectively balanced on either side by standard classical windows. Above unusually, there are only four standard windows as against this five. A heavy cornice, low parapet and balustraded parapet above complete a quite complex composition later marred by the subsequent imposition of a continuous dormer arrangement on the roof. Returning round to the square itself Simpson reverted to his Aberdeen-type gable with a three-bay composition which is given an architraved and pilastered central arched doorway recalling the arcade on the front. Above the cornice however, the design really takes off with a very broad panel, recessed, and

The Clydesdale Bank: Huntly.

supporting a high plain chimney stack, supported by curvilinear scrolls in an ambitious accumulation of planes and panels built up very much in a tiered arrangement. Internally much original work also remains, with the cool banking hall, the most ambitious space, having been basically little altered although successfully enlarged. Upstairs the quite modest first floor rooms remain more or less as designed.

In 1843 we find Simpson again engaged with the problem of street design in the west-end of Aberdeen. Designs for terraces in Victoria Street at Nos. 7–11, 18–56, and 21–59 all came off his drawing board in quick succession, as well as Nos. 2, 6, 8, 10, and 16 Waverley Place before the end of the year. In fact it now appears that by his death (in only four years time), only Nos. 21–59 Victoria Street had been completed, with Nos. 7–11 commencing only after 1850. However, despite the delay and the involvement subsequently of others, this is one of the most impressive and pleasing streets in Aberdeen. Hardly damaged and composed of two-storey houses on the eastern side and single-

The higher east side of Victoria Street, Aberdeen.

storey with a storey and a half central range of six cottages on the west, the street is built basically also of granite rubble. As at Ferryhill, the margins are all dressed; stringers at ground, first floor and under the eaves give unity and contrast, while some doorways and window heads are decorated with cornices and consoles. One door even allowed the owner to boast pilasters and an architrave head, and whilst most windows are designed to the standard Georgian type, the two-storey range to the northern end still sports Simpson's alternative horizontal pattern. The storey and a half block was further embellished with unusual plain architrave sides and a pointed granite notional pediment placed around each doorway. While many of the houses have basements, this is not universal, and within the high pitched slated roofs, all have bedroom accommodation, expressed by a regular rhythm of typically canted and piended dormers. The overall pattern now seems to have been established that streets were to be built in various sections and to an overall plan perhaps, but still allowing individual client freedom to choose between various distinguishing details. Despite some of the more prestigious streets subsequently adopting full architectural integration, this pick and mix arrangement became the norm for the west end of Aberdeen well into the twentieth century. Indeed even today a number of house builders in the city still adopt this particular sales tactic so that their customers can personalise the design of their individual dwellings.

The west side of Victoria Street, Aberdeen – more linked classic cottages

Simpson was also invited back in 1843 again to the Lunatic Asylum, requested to design some additional patient accommodation and link corridors, attached to the back of his earlier buildings. The work certainly appears to have been of a fairly mundane character however, and was probably only phase one of a subsequent proposal to provide balancing wings to be built eventually on either side. A west wing was commenced in 1848, to be swiftly followed by an east wing in 1852, and by 1855 with the addition of a new chapel, the main Mental Hospital building complex was virtually complete. As previously noted however, Simpson's Asylum has been subsequently greatly enlarged again and what with further more modern additions (Cornhill and Elmhill Estates having been absorbed into much enlarged grounds in the process), the massively expanded site is now largely strewn with an array of different buildings of various shapes and styles, rather akin to nearby Foresterhill. Now a development opportunity however, the Asylum and its site are apparently up for grabs.

The extension to the Lunatic Asylum, Barkmill, Aberdeen.

1843 also witnessed the revival of an Aberdeen proposal to build a new thoroughfare from the Castlegate down to the Links. This initiative had first been put forward as an idea by the Council itself in 1840, but the usual inertia, the difficulties involved and the anticipated cost led to its fairly swift abandonment. However, a new scheme was quite quickly put forward, public but "outwith the remit of the Council", to revive the idea, proposed "to promote the health and better the conditions of the working classes". The improvements as envisaged by Simpson involved the demolition of many areas of dreadful slums, in order to create an entirely new street from the south-eastern corner of the Castlegate, taken in a great sweep across the front of the Castlehill Barracks to a junction with Commerce Street and a new bridge then thrown over the Aberdeenshire Canal. From there, the thoroughfare headed straight for the beach front where a "Marine Parade" was intended. Despite the fact that the initial cost of this improvement was only £1,500 the initiative again failed, the opportunity to properly plan this part of town abandoned until the emergence of some dubious, rather more recent efforts. It would also take a further one hundred years before the Beach Boulevard itself, the natural successor of this scheme, actually got off the ground. Judging from the almost total lack of unity, style or purpose along much of its indifferent length until only fairly recently, apart from its apparent attractiveness to the "Bouley Bashers", one wonders if it was worth all the trouble.

In the following year Archibald Simpson was extremely busy with new commissions in the aftermath of the Disruption within the Church,

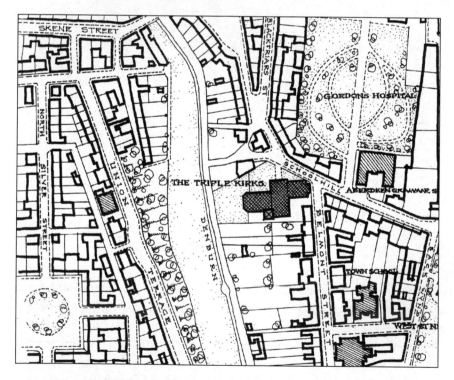

Simpson exploited the old site of the former brick factory to its full potential for his 'Cathedral of the Disruption'.

undoubtedly the most momentous event occurring in 1843. The ministers of the East and West Churches of St Nicholas, accompanied by their colleague from the new South Church in Belmont Street, walked out in defence of the spiritual independence of the pulpit, setting their faces very firmly against the interference of central Church authority. Simpson was immediately approached and recommended the building of a Triple Church arrangement to be built on the prominent industrial site, formerly suggested for his Grecian University complex, at the north end of Belmont Street at Schoolhill. The financial offer for this site was apparently accepted only minutes before someone from St Nicholas came in, only just slightly too late, with a higher amount in an attempt to gazump the deal. The old factory and some brick houses were immediately removed, and given the extreme scarcity of funds for the new buildings, much of the rubble and brick demolitions were set aside for eventual reuse.

Integrating his general design into a whole, he embraced the East, West, and South Churches under one roof in a Z-shaped arrangement fully exploiting the site, the fall to the Denburn and its almost pivotal location in the north of the

The Triple Churches seen from the Denburn, immediately to the north of it prior to the construction of the viaduct which resulted in the removal of the foreground slums as well as much else in the vicinity of lower Rosemount.

city centre. Further emphasis, if that were needed, was provided by a soaring, elegant spire, only the second such but by far the highest then in town. This, frequently referred to as the "Cathedral of the Disruption", was one of Simpson's greatest and most ingenious efforts. The fact that his final portrait shows him seen against the background of the Triple Churches with his Infirmary Building just beyond, suggests that he and his friend James Giles held these to be his greatest city architectural achievements.

With only £5,000 available to be spent on such a considerable project, economy was obviously the first priority, and in consequence the decision was taken to build in granite rubble, relieved by brick reveals and very limited Dundee sandstone dressings. The manner chosen was also restrained, being ecclesiastical Gothic, using the Early Pointed style. The various facades were set on a ground storey expressing the gallery with, as in the case of earlier East St Nicholas, square inset sandstone windows under a continuous sandstone stringer. Above this soaring narrow lancet windows broke up the elevations in bold rhythms, complete with brick reveals and sandstone hoods. Crocketed finials further enlivened and strengthened the buttressed corners. A broad fairly low slated, almost classical roof overlaid this, broken dramatically in the north centre by a three-lancet windowed gable, complete with pointed parapet. To the western edge of the site where the ground very steeply fell away down to the Denburn itself, Simpson marshalled all his elements with additional basement accommodation to present to the valley a tremendously dramatic interplay of receding verticals, culminating in his noble brick spire. Built around a basic granite core, brickwork was used here to maximum effect. The spire is of the Deutche Helm type, modelled on that of the Elizabeth Kirke in Marburgh and given a tall square belfry section with slim corner buttresses terminating in a perforated parapet before transforming into an octagonal spire soaring up to an elegant finial. The transition between tower and spire is masterfully achieved by tall corner pinnacles set above the buttresses controlling, on the main facades, four high pointed gablets provided with central openings.

The interiors of all the churches below were however designed very much to minimal standards, nonetheless still achieving an appropriately august and dignified impression on entering. Despite the strict financial constraints they also all boasted internal galleries with good woodwork, pews and pulpits. Evolving over time into East Belmont and Albion and St Paul's Churches, the East Church was much altered by Dr William Kelly when the old South Church next door was modified to become its hall. Sadly the emergence of extensive dry rot problems in the 1960s led to the eventual abandonment of Albion and St

Paul's with East Belmont lingering on as a pub-restaurant and a meeting hall above formed at the old gallery level. Despite various efforts to save the remaining fabric as offices and even schemes for flatted housing developments implanted within the retained shell, all this architectural activity has over the last forty years come to absolutely nothing. In the meantime the attentions of the Council's Roads Department and their apparently unnecessary Denburn dual carriageway, have all played their part in the final desecration of Simpson's ecclesiastic masterpiece. How such a uniquely impressive building could find itself in such a ruinous condition in the very heart of the Oil Capital of the Northern Hemisphere, given its original listed building status and supported by an army of planners and publicly paid protectors, is simply beyond understanding, but I suppose even in its present grim condition it is still ahead of the New Market which has absolutely gone for ever. The most recently published proposal also to create an office complex along with an Architectural Heritage Centre within the remaining gaunt shell, extends at least the possibility that this building's troubles might shortly be over. It is now at the stage that

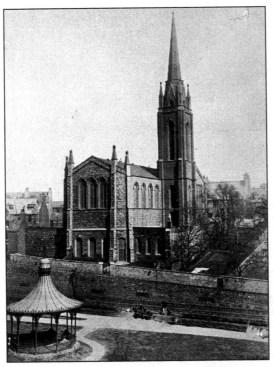

The Triple Churches from Union Terrace.

almost any solution would be better than nothing at this pivotal location and now that the new glazed theatre extension opposite is well underway, hopefully its intended patrons might someday expect a much improved view to be provided in the immediate foreground. We can only but hope.

Meanwhile in far-off Rothesay on the Isle of Bute, Simpson also commenced another monument to the Disruption this year, with the design of a new Free Church there, to a budget of just over £3,000. The completed church was opened for worship on the 13th July 1845, the first sermon being given by Dr Thomas Guthrie of Edinburgh. The first minister was the Rev Robert Gray, and it was he, who in June 1843 had left the Established Rothesay Parish Church with almost his entire congregation to establish a new Free Church. A single statement, but acknowledging something to its Aberdeen Triple Kirk's predecessor, Simpson's modest freestone Early English Decorated rectangular box is dramatically concentrated on the front gable and distinguished with a tall, centrally placed elegant ashlar spire, proudly proclaiming the entrance. Similar in type but not in scale or indeed even in point of elegance with his original in Aberdeen, the high corner buttressed box

The Free Church, Rothesay, Isle of Bute.

tower is set with four decorated corner pinnacles to emerge perhaps rather too suddenly as a simple octagonal soaring spire, somewhat relieved by four ogee double curvature openings inset into its four principal facets at the base. On either side of the main doorway below, lower splayed corridors giving access to the double aisled church interior behind, also terminate in balancing subservient buttressed pinnacles.

Inside the note of solemnity is immediately struck with another extremely restrained, five-bay interior brought about in that severely understated manner which Simpson managed to make all his own, while still succeeding in creating an appropriately memorable space. Provided with a continuously raking sloping floor and a single bay gallery to the rear, the still evident original plainness is relieved with a dramatic pine pulpit under the three windows high on the end gable. Rows of pews and a high arcade-moulded dado all round the church below the tall lancet windows, reflected also in the treatment of the balcony front of the gallery, provide additional interest. The original trussed roof overhead also upheld a flat plastered ceiling with short sloping sections all round the edges, left exposed under the level of the main roof tie. How comfortable southern congregations were with such spartan north-eastern rigour however remains unclear, except it is evident that the plastered walls were originally painted to simulate stone with a lighter stone effect treatment at all windows, further elaborated with a deep stencilled decorative band taken all round at the level of the springing of the arch-headed lancet windows. Attached to the church at the rear, the offices and vestry building could also have been designed by Simpson, but appear to have been erected slightly later than the main building itself.

In 1904 the first organ was installed, removing at a stroke the need for a precentor, and also boldly adding two organ cases at either side of the pulpit access stairways, successfully adding to the drama of the main end. Tragically however, virtually the entire church roof collapsed without any warning in August 1907, but as the premises were not in use at the time, no one happily was injured in the event. Within twelve months an entirely new roof was installed to a powerful hammer beam design, all finely executed with timber beams and inset panelling, necessitating also the raising of the main wallhead by some three feet to accommodate its increased depth, with the end beam drops and the new supporting internal stone wall-brackets. The resulting beamed roof certainly adds considerably now to the overall success of the interior.

The three principal end windows, together with the first flanking windows to both sides have also been fitted up with stained glass, which also successfully

The Free Church's roof collapses in August 1907.

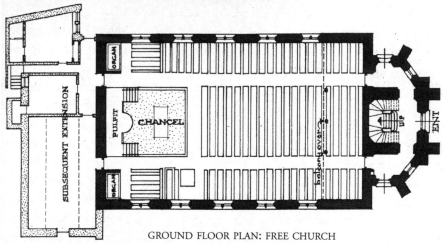

GROUND FLOOR PLAN: FREE CHURCH

The restored interior of the Free Church, Rothesay today – note the introduction of roof trusses as well as wall bracket supports between the Gothic side windows.

introduces a note of luminous colour. The main centre windows, to a design by Mr Oscar Patterson of Glasgow, are a memorial to the fallen in the First World War, while the Second World War is commemorated on the east side by a window designed by Gordon Webster, also of Glasgow. The corresponding window on the west is dedicated to the Munn family, and Provost Munn himself, who regularly worshipped in the church.

In 1988 a new impressively sounding digital organ was installed, and currently plans are being prepared in order to free up the communion area, thereby creating a more flexible useable space, whilst at the same time better accommodating the choir and disabled members of the congregation. For long renamed the Trinity Church, the old Rothesay Free Church is now most certainly in a considerably happier state of preservation than its northerly cousin in Aberdeen, which did so much to inspire it.

At the other end of the Region deep in the heart of Nairnshire, in an enviable position set on a promontory overlooking the valley of the River Findhorn far below, Simpson also embarked on the erection of another late, great design, that of the mansion of Glenferness House. Set in the middle of a magnificently wooded estate, the house, built to what was described at the time as "a fine Renaissance structure with an effective low square tower", is still very discernibly embedded within an ensemble embellished with a number of less happy later extensions and additions.

The property originally formed part of the ancient Lands of Brodie, which extended all the way up the valley of the River Findhorn. Acquired in the 1820s by a Mr Cunningham, he envisaged building a large castellated house on a summit within the higher ground immediately to the north and east of the present house. Nothing came of this adventure however, until the property was sold to a Mr Dougal, who commissioned Archibald Simpson to design his house in 1844. Ostensibly completed in the following year, Simpson created a quite compact block of reception rooms about a noble entrance hall, extending off to the north with a service wing, again making possible an agreeably asymmetrical composition. A note of symmetry however still lingered at the entrance, where the front five-bay broad horizontal projecting porch was very firmly held between his very typical gabled and slightly advanced wings. Designed in his light and airy, very understated style, a memorable sequence of rooms unfolds around the vestibule and its adjacent pitch pine lined stairwell, including the elegant library, originally en suite with an imposing drawing room complete with a broad canted bay facing directly south, and a fine dining room confronting the western garden terrace and the magnificent river view. On the

GLENFERNESS HOUSE

Unfortunately most of what is seen today on the entrance front of Glenferness is either rearranged or the result of considerable later alterations and extensions made to Simpson's original Italianate design. The house however, the delightful home today of Lord and Lady Balgonie, still retains sufficient of its originally conceived charm to be readily recognisable by its initial architectural designer.

The rear elevation of Glenferness has survived better than the front, except for the rather unfortunate late extension of the three bay dining room and bedroom elevation which damages Simpson's original. He also carefully positioned his front to take advantage of a truly spectacular view down the Findhorn.

other side, this is balanced with the business room and the housekeeper's room, in conjunction with the service areas, the kitchen, and some limited basement cellarage. The floor above is distinguished with five good bedrooms with the master bedroom set directly over the dining room, also commanding the finest river view. Most of the bedrooms are furnished with their own dressing rooms, positioned immediately next door, and a recognisably modern toilet and bathroom make an early appearance. Above the adjoining service wing, a nursery and maidservant's room was also provided, along with an adjacent drying room.

The design perhaps owes something of a debt to Playfair's nearby drama at Dunphail, completed some fifteen years earlier, but realised on a smaller, more compact scale, developing clearly from Simpson's recent rather informal, astylar residential experiments. To the south, a resolutely off-centre full-height canted bay makes its appearance in preparation for the west façade, where gables, flat ranges and an elegant tower, vie with one another to produce a delightful truly informal composition. This is further underlined by the service wing accommodation extending off northwards. The walling throughout is of basically granite random rubble, originally entirely rendered except for exposed margins, ashlar stringers, a basecourse and under-sill inset spandrel panels. For contrast the walling to the back and sides of the entrance porch were carried out in smooth granite ashlar, as are the various chimney stacks also with their decorative flourishes. Apart from the numerous gables disposed on all elevations, a particularly notable feature of the design is the projection of the low pitched roofs over and beyond these gables, supported on modillions with carved decorative ends. This treatment has also been used to embellish the supports of the small slated pyramidal roof set over the charming little rear tower.

Simpson, whilst active at the House of Glenferness itself, also produced designs for the small stable block north of the house, the half-moon walled garden and adjoining cottage, Glenferness Home Farm, various cottages within the estate, and the main gate lodge, all of which were actually executed on site. However the house was barely twenty-five years old before the property was acquired by the Earl of Leven, head of the Leslie Melville Family who after 1869 subsequently embarked on a number of alterations and extensions, some proving to be rather happier than others.

Almost immediately the dining room and master bedroom above it were much enlarged by pushing out the relevant part of the west front, thereby sadly damaging the integrity of the original adjoining gable, and completely compromising the dominance of the adjacent tower on the other side.

Internally, the extension to the dining room was actually well enough handled however with the introduction of a bold ceiling beam supported on end brackets, although the unfortunate and quite unnecessary alteration to the spacing to the windows irrevocably damaged the master bedroom on the floor above. The next alteration appears to have been a relatively small extension to the servant's quarters, with a wholly compatible wing and gable added very much in the style of Simpson, whilst on the front a new three-bay porte cochere was erected immediately in front of the existing linear porch, providing further protection to the main entrance porch.

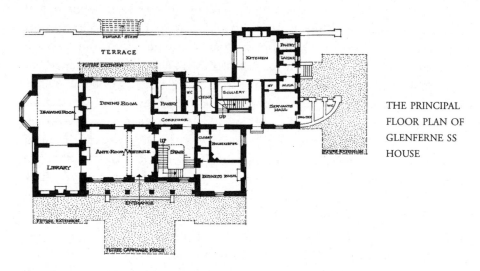

THE PRINCIPAL FLOOR PLAN OF GLENFERNE SS HOUSE

By 1894 a very remarkable and impressive pre-made timber billiard room was constructed with logs emanating originally from Norway, and linked back to the library with a short passageway, also executed in timber. Its establishment on an angle introduced a slightly wayward diagonal into the overall composition, which was matched with the erection of a balancing little timber outbuilding on the other side of the house, slightly to the north-east of the service wing. This was shortly joined by a much more magnificent neighbouring timber building attached to it, with a further building, now used as a squash court, situated slightly behind. By 1901 the old front gables of Simpson's house had also been pushed out, enlarging at the same time the library, the business room and bedrooms above, while embracing a new rather handsomely glazed front vestibule, which now occupied the old site of the carriage porch, much expanded for the purpose. In the event also, the old porte cochere itself was re-erected in front. This particular enlargement is distinguished by the very

Glenferness today as revealed from the entrance drive. Despite the retention of the original character and materials of Simpson's design, almost everything visible in this view of the house is the result of much later extension and rebuilding works carried out in the latter part of the nineteenth century.

Simpson's garden front at Glenferness, spoiled by the later advancement of the dining room and master bedroom range, immediately adjacent to the tower.

The delightful little Gardener's Cottage, adjacent to the walled garden at Glenferness.

considerable internal use of teak, which was also enthusiastically introduced into the woodwork of Simpson's adjoining (now inner), anteroom vestibule hall.

Despite various scribbled alterations over Simpson's old sections and elevations proving that that at least sometime, probably early in the twentieth century, someone had contemplated adding a further floor of bedrooms to the house, this temptation was obviously resisted. In the 1930s, Simpson's external coat of rendering was sadly totally removed, at least however allowing the added interest of the various colours and textures of the rubble stonework underneath to be revealed to quite good effect. This has been followed by the more recent removal of an unnecessary and also offending corridor, apparently intended originally to screen off the side entrance to the servants' entry. Notwithstanding this quite colourful history of building works since its completion in 1845, resulting in the almost total reconstruction of the main entrance front and the complete loss of its original all-embracing external rendering, Glenferness would still however be recognisable by Archibald Simpson today, remaining a remarkably satisfying and quite delightful mansion house beautifully embraced by its breathtakingly dramatic highland setting.

The Stable Block, Glenferness.

The year concluded with Simpson called back by the Managers to erect a separate Fever Wing at the rear of his Woolmanhill Infirmary complex. Built on the side of Woolmanhill itself, on land originally intended for his colonnaded gardens, the simple two-storey building, economically planned and simply elevated with end gables set under an oversailing eaves, did not in any way detract from the dignity of his original Infirmary. The new wing remained in use for only about thirty years when this facility was eventually more appropriately rehoused in the City Hospital opened in Urquhart Road. Simpson's building was subsequently demolished later in the nineteenth century to make way for further ambitious buildings, as a large and still existing courtyard complex of related hospital facilities developed on the site.

In addition to the Fever Wing, Simpson was also asked to provide the Infirmary with a separate Porter's Lodge, situated along side the main entrance gateway towards the front. Subsequent alterations, and the building of the rear courtyard accommodation, eventually forced a change of entry into the site to the back of the original Infirmary. Consequently the Porter's Lodge was dismantled and re-erected on a new site nearer to the new vehicular entry where it still stands to this day, albeit the entry now functions as an exit. Simple, square and carried out in rusticated ashlar with double recessed windows on three elevations and a door on the other, a bold cornice and a low parapet completely conceals the roof of this minimalist geometric box.

The Porter's Lodge and the gable of the Fever Wing just beyond Simpson's Infirmary block.

In 1845, back in the city centre, Simpson became concerned with the intended building of the Mechanics' Institute, to be built on a prominent site on the west side of Market Street, virtually opposite his newly built New Market. Claiming that it could not afford to employ an architect of Simpson's standing, and as his assistant William Ramage was already in their employ in the evenings as a drawing master, the Institution seem to have approached Ramage as their designer, based on something of a nineteenth-century "homer" basis. Ramage very correctly immediately wrote to his architect employer, requesting that he be allowed to carry out the commission, and Simpson actually readily agreed. Indeed he wrote back to the Institute itself, offering his own services absolutely free of charge as his personal contribution to the building fund. The initially preferred site in question, south of the New Market and on land now earmarked for the proposed future Railway Station, had to be abandoned and an alternative location on the eastern side of Market Street opposite Hadden Street was offered instead. While William Ramage with his particular inside knowledge prepared the general floor plans, Simpson busied himself designing the very imposing frontage of what would prove in the event to be his last major contribution to a public building built within the city of Aberdeen.

The Mechanics Institute terminates the axis of Hadden Street, Aberdeen with the flank of Simpson's splendid New Market Building prominent on the left of the picture.

The Institute, comprising various meeting rooms and lecture rooms around their considerable library, was accommodated within a broad, deep block, apparently only single-storey on the front above a commercial ground floor. The powerful, still Grecian-inspired façade, controlled under a bold black painted frieze carrying a modillion cornice and high parapet, has pairs of long windows with architrave cornices supported on narrow side pilasters, set on a broad banded parapet base, either side of a central feature, borrowed for the purpose from the ancient Arch of Hadrian in Athens. This drama, successfully terminating the axis of Hadden Street opposite, comprises a central window, balanced by half windows on both sides, all embraced between columns supporting a broad pediment overhead in the manner of an attached portico. Below this on the ground floor within a rusticated base, a powerful arched doorway is implanted. On either side architraved and pilastered four-bay arcades complete the ensemble, allowing originally two pairs of shops on each flank. Very sadly one side of this arrangement has been quite ruthlessly damaged in the creation of a modern shop front. The remainder of the building however has fared much worse when the Institution eventually departed the premises altogether, as it greatly expanded into Robert Gordon's Institute of Technology and subsequently Robert Gordon University. The vacant property was initially successfully converted into the Bon-Accord Hotel, which operated for some time, and despite the basic bones of the building surviving this considerable alteration to its circumstances, the subsequent further internal refurbishment necessary to reinvent it more recently into the Metro Night-spot,

The Mechanic's Institute today, badly disfigured both inside and outside.

has resulted in very little of any architectural merit surviving now within the walls. Only the ghost of the originally impressive principal library apartment exists, now used as the gaudy nightclub itself, still overlooking Market Street below. Notwithstanding its subsequent internal decline, on the 13th August 1845 all this was very far in the future, as a company of civic dignitaries almost a mile long processed through the crowded city to the site to lay the foundation stone, with Archibald Simpson proudly holding a copy of the rolled up plans firmly in his hand.

Meanwhile to the west of Aberdeen above Cults, the developing little suburb there witnessed Simpson engaged on the erection of Morkeu, a house built for George Collie, a successful local merchant. Constructed on a high bluff overlooking the River Dee valley below, the mansion, designed in a compact but expanded informal cottage style, far removed from Simpson's normal classicism, combined high slated roofs with various pointed gables, chimney stacks, diagonally set chimney pots and shaped timber barge boards. Various bedroom windows also half break into the main roof with little dormers, and a single-storey canted bay window enlivens a design created within a generally rendered granite rubble construction, complete with dressed stone margins. Even the rendering was unusual however, with small pebbles individually set into the mortar finish. Relatively small scale also inside, the plan unfolds about a low broad vestibule and central hall with a fine suite of reception rooms taking full advantage of the magnificent southern aspect available. The spacious drawing room, dining room and library all face south with only the morning room and kitchen-service accommodation on the other side. In addition a fine central timbered galleried staircase accesses the extensive suite of five principal bedrooms arranged on the floor above. Outwith the house, the farm and stables buildings were also much expanded and a great walled garden was formed below the house occupying a natural suntrap.

The estate, formerly extending to some twenty acres, originally belonged to the ancient family of Menzies of Pitfodels. The land was presented to Priest Gordon in 1838, and he erected a small house and some farm buildings on it. Finding the location inconvenient for the carrying out of his pastoral duties, he sold the property to George Collie. Mr Collie had a brother, a surgeon Lt. Alexander Collie, who whilst on duty in Western Australia, was saved from drowning by his faithful servant, an Aboriginal by the name of Morkeu. This far-off event was responsible for the name of the house. In 1873, on the death of George Collie, the house was purchased by Alexander Forbes. His only notable contribution to the fabric was the insertion of French windows into the dining room so that his horse could freely

Simpson's original front: Morkeu.

THE PRINCIPAL FLOOR
PLAN: MORKEU

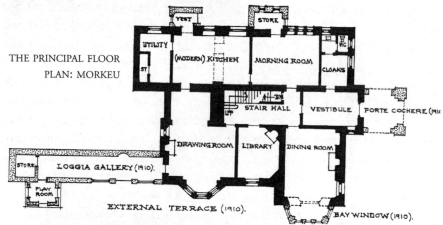

Simpson's design, heavily over-laden by George Watt, just manages to hold
its own against the much later ashlar Lutyenesque extensions added in 1910.

enter and enjoy dinner with him. Apparently Mr Forbes believed that his horse was the reincarnation of his late father. He left the house to his niece, who died in 1909 and the property was then bought by Lt. Col. Alexander Findlay Milne, who in the following year called in the local architect George Watt to implement a number of very significant changes.

He added the rather too grand porte cochere to the existing entrance front, which together with a long extended Tuscan Loggia gallery and some considerable balustraded terracing across the south front all carried out in a cool crisp granite ashlar, is somewhat at odds with Simpson's original understated air of simplicity. Additional oriels with red tiled roofs were also inset here and there, and various internal alterations were carried out at the same time mainly to the kitchen and service arrangements, which also acquired a square tower rather unexpectedly capped by a red tiled pyramidal roof. A garage block was introduced as well, along with a separate servant's flat carved out within the existing first floor accommodation. Internally however the house was still quite well preserved with most of the fine original rooms remaining. The character of the circulation was quite dramatically changed in the process, with the introduction of much dark wood panelling and Art Nouveau stained glass. In consequence, within and without, a not unsuccessful hint of Sir Edwin Lutyens has rather blurred Simpson's original much simpler tone.

Following its sale in 1918 after Lt. Col. Milne's death, the house was occupied for a short time by Alexander Benzie, before being purchased in 1934 by Mr George Duncan Collie of the notable local legal family. Mr George Francis Collie inherited in 1949 with the intention of converting the farm buildings to the north of the house into a modern family home for himself. The name Little Morkeu was therefore used for a time for this converted house. In 1954 on the death of his mother, Mr Collie sold the original Morkeu to Mr Thomas Carr, with the name being permanently changed to Greenridge, Morkeu reverting to the former stables house which was again considerably altered and enlarged. It was sold again in 1958 to Mr George Webster who was responsible for carrying out extensive internal alterations; he also acquired the old walled garden in 1963, which was eventually restored. Since 1974 the old house and its immediate surrounds of three and a half acres has been the property of British Petroleum, who originally bought it for their Area Manager. Much restored and beautifully refurbished within and without, they now use it as a conference and corporate entertainment centre in connection with their oil business.

North in the Aulton meanwhile, on a site at the head of the High Street itself, Simpson was engaged to design a church for the extremely hard pressed Free

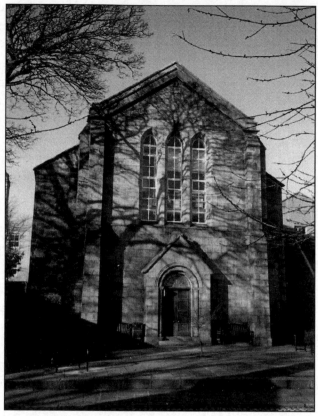

The Free Church, High Street, The Aulton

Congregation anxious to very quickly establish themselves there. Becoming something of a Simpson speciality, he created for them on a shoestring a nicely restrained six-bay "Gothic" building with most of the interest again concentrated on the front. Initially inhabiting a temporary wooden building specifically bought for the purpose, the congregation had the benefit also of the freely given advice of their builder, one William Henderson. Instigating a revision of the plans and a further reduction of the specification, the eventual building cost of £1,439 did not allow for much in the way of architecture. Forced to reserve any statement to the street, Simpson arranged his favourite three independent lancet windows over a projecting arched central doorway within a reduced high gable in ashlar, contained between corner buttresses, emulating in both plan and form his previous front treatments at both Kintore and Drumoak. The remainder of the building was built in pinned granite rubble, with the six pairs of upper side windows, unexpectedly round headed. The windows below, lighting under the gallery, have all been subsequently enlarged. The axial galleried interior was as always noble to the point of severity, but coming in on budget, the congregation were extremely pleased with the result, which was consecrated on the 1st July 1846. For some considerable time now however, the former church building has been converted into classrooms and lecture facilities linked by an overhead bridge to Aberdeen University's modern Geography Department, which was erected on the other side of the lane. This department also of course occupies the massively altered church premises and unfortunately in this process, virtually nothing of the former interior survived the reconstruction.

This same year, Simpson was called back again by the Principal of the University to carry out urgent repairs to the Surgical Museum at his Marischal College, following an outbreak of fire there. While involved in that restoration he was also asked to prepare plans for the installation of a new Natural History Museum to be created within the confines of the original premises. His quickly prepared initial ideas, designed to be incorporated within a refurbished arm of

Simpson's original design for the Natural History Museum, Marischal College, Aberdeen.

the main building range, which were unfortunately duly costed at the sum of £1,000. The necessary funds not being either available or forthcoming, his museum was eventually fitted up but at only a fraction of that cost, following a nonetheless most generous contribution from the City Council's coffers. Their only condition was that access to the museum had to remain free in perpetuity to the general public.

In 1845 Archibald Simpson was also invited to submit design proposals to the Incorporated Trades for their new premises in Union Street, Aberdeen. Having decided slightly earlier to abandon their very historic but now completely inadequate premises occupying the site of the ancient Trinity Friars down by the Green, both Simpson and Smith were consulted to advise on the best suitable new location. The qualities of three different sites were examined in detail, one being beside the Canal Bridge in King Street, a site beside Simpson's St Andrew's Chapel in King Street, and also a site on Union Street itself against the south-eastern abutment of the Union Bridge. At the end of the day the most prestigious Union Street site was unanimously chosen and probably due to divisions and the usual internal machinations, the eventual design competition was thrown open. Although Simpson and Smith both submitted their designs, others in the field did also. Mackenzie and Matthews even went so far as to submit proposals free of charge to the Incorporation, unless of course they actually won the competition when remuneration was expected. In the end Smith's proposals were selected, his being calculated to be £2,000 cheaper than Simpson's, obviously an important consideration. It would be also instructive to know exactly what part Smith's young son William had in the production of the successfully built design. It is certainly the case that the architectural success of Trinity Hall helped William Smith win the commission to design and rebuild Balmoral Castle, (with Prince Albert's help of course), in a just a few years' time.

Sadly Simpson's scheme is lost, but from fairly inadequate descriptions of it at the time, it appears to have been executed "in the style of the street", obviously still in a thoroughly neoclassical manner. It was becoming increasingly obvious however that there had been a distinct shift away from classical formality towards a Romantic Historical revival, and by the end of the decade, despite the fact that it would take a further twenty years to complete Union Street itself, it could be said that for all practical purposes the era of pure neoclassicism was distinctly on the wane.

Simpson had also become very actively involved again with Adam and his old client Anderson, who between them since as early as 1838 had been eagerly anticipating the arrival of the railway. Of course the entire country was gripped with railway mania at the time, fortunes were being invested and many fingers were going to be burned. However in these early days, after having been denied the possibility of acquiring the New Market for possible conversion into a railway terminus, all eyes settled upon the site next door between Hadden Street and Guild Street. The imminent removal also of the Incorporated Trades from their old premises simply made the prospect even more attractive. The idea of a railway station on this site was however to occupy Simpson up until his death in 1847. In the event of course, the collapse of a section of the railway viaduct, a late change of plan, and the obvious advantages of aligning the railway for the possible future use of the Denburn valley won the day, and the station was eventually built on Guild Street much further to the west.

This fine view of neo-classical Aberdeen from Torry, illustrates the proposed railway viaduct intended to terminate at this time at a station situated at the bottom of Market Street, in the centre of the picture.

By 1846 Simpson was also already involved with the design of Woodside New Parish Church, another late masterpiece. The church was built on a site at the head of King Street in Woodside, on ground belonging to Leys Masson and Company of Grandholm Mills. Simpson was duly appointed and requested to design and build a church to accommodate a thousand parishioners, in a "Gothic" style, and at a cost not to exceed £800, if possible. The design, much more Tuscan than Gothic, was very quickly agreed and on the 10th February 1846, the foundation stone was

Woodside New Parish
Church

The New Parish
Church from the
front.

duly laid. Having already successfully captured the market in the design of impossibly cheap churches, it is truly remarkable that this particular one, actually cheaper than all of the others, should make such a notable and noble statement. Planned and executed in the full spirit of economy, the church was conceived as a great rectangular box, built entirely in granite rubble, with dressed margins and as little dressed ashlar as possible. A low pitched slated and greatly overhanging roof at the eaves is abutted at the northern end on to a high box-projection containing the sanctuary, set between broad end plain pilasters, and carried up to a parapet out of which grows a remarkable tower (recalling something of his earlier doocot towers on various stables buildings), and still by far the finest monument on the Woodside skyline. From a stubby square base with a Diocletian window, an octagonal tower rises up through a tall belfry section to a heavy cornice above which a short cylindrical drum with four clock faces prepares the way for a slightly pointed copper dome. The clocks were actually added in 1867 at the instigation of the distant mill workers, so that they could have permanent visual access to an independent timepiece. On the reverse, actually the entrance side of the church, the basic Tuscan character is further reinforced by the provision of a single-storey vestibule and two terminating staircases up to the gallery level, which are also contained under broad-eaved roofs and low pitched gables in a most unusual but striking composition.

The very severely restrained interior as completed by William Ramage in 1849. Note that the archway was introduced when the organ cases were repositioned.

Internally the typically simple but august note is again struck in a four-bay long arrangement of very restrained dignity. Drama is allowed by the gallery running round three sides of the interior supported on slender cast iron columns, the four high arched windows marching down both sides, and the strong axial treatment terminating in the sanctuary, contained within its subsequently introduced archway. The wall and ceiling plasterwork treatment is extremely plain with just a simple cornice. The originally axial pulpit has been brought forward to the western side of the archway, some pews have been taken out from under the rear gallery opening up a milling space there, and a small kitchen has been tastefully introduced at the rear. Above where the pulpit used to be, an illuminated stained glass panel very effectively dominates the northern end wall. In addition also the pine timberwork to the all embracing high dado, the pulpit, pews and upper gallery, considerably adds to the general feeling of light and airy spaciousness. This commission however was actually completed in 1849 by William Ramage, well after Archibald Simpson's untimely death, and much of its success is obviously due to him. Happily also for the present this church still enjoys a very healthy congregation.

In a quite remarkably distant exercise Simpson was invited to prepare a design for the Union Bank of Scotland in Lerwick on far-off Shetland. It remains unclear if Simpson ever visited the site himself, which would seem unlikely given his other considerable commitments, but a design was definitely prepared, drawings sent north and a building erected in Commercial Street, Lerwick as planned. Unfortunately there is no evidence surviving today to verify the appearance of the building (although it seems most likely to have been in his plain and simple neo-Jacobean style), and as it was completely demolished in 1873 in any case to be replaced by a much larger crow-stepped gabled affair,

The Bank Manager's house, Lerwick – a Simpson design?

we shall probably never now know. Even this replacement Bank was destined to completely burn down in 1903 and was subsequently rebuilt in a more Classical Renaissance style to a design supplied by Burnett.

Interestingly there is just the chance however that a house built to a Simpson design still exists in Lerwick today at the top of the hill. Now operating as a guest house, Alder Lodge at No. 6 Hillhead, Lerwick, possesses very distinctive Simpsonian style dormers within an otherwise simple three-bay basic design. I am indebted to Mike Finnie who has advised me that this style of dormer is not found on any other building in Shetland and the possibility certainly exists that this property was designed and built originally as the Bank manager's house. In its general bearing and with three bays and spiky dormer window heads, the house definitely suggests a probable reworking of Simpson's Mains of Dyce design of a decade earlier. Unfortunately however for the building, the frontage has more recently acquired a new and very intrusive entrance cum porch extension, complete with an array of quite inappropriate replacement windows, which do little to either complement or indeed enhance its original appearance.

Almost as far away as you could get from Lerwick, at the bottom of the Royal Mile in Edinburgh, the Good Duchess of Gordon latterly employed Simpson again on what turned out to be his only architectural commission in the Capital. Designing a suitable charitable school for the local children living just a stone's throw away from the Palace of Holyrood House and built simply of sandstone ashlar in Simpson's neo-Jacobean style, typically long architrave-surrounded windows are compressed into a short gabled frontage of some distinction. A ragged eastern end to the lower linking wing at the entrance also suggests the distinct probability that Simpson may well have been contemplating a design for the subsequently built adjoining church as well. The building is rectangular, compact and of three storeys, with a steeply pitched slated roof overhead concealed on its principal five-bay return elevation by a parapet, enlivened with a continuous stringer, brought to a peak over each of the top floor windows with a fleur-de-lys breaking up through the parapet top coping stone. Simpson's favourite little ogee pediment heads are placed over the rather longer first floor window cornices, all of which sit on a moulded stringer taken all round the building at sill level. Below a similar rhythm of arch-headed full length windows make up the ground floor. Two projecting out, slightly lower links at the front and rear of the main block accommodate access stairways serving all floors. Although Simpson most probably also intended completing his design by providing a scheme for the Church immediately next door, his death unfortunately resulted in the commission being subsequently given to the local architect John Henderson in 1850.

THE QUEEN'S GALLERY

Simpson's Duchess of Gordon's School building in Holyrood Road, Edinburgh,
has been splendidly reinvented as the Queen's Gallery along with the church
immediately next door. While the outside has been well respected, the interiors of both
buildings have been totally reorganised and refurbished to create a marvellous new gallery
for the City of Edinburgh.

Both these buildings have long been brought within the curtilage of the Palace complex itself and used historically mainly for general storage purposes. They have however only quite recently been rescued and beautifully converted and refurbished into Her Majesty's truly superb Scottish Queen's Gallery. The old interiors of both buildings have been boldly opened up into one another, especially on the upper level, and have been rejuvenated in a marvellously imaginative modern arts and crafts style involving the conspicuous use of wood, glass and a deep blue fabric on the display walls. The ground floor of Simpson's block also accommodates the excellent Royal shop. Opened in 2002, this gallery promises to be one of the unmissable artistic venues in the Capital for the future, with many marvels from the Royal Collections regularly put on show. Simpson I think would have been very pleased with the result.

As he removed from his office-home at 15 Bon Accord Square into a new house at No. 1 East Craibstone Street (also designed originally by him), this year witnessed Simpson involved with Smith and Matthews in the production of plans as part of a major report for the Aberdeen City Council on various necessary Civic improvements. Recommending the creation of a Public Board to execute the entire scheme, it was envisaged that the Bell and Petty Customs would be abolished, the New Market would be acquired for the Town, a new Cattle Market and Slaughterhouse would be built, the Gas Company's undertakings would be publicly acquired and a programme of new street building would be undertaken. His first new street proposal was to construct a bridge-street from just opposite Back Wynd, over the Green below on arches, to terminate on Guild Street to the south. In addition a new thoroughfare was proposed from the SE corner of the Castlegate directly south-east, to connect with Waterloo Quay and at the same time making possible the clearance of very inferior housing in the area. In the same vein he also proposed the widening of Justice Street on the Castlegate's other eastern corner. As well as attempting to revive his St Nicholas to Marischal College cross street, he also envisaged extending Queen Street westwards to join with St Nicholas Street where he proposed the creation of a major civic space giving on directly to Union Street itself. He also advised the upgrading of St Paul Street and its continuation westwards to connect with Skene Street, although he did envisage probable opposition to this proposal by Gordon's Hospital, through whose grounds the road would inevitably pass.

As well as reminding the Council of the benefits of carrying into execution his previously designed road to the Links, he also anticipated the planned development of a number of new streets off the Gallowgate in northern

Aberdeen. To the west he suggested what would slightly later be carried out as Bridge Street, with also a lower Denburn Road, removing at a stroke very unsightly buildings still existing in the Windmill Brae and College Street areas. These he intended would be replaced by a tiered terrace, one envisaged to accommodate and largely conceal a possible future railway line which would extend through to the north. Further suggestions were also made for various new streets to be laid out in the Ferryhill district, and he finally proposed a new link route cut directly through from Holburn Junction to connect with the old Skene Road in the north.

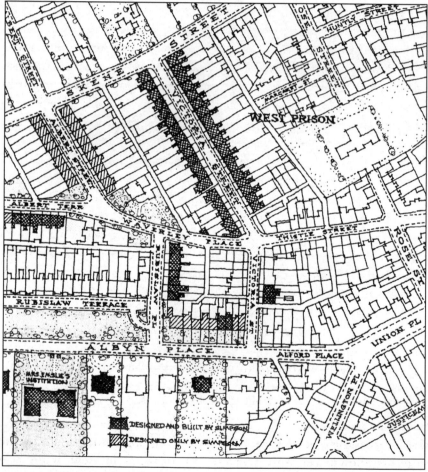

The developing West End of Aberdeen beyond Holburn Junction.

At a public meeting in Marischal College at which about five thousand interested parties attempted to attend, the necessary bill to execute these proposals was rejected completely out of hand, such was the force of local opposition. Simpson, Smith and Matthews who were all involved, asked that the meeting be reconvened later and that £100 be voted by the Council to meet their expenses and allow for the production of a revised and reduced set of proposals. The Council in eventually declining to do so ensured that none of these very worthwhile improvements were carried out. That the majority of them have been subsequently executed in the last one hundred and fifty years, simply illustrates just how far Simpson and his colleagues in the profession were ahead of their time in the field of civic planning.

On a more mundane note, this year also found Simpson back at the Lunatic Asylum in order to provide additional accommodation for the patients to involve them in more useful work and creative pursuits. The buildings, which probably still exist at the rear of the present complex in a section distinguished

The rear of the Lunatic Asylum, Barkmill.

with broad over-sailing eaves and occasional groupings of arch-headed tripartite and paired windows, certainly suggest his hand. The new wing also incorporated the erection of a small chapel and a colonnade, which has subsequently been removed along with much else probably, replaced by the vast eastern extensions carried out only slightly later in the century. It is very sad that despite Simpson's very active periodic involvement in the construction of this considerable complex, spanning virtually his entire career, very little of his actual creation seems to have survived unscathed in the process of the building's subsequent expansion at the hands of Ramage and Kelly. Obviously still fired by the perceived need to spend as little money as possible on the poor unfortunate patients however, even the vastly enlarged complex exhibits a distinct lack of quality which seems to have plagued this project from its very inception.

The year ended with Simpson's involvement with the design of the West Parish Church School of Aberdeen, situated in George Street just beyond its junction with John Street. It consisted of accommodation for five hundred pupils, with the boys to the northern end and the girls to the south. In a rather revolutionary open plan arrangement for the time, the two spacious schoolrooms formed were entirely open and designed in such a way that the headmaster in the centre could easily oversee the behaviour of the pupils. What this actually looked like externally it is now difficult to determine but whatever, the complex was subsequently hugely altered when it was completely absorbed within the subsequent rebuilding necessary for the Aberdeen Training College, itself now very successfully converted into various apartments.

In 1847 Simpson was primarily still engaged in much groundwork in connection with the eagerly anticipated railway, which had actually commenced construction with a Forfar to Aberdeen line. With the site of the final terminus not even settled and different interests investigating various options, these were exciting times indeed.

However Archibald Simpson's first task at the beginning of this year was to design an extension and carry out some alterations to Skene House. James Duff MP (later the 5th Earl of Fife), had just married Lady Agnes Hay, the daughter of the 17th Earl of Erroll in the previous year and they were both anxious to alter and modernise their house. Simpson's proposals envisaged an extension to the Georgian wing to create a large new dining room with butler's pantry beyond and the transformation of the old dining room which was combined with the bedroom immediately above it into a splendid new double height library. The existing archway and belfry at the old entrance courtyard was also re-sited to allow the formation of an impressive new entrance to the house itself in addition to a new grand internal stair complete with strapwork balustrades. The old archway was of necessity relocated to one side within a screen wall terminating in a splayed corner lead-capped tower, screening the new service court beyond. The house entrance, placed dramatically between two tall twin cylindrical towers, alongside the spirited high gable and adjoining ogee lead-

SKENE HOUSE – SIMPSON'S FINAL COMMISSION
Simpson's bold entrance front embraces Renaissance elements.

capped tower of Simpson's new south facing extension, gives on to an elongated Jacobean entrance hall also of considerable distinction. To the rear of the mansion, a small further compact family wing was also created. The overall design both internally and externally successfully combined many elements of 17th- century Scottish Renaissance work. In addition the picturesque nature of the enlarged ensemble was considerably enhanced also by the juxtaposition of rough masonry with smooth ashlar details and features, revealing again his abiding interest in the exploitation of textural effects. The work at Skene however would not be completed until 1850, and in the event of Simpson's early demise, his ideas were to be faithfully carried out and executed by his assistant William Ramage.

The south front of Skene House, as subsequently completed by William Ramage in 1850.

The east side of Albert St, two storeys with basement and attic

The final flourish as Mackenzie and Matthews realises Simpson's last street design with this typical rendering of the neo-classical Aberdeen street in the West-end.

The storey and half west side of Albert Street, Aberdeen.

In March 1847 Simpson attended a meeting of the Police Commissioners about various necessary repairs to Union Street, a slight narrowing of the pavements and the installation of better quality kerbstones. Following swiftly after that, he also put forward for auction a number of wooden models he had in his collection, including those of many of his own built and also unrealised projects. Sadly none of these now seem to have survived. Having been called away south to Edinburgh and then to Derby on business, he returned to Aberdeen shortly complaining of having caught a chill. Becoming feverish, his condition suddenly worsened and within the week he was dead. He died on the 23rd of March 1847 at his home at No. 1 East Craibstone Street, Aberdeen. He was only fifty-six years old.

Following his untimely death, his assistant William Ramage was able to carry on the practice reasonably successfully, completing Skene House, Elmhill House, large extensions to the Lunatic Asylum and the Military Barracks in King Street, as well as completing some country house work as well. Ramage does not appear to have been quite as diligent as he might have been however, allowing the firm of Mackenzie and Matthews to become Simpson's true successors in the City of Aberdeen's west end at the end of the day. Here they successfully completed, among much else by their own hand, the construction of his Victoria Street, Albert Street and Albert Terrace.

Immediately after Archibald Simpson's untimely death, his great friend John Ramsay penned the following public notice:-

"Although Mr Simpson was latterly eventually successful, his professional

The neo-classical city of Aberdeen complete

THE CASTLEGATE
Looking West.

UNION BRIDGE
Looking East.

UNION STREET
Looking West into Union Place.

UNION PLACE
Looking East into Union Street.

career was by no means unknown to early struggle but from the time he obtained an opportunity of displaying his taste and talents, his business progressively increased, and he at length reached the highest status in his profession.

His genius was as versatile as it was refined. He succeeded in all styles of Architecture, the Classical and the Gothic, the Ecclesiastic and Institutional, Baronial and Domestic. Of these, numerous and splendid specimens are to be found in this City and County and in various parts of the Kingdom. To enumerate them all is impracticable. We give the list of the principal – in the City of Aberdeen; Marischal College; The County Rooms; Royal Infirmary; New Markets; Town and County Bank (must have been his first building); North of Scotland Bank; Lunatic Asylum; Hall of the Medical Society; St Andrew's Church; Free Churches in Belmont Street; Oldmachar Free Church; the Post Office; Orphan Asylum in Albyn Place; North of Scotland Inverness Branch; and the Bell's Schools. He also planned BonAccord Square and Terrace. Mr Simpson was also first to give the outline of the recently contemplated City Improvements, and his ideas will doubtless be found to be of great value when circumstances favour that improvement undertaking.

Mr Simpson was also the architect of the beautiful Church of Elgin, General Anderson's Institution there, The Duchess of Gordon Schools at Huntly, the rebuilding of part of Gordon Castle, and the Chapel attached to it. He planned and executed the mansion houses of Boath, Morayshire; Stracathro, Forfarshire; Newe, Murtle, Meldrum, Heathcot, Park, Durris, Druminnoir, Putachie (Castle Forbes); etc. in Aberdeenshire.

Latterly he planned the beautiful Free Church of Rothesay, the additions to Skene House, and at the time of his death he was occupied with the plans of the Railway Terminus of this City. In addition to the works above enumerated, we must not forget to mention Mr Simpson's rebuilding of the bridge across the Spey at Fochabers, which is a signal proof of his skill in engineering.

The extensive business, which Mr Simpson thus enjoyed, was entirely the reward of his undoubted genius and taste. He was imbued with the warmest enthusiasm, and the finest feeling for art. He had great tact in the adaptation of his business to any given circumstances, and where difficulties occurred, no man could display more adroitness in surmounting them. He was particularly happy in connecting the style of his works to the purpose to which they were intended, and to the character of the situation in which they were placed. Thus when at one time it was proposed to place the new Marischal College on the site now occupied by the Free Churches in Belmont Street, he designed a magnificent Classical building with an expansive and imposing front, and lofty dome admirably calculated to bring out the greatest artistic effect of which the situation was susceptible. But when this site was abandoned for that on which Marischal College now stands, his was altogether different. Then he chose the Cloistral or Monastic Style, which was unquestionably the best adapted to the peculiarities of the retired site of the building, which it harmonised with the character of an academic institution. In process of time however the old site in Belmont Street was again to be occupied by a Public Building, comprising three of the Free Churches. In this case the funds were rather limited. An erection in the Classical Style was impracticable. Such a building as Marischal College would have been sadly misplaced but true to the genius loci, Mr Simpson adopted the style of Ecclesiastical Gothic, so moulding it to circumstances as to take advantage of the very peculiarities of situation, which have given so much effect to a building of the Classical Style.

Mr Simpson's character was marked by all those peculiarities not to say eccentricities, which are normally found in men of quick and keen perception and susceptible temperament. Those who were privileged to enjoy his liberal and tactful hospitality, when he drew around him his friends of congenial sociality, appreciating his real merits, and liking him all the better for occasional eccentricities, traceable to genuine simplicity of heart, will not soon forget the many happy hours alas now fled. When none more apt than he to circulate the round of wit and humour and when which, however prolonged, left his guests, even those of a most domestic mind, still chiding the stealthy stupidity of time. On these occasions when he was in the vein, he would delight his friends with specimens of his exquisite taste and masterly skill in music. In his hands his favourite instrument (the violin), attuned to some of our unimaginable national airs, would charm forth the whole spirit of their touching melody. The merits of his genius, skill and taste will long survive both him and they who must soon follow him. To these may the testimony of his Professional merit be well entrusted. Our own intentions will have been realised of what is written shall gratify desire, or enkindle emulation, when, happily in aftertimes some kindred spirit may inquire his fate."

ARCHIBALD SIMPSON'S FINAL PORTRAIT

Completed by his friend James Giles shortly after Simpson's death, the portrait shows
Simpson seated with two of his greatest City monuments placed in the background.

THE TRIPLE CHURCHES TODAY

For far too many years, Simpson's 'Cathedral of the Disruption' in its now severely fragmented condition, has disfigured this very pivotal position within the City centre. It is to be hoped that recent initiatives envisaging the development of the site and the restoration of the soaring brick spire, may be more successful than the many previous failed attempts at resolving this particular problem.

The Simpson Achievement

Archibald Simpson could be said to have been particularly fortunate to have been born into Aberdeen when he did at the end of the eighteenth century, just at the beginning of that explosion of economic growth, population and building activity which would leave us with the city centre we largely still possess today. He would not be however alone, and it must be said that his slightly older rival John Smith, certainly did as much to create a great deal of the city of that era. It is also very likely that had it not been for the industry, imagination and flair of both these extremely gifted architects, Aberdeen's principal streets and thoroughfares might easily have resembled those of George Street or Holburn Street or even worse, with successions of variously designed and ill-connected buildings just lining streets in the manner of many another provincial town or village in Scotland. With their talent and determination to aim much higher, they provided the vitally important inspiration and example, which did so much to lift the aspirations of the citizens above the usually acceptable norm. However we must not ignore either the attitude of the Council or the Trustees who, in the face of financial disaster, stuck firmly to their building specification for buildings in Union Street, when the pressure to abandon their high standards would have been perhaps a deal more sensible at the time. It is obvious too that many of the leading citizens at the turn of the eighteenth century were acutely aware also of the architectural shortcomings of Aberdeen, and were quite vocal in their desire to see their burgeoning city match the graciously planned new towns of both Edinburgh and Glasgow.

Much has been said in the past about the difficulties of cutting and working with granite and there is no doubt that this factor had a very strong influence on the native architectural character of this region. Much has also been made of this in explanation of Simpson's severity of style, failing perhaps to understand that severity and neoclassicism, the architectural style then prevalent over the entire European dominated world, were in fact the two faces of the same coin. Similarly his apparent ability to achieve a work of real architecture out of very little, and indeed frequently for very little, generally made the use of the simplest and most spartan of architectural approaches a virtual necessity. Of course many visitors coming to Aberdeen for the first time, unprepared to find a city built almost entirely of one material, grey granite, and unschooled in the local nuances of both history and style, tend to see a city of considerable sameness, not to say even monotony. Some in fact, more used apparently to the multicoloured extravagances of the south, can hardly see any merit at all in buildings where only exquisite proportion, scale and balance say it all. It appears that eyes now attuned to later and greater dramas with increased levels of superfluous decoration can frequently miss the basic merit of simplicity, in a world increasingly acclimatised to largeness of scale, vulgarity and extravagant show.

Simpson's own personal architectural simplicity came from his deep seated north-east roots, a combination of his own profoundly felt feeling for the rightness of it in itself, and his consequential almost magnetic affinity with the current neoclassical style which has simplicity as its most basic ingredient. This style of course was in his youth then enjoying its most fashionable vogue when he was in London as an impressionable architectural assistant. Also his innate sense of classical balance, his natural gift for proportion and restraint, and his tendency to reduce everything to pure geometric forms, smooth surface treatment and minimal simplicity, ensured that his designs, executed in the main in either granite ashlar, rubble or stucco, all possessed a natural quality of monumentality, elegance and grace. A pure neoclassicist through and through, he would also very naturally aspire to incorporating Greek pediments and porticoes into his designs whenever and wherever possible. This personal eclecticism has for some however been seen as the work of a mere copyist.

It is also noticeable that even before he had realised some of his most sublime Grecian statements, he had already executed a tolerably good neo-Jacobean extension, erected an accomplished early Gothic church, and completed a dramatically Perpendicular Gothic chapel in Aberdeen, at the very least indicating a versatility of style and a breadth of knowledge which was impressive for one so young. His noble but professionally disastrous early attempt at the picturesque castle style was never repeated, understandably perhaps abandoned in favour of a future neo-Jacobean style which allowed him perhaps greater personal inspiration, scope and freedom. This could also be explained of course by the unjustified adverse criticism his castle design attracted in some quarters, and the dreadful memory of the structural difficulties, which had led directly to his removal. His exploitation of a very personal version of neo-Jacobean however, albeit always with a definite dash of classical rigour, more than made up for this omission with efforts such as Lessendrum and Newe, being among the very finest and innovative of his compositions. He also showed that as well as an early debt to his rival John Smith and his mentor Robert Lugar, threads in his work indicate particularly the influence of Dance and Soane which would remain with him virtually all through his career. Also his later commissions illustrate that he was equally well aware of the pioneering works in Scotland of the likes of Wilkins, Burn, Graham, Elliot and most especially Playfair, whose innovations in planning and style he showed he could equally match. Of course, here in the north-east the availability of larger scale commissions was very much less than in the south, the lesser requirements of a much smaller population being the most obvious reason. However it is striking that when he was commissioned to furnish a design for whatever purpose, scale, or price, Archibald Simpson always managed to create a real and monumental work of architecture, large or small.

It is perhaps unfortunate that much of his efforts in Union Street itself are only accredited to him, or even sometimes style of Simpson, when his work and influence here upon this street was of the utmost significance for its eventual overall success. Despite the rejection of Young's initially proposed palace façade approach, Simpson achieved the first and last such triumph with his integrated design for Union Buildings. Sadly this success did not apparently warrant emulation, but his more standard block set the norm for most of the eastern end of the thoroughfare. Centrally planned and dignified usually with five-bay frontages, these buildings were established with usually two full floors and a lower top floor, set above a commercial and arcaded ground floor, itself built frequently above one, two or even three basements below, emulating the multi-layered approach pioneered earlier by Robert Adam in London and particularly Edinburgh. Although in principle also much indebted to the earlier city work of Burn, Fletcher and his greatest local rival John Smith, Simpson by the inclusion of stringers at first floor and top floor sill level, personal cornices, block or low parapets, broad wall-head decorative panels, and where possible, dramatically blocked and stepped chimneyed gables, always managed successfully to give his creations his own very personal stamp. This of course was underpinned by his innate ability to create a sense of dignity within beautiful overall proportions and always a dominance of solid over void which if anything exaggerated the monumental qualities of his work. Simpson also had a noticeable preference for very long narrowish windows, which he tended to use throughout his entire career. Frequently taken right down to the floor, or with a low recessed inset spandrel panel below sitting on a basecourse or stringer, these very elongated openings might even have been suggested initially by John Smith's own early work, as he was also extremely fond of such elegant window proportions. In addition Simpson sometimes liked to outline the importance of the more major window openings in his designs, in all types of commissions, with usually extremely refined architrave surrounds and occasional cornices. These could also be included in a simpler more minimalist form, even in his most modest and quite rustic commissions.

Another pronounced feature of Simpson's work was his slated roofs, almost always extremely low pitched, piended and just peeping over the top of a low parapet. Conversely he was not at all opposed to using the same roof very boldly exposed, with broadly overhanging eaves taken frequently all round, a solution he adopted very successfully in many of his later villas, cottages and even churches. He also almost always lowered the height of his top floor, most especially in his domestic work, and invariably in some of his early civic work as well. Interestingly however this tendency is not at all apparent in almost all of the streets of terraced town houses he built in Aberdeen, the main two storeys above basement treatment utilised, precluding the successful use of this device. Lower scale top floor windows are however still evident in Union Street itself where his two existing town houses at the far west end are uncharacteristically three storeys above basement high. In his most Grecian phase also his attention to classical balance, his reliance on sophisticated surface treatment, plainness and purity, further emphasised the monumental quality of his designs. He also almost completely eschewed the use of decoration or any unnecessary elaboration in most of his work, particularly earlier, depending wholly on geometric mass, simplicity of form, proportion and refinement for the creation of his effect. Indeed it is precisely these qualities which enable a Simpson design to be so readily noticeable and appreciated in the first place. Where also he did occasionally incorporate some minor and judiciously placed embellishment, this actually managed if anything to emphasise the smooth plain sophisticated simplicity of the whole.

His very obvious preference also for tight, efficient planning, coupled with the use of simple H- and T-shaped basic forms, also developed into a fondness for the expression of advancing his ends as usually one, two, or sometimes even three-bay terminations. This tendency is even noticeable in his most rectangular of buildings where he would frequently slightly advance his ends just to provide an excuse to incorporate one of his favourite Greek pediments overhead. In his domestic work also he almost always emulated Smith's fondness for en suite arrangements of two or three principal reception rooms, allowing for the introduction of an external swelling-out segmental bow or bay placed normally in the centre. From the early days too, Simpson also rarely departed from symmetrical plan arrangements, about one or even two axes, even in his most humble farm complexes and stable blocks. These less prestigious commissions however, in concert with many a gardener's cottage and gate lodge, provided him with very important opportunities for experimentation particularly in the cottage-orné style, at which he became extremely adept. These small scale commissions also gave him the possibility of developing expertise with informal asymmetrical groupings which he would eventually successfully exploit in his later more prestigious domestic work.

For the eclectic in him also, doocots in the form of central octagonal towered features could be easily translated and expanded into gatehouses or church towers, just as effortlessly as the Monument of Lysicrates in Athens, the Tower of the Winds, or even the Elizabeth Kirke in Marburg. He always however succeeded in making his borrowings his very own with an individual personal touch or interpretation. Domes were also a favourite form, but realised most frequently only internally in their shallowest manner. His very notable Aberdeen Infirmary success with one external dome, achieved possibly his most profoundly pure neoclassical statement in a civic public building. His superb domed compositions however at both Murtle and Letham Grange originally in the domestic field, also demonstrate his full appreciation of the dome as a very effective monumental cap to his more ambitious classical designs. Simpson also had a frequent desire to incorporate a sculptural group into his buildings, most usually above the parapet in the centre over the principal entrance. This is very noticeable in many of his preparatory perspectives, and even in his Infirmary design the main pediment is filled with sculpture on his front elevation. Sadly, very few of these artistic initiatives became a reality, for despite considerable advances in the quality, working and cutting of granite, the first granite statue in Aberdeen emerged as we have already seen as late as 1844 with that of George Duke of Gordon in the Castlegate. However, as usual the saving in statuary was most probably down to economy and cost cutting at the end of the day.

Internally Simpson's handling of space itself was also innovative, frequently achieving remarkable results again for very limited actual expenditure. However where sufficient funds were available he always demonstrated his considerable ability in creating rooms and relationships of great diversity, simplicity elegance and restraint, very often electrified by the dramatic imposition of domes, screens of columns, and top lit lighting effects. At the Anderson Institution in Elgin in particular he managed to combine almost all these elements together with Diocletian windows into an internal tribune of Roman gravity. He had obviously absorbed much from the earlier pioneering efforts of both Robert Adam and John Soane, although he was obviously not blind either to the previous local architectural achievements of his rival John Smith. In most of his domestic work particularly, sophisticated designs for compartmented ceilings, wall panels, his favourite Greek key decoration, exquisitely detailed woodwork, folding doors etc. allowing the possibility of throwing the principal reception rooms altogether, were all part of his normal repertoire. Although he could on occasion exhibit considerable richness when demanded, especially in his Graeco-Roman phase, his general feeling was certainly much more for serene elegance and understatement. Indeed any use of decoration by Simpson was normally, as we have already seen, simply a device to emphasise the intrinsic smooth quality of the surrounding wall surface in any case. His general restraint was also almost always achieved by an overall lightness of touch, simplicity of approach, basic unity of design, and an all-pervading sense of interrelated internal space and form, coupled with exquisitely realised overall proportions.

Even as the initial excitement of the Greek phase began to wane, Simpson had rather perfected his typically cubic or rectilinear planned astylar box house, which as asymmetry suddenly became the vogue, could be almost effortlessly attached to a lower scaled service wing to instantly create the desired effect. This also had the benefit of removing the necessity for basement accommodation, with all its attendant functional as well as constructional and water ingress problems. His ability too, to use cheap granite rubble, squared rubble or even on occasion common brickwork, all rendered or stuccoed as necessary or desired, must have appealed to the narrower pockets of very many of his clients, interested in achieving the greatest effects as cheaply as possible. His rendered rubble work in various home farms and stable blocks is also very remarkable for its considerable design quality in buildings not generally thought worthy of such architectural attention except of course for clients used to living in the most august and wealthy of circumstances.

In his Town House commissions he was always prone to favour regular rhythms of elegant openings within smooth ashlar walls under an all-embracing cornice for this type of work. In Golden Square and later in perhaps Crown Street and most definitely in Bon Accord Square, Terrace and Crescent, he fully exploited serenely cool classical monumentality of this sort to the greatest possible advantage. This manner however was quite expensive, so on the periphery at both Ferryhill and the initial west end, early and cheaper experiments carried out in rubble and squared rubble with dressed margins were skilfully introduced. Dressed stringers and very minimal decorative features also became more noticeable, possibly even at the request of the builder developers themselves. Simpson became very adept at this kind of economy throughout the rest of his career, as designs utilising the most minimal amount of dressed stone possible made an appearance in various streets and churches the length and breadth of the city of Aberdeen. Here was a remarkable instance of Simpson turning an apparent defect into a triumph of contrasting colours, forms and textures to frequently delightful effect. However he was very much less successful in promoting the much more sophisticated palace façade solution for street architecture, despite some valiant attempts. Given the apparent initial failure of his finest integrated street design at Belvidere Terrace in Ferryhill (now Marine Terrace – the eventual completion of which rather languished during his lifetime), it is perhaps quite   understandable that this overambitious early experiment was not repeated again. It seems as if the relatively rich in Aberdeen at that time were just not quite ready to pay that little extra for the necessary degree of additional cost and control, or indeed perhaps to sublimate their own individual sense of personal importance within a overall unified development, just for the possible furtherance of some greater architectural good, whatever they might have understood that to be.

There has also been a tendency for some to unfairly criticise Simpson for his undoubted willingness to concentrate much of his architectural effect on the fronts of his buildings. Although there is certainly some truth in this, particularly with regard to his churches, most of these were actually built gable-on to the street on tight sites, which obviously favoured this approach. Also the extreme financial restrictions nearly always present in these commissions, generally elevated the interests of the interior over the exterior in both Simpson's and the congregation's minds. Given some of the paltry sums of money Simpson was also asked to work with, his churches are in fact an object lesson in his most economic style of design at its most extreme. Of course it must never be forgotten either that the phrase "Queen Anne front, Mary Anne behind" could almost have been first coined in this area, as the majority of clients were perhaps understandably not too inclined to spend money unnecessarily on building effects not publicly very visible. It is also perfectly clear that when the occasion arose and he was given sufficient funds to work with, his ability to take his architecture all around is self evident and undeniable. His considerable public building masterpieces such as St Giles Church and the Anderson Institution in

Elgin, the Assembly Rooms, Royal Infirmary, North of Scotland Bank, Mrs Emslie's Institution and the Triple Kirks all in Aberdeen, are very accomplished completely in the round essays, rarely matched anywhere for their skill, style and overall quality of their design. His very considerable successes also with various finely honed designs in the field of grand domestic house architecture is equally well pronounced, complete with their numerous attendant adjacent stable complexes and home farms buildings.

When the shift to other more flexible styles gained momentum Simpson also frequently proved himself equal to the task, and quite capable of moving with the spirit of the times. However it must be said that the more classically inspired the style, the happier he seems to have been in employing it. His incursions into the Tudor, Jacobean and Gothic styles are noticeably less bold and dramatic than his local rival, who succeeded virtually in cornering the "Tudor" market as his very own. Simpson's efforts in his own version of neo-Jacobean and Gothic, display sometimes a stiffness and indeed coldness of execution, which coupled with a tendency to employ rather too discreet stringers and details, works against the overall success of the whole. Even in this area his Pointed Style work was much in advance of his more timid "pure" Gothic designs, where by his retention of a considerable dominance of solid over void, he frequently managed to create an impressively bold monumental whole. It is certainly sometimes true that you feel in some of his more Gothic work that his heart just wasn't completely in it, with on occasion even the appearance of round headed windows and various other rather classically inspired details creeping in. His tendency to provide also a frequently tied roof structure complete with a central internal flat plastered ceiling in his churches and chapels, whilst commonplace at the time, seems hardly in the true spirit of Gothic either. His ecclesiastical Gothic work frequently lacks the flair present in his neoclassicism, possibly in most instances due to severely imposed financial constraints being applied as well. His institutional and collegiate Perpendicular design work is usually rather more successful however, especially internally. With its insistent verticals, hooded windows, flattened arches, concealed roofs and occasional octagonal towers and turrets, the style was probably much more in accord with his innate classically inspired understanding in any event.

As Simpson's career progressed into its final phase it must be noted that considerable improvements in granite working technology, together with an overall increase in the quality of granite quarried, had led to a parallel movement in favour of increased embellishment and decoration, particularly in the City of Aberdeen. Smith in his Ionic Screen and Advocates Hall in Union Street perhaps introduced the more showy mood, but many clients were increasingly prone to request a greater degree of architectural drama than that now traditionally achieved by the standard neoclassical town block. This was particularly true of the Banking buildings, which were suddenly springing up throughout the region and where a certain competition culminating in Simpson's magnificent North of Scotland Bank in the Castlegate was obviously well underway. This trend manifested itself not only in Aberdeen of course, as fine examples of the genre by Simpson in both Huntly and Fraserburgh will readily testify.

Despite his very considerable fame and prestige, one area perhaps where Archibald Simpson had a bit of a blind spot was in the appreciation of the architectural and historic qualities of old buildings. This was of course not at all unusual at this time, a period which was extremely anxious to put the troubled past behind it in order to sail on into the golden promise of tomorrow. Many of Simpson's clients were to sweep away their old castle or mansion house in order to replace or extend it with some streamlined Greek or Tuscan creation in the most up-to-date manner. It did not seem to occur to any of them that the "modern style" was actually over two thousand years old itself, but at the time it was ultra-modern and international into the bargain, and that was all that mattered. It was John Smith's feeling for the past, which was if anything unusual (although Lord Cockburn was certainly with him), and with his restoration work at St Machar's Cathedral, King's College, Craigievar Castle and the widening of the Bridge of Dee, he proved that he was considerably ahead of his time in point of historic architectural appreciation. Archibald Simpson on the other hand found it easy to acquiesce in the destruction of the old Church in Kintore, the Auld Kirk in Elgin, and the East St Nicholas Church in Aberdeen, provided that he of course was commissioned to erect the modern replacement. Simpson's proposal also to re-clothe the old Bridge of Dee in modern granite ashlar garb is yet another instance of his almost complete unconcern for the integrity of a very ancient and beautiful bridge of considerable historical significance, even at that time.

Simpson's main intellectual concerns always seem to have been the present and the future, and their realisation in the form of newly planned improvements to the city, the intelligent laying out of peripheral areas on the outskirts, and the design of modern churches and Institutions of all complexions symbolically enlivening the whole. In this context he always preferred where possible to work on a blank canvas, the better to display his remarkable talent. His pioneering activities with the New Market project, and his ground work in connection with the Aberdeen Railway, all illustrate a man of the moment concerned very much with the problems of the present and the future. Indeed Simpson, like other local leaders of the profession at that time, appears to have been very far ahead in his genuine aspiration to create a much better planned city for the betterment of all its citizens. He could plainly see that in doing so of course, some of the most obvious areas of slums and deprivation could be readily swept away in order to create a considerably better planned environment in its place for the poorer citizens living there to enjoy. However it would be many years after his untimely death before the Municipality itself would be prepared to properly shoulder this particular burden in a really meaningful way. It would be much later in the century before slum clearance in earnest really got underway and even so, many quite insalubrious streets and areas within the city centre survived undisturbed until as late as the 1960s, despite having made their initial appearance in Simpson's list of demolition proposals, a hundred and twenty years previously.

One characteristic Simpson had in considerable abundance was like all great architects he had a remarkable understanding for the intrinsic qualities of his site. This is very noticeable in his location of buildings within their landscaped settings, particularly mansion houses, where he always exploited the best position and its most obvious qualities. His development also of a very personal reduced neo-Jacobean style for many of his more rugged highland sites, would seem to indicate that he intrinsically felt that cool Grecian or Italianate villas were not always entirely appropriate in such dramatic settings, requiring possibly at least a ghost of something borrowed from the illustrious and more romantic historical past. His powerful architectural displays at both Newe and Lessendrum in this genre (tragically both now no more) clearly illustrate his gift in this direction. His utilisation also of many a high knoll, bluff or natural prominence, in many of his commissions, frequently greatly contributes to their overall architectural success. Perhaps his greatest triumphs in terms of effect of site on design and form were his very remarkable Triple Churches complex brilliantly engineered to fit its very pivotal location, as well as the superb sweep of Bon Accord Crescent hugging the very edge of the Howe Burn valley. His positioning also of mansion houses such as Park, Murtle, Newe, Glenferness and Morkeu are also particularly exciting, fully exploiting the drama of their magnificent natural settings.

We have to return to his Greek phase however to find many of the basic qualities of his style developing which he would take with him right throughout his career. His particular fondness was for low-pitched roofs, sometimes set behind a parapet but also cantilevered out beyond it with broad eaves, frequently suggesting in addition an excuse for Greek pediments on the gables or a swelling bow implanted in the centre of his façade. His incorporation of a usually Ionic portico, free-standing or attached, or some episode involving columns both externally and internally, found their way into very many of his architectural commissions and in building types not previously thought sufficiently worthy of such attentions. In this manner Asylums, Hospitals, Educational Institutions and even some of his Churches were all embellished with Greek forms and detailing, both inside and out. Even Simpson's most humble stables and farm buildings could frequently boast a reduced version of an attached portico or some august triumphal entry or other, even if it was only to facilitate access for the beasts into the farmyard behind. The most modest lodge or cottage too, did not escape his attentions with many porches, reduced porticoes and cottage-orné flourishes successfully combined in beautifully considered building, designed and created nearly always with an eye to economy of function, planning, material and price.

Although Archibald Simpson was undoubtedly a supreme neoclassicist at heart, producing in his early career a succession of magnificently monumental Greek jewels, even he could not hold back indefinitely the inexorable tide of change. We have seen how when required he could diversify into a respectable Gothic or Perpendicular design for ecclesiastical, institutional or educational purposes. Even in the field of house design, whilst his basic classic terraced town house remained virtually unaltered throughout his career, the same cannot be said about his individual mansions. As his early totally symmetrical Grecian manner became diluted by the client-led requirement for more informal planning arrangements and compositions, it is very noticeable that he usually still produced a basically formal, externally symmetrical main block on all its elevations, whilst relying on an attached service wing to introduce the required note of informality into the composition. Even almost to the end, he would frequently incorporate blank windows into his elevations just for the sake of balance, and even frankly fake windows, if absolutely required to maintain a classical sense of order. On the occasions when he chose to exploit his own version of the neo-Jacobean, his instinct was still to achieve an overall sense of basic harmony and underlying classical balance through symmetry, as illustrated in his most dramatic incursions into this style such as Castle Newe and Meldrum House. It is apparent also that his most successfully informal, late asymmetric compositions were most frequently arrived at when he was employed to extend some already large and existing mansion, where the achievement of classical balance was entirely out of the question. Hence his undoubted successes such as Pittodrie, Lessendrum and Thainstone were due in no small part to the relative smallness of the extensions he built in all these cases. The natural classicist in him could even on occasion burst forth quite late in the day, as the charming but resolutely old fashioned enlargement of Devanha House in Aberdeen would readily testify. Remarkably this design was executed in exactly the same year that he commenced the enlargement of Thainstone House, certainly one of his most monumental and serene astylar and asymmetric designs. Glenferness also, despite the retention of a still classically balanced main entrance façade, disturbed only by a subservient service wing and off-centre little tower emerging behind, instantly develops on its other elevations into a notable asymmetrical composition of an advanced Italianate type. The following year at Morkeu, he even experimented successfully with the mid-Victorian cottage type, rather courageously involving the complete abandonment of his classical vocabulary altogether. His last domestic statement was a remarkable reworking and extension of Skene House, a final flourish in his neo-Jacobean manner shot through with a dash of the Scottish Renaissance, acknowledging also now the imminent triumph of a more full-blooded Scots Baronial Revival.

Another aspect of Simpson's career worthy of note is his sheer capacity for hard work. We have noted the speed with which his office recovered from the disastrous fire on the premises in 1826. However the scale and breadth of his workload throughout his entire career always pays homage to his efficient production as well as his architectural stamina. All his available remaining drawings are without exception immaculate, beautifully presented and noted. His frequent travels in the supervision of his commissions involved him in journeys as diverse as Rothesay, Edinburgh, Glenferness and almost everywhere in between within the north-east, at a time when travel was still extremely slow and overnight accommodation could be very problematic. How he and his assistants coped with many still very poor country roads in all kinds of weather conditions can now only be guessed at. How too it was possible to actually build some of his more sophisticated designs using contractors and builders not usually schooled in the rigorous requirements of any style let alone the neoclassical, is perhaps his greatest achievement of all. Undoubtedly also Simpson owed a considerable debt to his assistants who must have carried out many of the more onerous visits, and to various appointed site agents who would also have been employed to keep a regular eye on the successful execution of the work.

Archibald Simpson of course also owed a considerable debt in the design field to the earlier pioneering works in the Greek Revival style of his great competitor John Smith. His rival had gained an eight year advantage over him, and although probably slightly less aware of the latest up-to-the minute London trends, Smith even in his early works in the city and surroundings had illustrated a firm grasp of simple direct planning and august monumentality. He had also pioneered the simple classical neo-Greek box and the small classical villa type as well as introducing into most of his houses the interrelated arrangement of three reception rooms with the central principal drawing room expressed externally with a canted bay or segmental bow. His early Tudor Gothic churches also may have provided Simpson with a model on which to build his own particular versions in the emerging Gothic Revival style, although Simpson never incorporated the box-tower, which in itself almost became a Smith signature. Smith in his classical work also virtually always favoured the use of the Doric order at least externally, whilst his rival distanced himself by preferring to use Ionic most frequently, both inside and outside.

Studying the professional lives in Aberdeen of both Archibald Simpson and John Smith, it is extraordinary just how parallel their careers actually were. The instances also where they were both consulted on the same project are very remarkable, when this frequently required the production of a well-considered scheme, probably also augmented by a fine perspective sketch of their proposal into the bargain. In the competition stakes, including proposals for such buildings as St Andrew's Chapel, the Assembly Rooms, the Infirmary, Gordon's College Extension Wings, the new Town School, the Hamilton Monument, the East Church of St Nicholas, the widening of the Bridge of Dee, the Wellington Suspension Bridge, the North of Scotland Bank, the Workshops for the Blind and the Incorporated Trades Hall, Smith on balance came out slightly ahead. It must be said also in fairness that this was usually because his scheme was actually slightly cheaper, and because he was certainly an equally gifted architect, the client perceived this as a double gain. Despite all this competition however there seems to have been no animosity between the two men, and occasionally one would conveniently withdraw from a scheme, to allow the other a free reign. On certain commissions such as at King Street and Market Street, they proved how successfully co-operative their combined efforts could be when this was to the overall advantage of the particular undertaking. The failure of the projected jointly designed church proposal at Holburn Junction however, ensured that posterity was denied a truly integrated architectural example of their talents, if ever such a thing was actually possible or even desirable.

It would be wrong however to imagine that Archibald Simpson was without his critics, and even within the field of neoclassicism, many prefer the slightly more robust and sober work of John Smith. While Simpson may strictly have been the better, more exciting and innovative classical planner, Smith could usually match him elevationally, displaying frequently a drama, boldness of composition and detailing, sometimes absent in some of Simpson's more severe work. One of his main preoccupations was of course always the exploitation of very plain surface treatment, a characteristic that at the end of the day even seemed to become a concern of John Smith also. Other critics have also found Simpson's work to be slightly derivative, and possibly even worse, rather cold and impersonal as well, exhibiting for them far too much simplicity, restraint and control for their particular personal tastes. It is of course impossible for any architect at any time to please everyone, and neoclassicism, even allowing for its attendant use of elegant and refined proportions, has always had its fair share of detractors, unable to see much merit in such an apparently alien and imported style involving strict allegiance to insistent horizontals and verticals.

Whilst acknowledging that the general antiquarian mood of the time and these very qualities of extreme order and restraint following the upheavals across much of Europe in the wake of the French Revolution had given rise to the Greek Revival in the first place, the necessary architectural rigour involved soon gave way to allow the possible use of the arch, various Roman, and even some Renaissance elements. This had the immediate effect of considerably softening the initial rather stark simplicity of the style. It cannot be denied however that Simpson's own personal sense of reticence and restraint, coupled with his considerable perfectionist streak, almost always erred on the more severe side of this particular balance. His reuse also of many elements and forms introduced into his designs from the distant classical past or reinterpreted through others is also marked and has given rise to more adverse criticism by some, as evidence of his architectural plagiarism. This rather ignores the tendency of all architects at this particular time to reuse various antique elements in exactly this same way, indeed wearing their sources of various porticoes, capitals, columns, details and arrangements almost as a badge of honour. Even his great local rival John Smith could on occasion be found guilty on this score.

Regarding the possibility of Simpson's wider influence, given his scale of operation and his location in the still rather remote City of Aberdeen, there was little practical opportunity for him to spread his wings and achieve an architectural presence in either Edinburgh or Glasgow at this date without him actually taking up residence there. Despite gaining late commissions in both the Capital, Lerwick and at equally more remote Rothesay, work at such a distance is difficult enough to carry off successfully even today. It would have been very different had his main base been Edinburgh or Glasgow and his greater fame might then have sustained him in the north-east. Presence in the locality and personal business connections however have always been essential in the furtherance of any architectural career, and this was as true in the nineteenth century as it is today for all but the most famous. This corner of Scotland in any case has always had something of a rather separate quality about it, consigned beyond the far Grampian Mountains, and probably happiest in and among its own. His abiding interest was simply the furtherance of his talent and to serve and meet the local architectural requirements as best and as often as he could. It is however as always regrettable, that like many another great provincial architect, had he operated on the larger stage, his name and reputation at the national level would undoubtedly have been considerably and very deservedly greater.

In an island which has always perhaps understandably gravitated towards its south-eastern corner in most aspects of its existence (including its architectural development), it has long been the received wisdom that the further north the location, the more primitive and uncivilised are likely to be the conditions. The architecture of Scotland itself has therefore suffered greatly from this southern orientated prejudice of an English-dominated island, a condition however also sadly present north of the border as well in a nation over-concentrating in the activities within its Central Belt. In a rapidly changing society witnessing the birth of the modern world, both Archibald Simpson and his great rival seized their opportunity to stamp their London attuned architectural ideals on the entire north-east region of Scotland, for once ensuring that Aberdeen was up with the big boys. They exploited also in the process the opportunities presented by the inexorable movement away from the old landed order towards a new urban based middle class with its considerably expanded domestic, commercial and institutional requirements. In so doing they laid the basic ground rules for all sorts of building types and initiatives which would last for well over a century and more despite some intervening changes in style, not only in Aberdeen but throughout the entire region. Fully acknowledging the indigenous and separate character of the area, the people and their buildings, they succeeded in realising their advanced neoclassical ideas in the full spirit of modernity whilst creating also for the first time the presence of a recognisably sustainable architectural profession in the area, which would in the hands of their pupils and successors continue their established traditions.

It is to be hoped that this study of Archibald Simpson's career may go some way to explaining his importance in the architectural development of Aberdeen and its surrounding area. His enviable ability in handling space, his capacity to realise his creations as monuments within their various settings and his intuitive employment of the most superb proportions in his work, were all conceived and built upon the triple pillars of simplicity, elegance and restraint. Hopefully also the scale, quality and breadth of his remarkable achievements throughout the entire north-east may also be more readily appreciated beyond the immediate geographical confines of the City of Aberdeen and the region that he served so long and so well.

* * *

The following article from the *Free Press*, dated 1877, is worthy of reproduction, setting out as it does a relatively contemporary view of Simpson's considerable architectural achievements, only some thirty years after his unfortunate demise.

ARCHIBALD SIMPSON

Our greatest local architect of modern times, and the man who Aberdeen owes the finest and most effective of her public buildings. The son of an Aberdeen merchant, Simpson was born in 1790 and was educated at the Grammar School and Marischal College. He studied his art in Aberdeen, in London, and in Italy, learned more than the theory, put his hand to practical constructive work in stone and wood, and gained knowledge that served him well in later years. Establishing himself as an architect in Aberdeen he had many early struggles to get through. One of his first works of any consequence was St Andrew's Church, King Street erected in 1817, at a cost of about £6,000. Some years after, and at the very outset of his career, his plans, sent anonymously, for the erection of the County Buildings (now the Music Hall Buildings) were selected in open competition. The fine open Ionic portico is one of the chief architectural features of the City, and, even if the Infirmary and Marischal College had not followed, his reputation would have been made. The County Buildings were founded in 1820, and cost £11,500. By and by other and greater work came upon him, and the results of his elegant architectural conceptions are to be seen all over the City and there are very few of our best public buildings which are not emanations of his fertile fancy and prolific pencil. There are the Royal Infirmary, severely classic in outline and imposing in its chaste simplicity (erected in 1832–40 at a cost of £17,000); the Female Orphan Asylum in Albyn Place, erected in 1843; Marischal College, so effective in its quiet cloistral style (erected in

1837–41, at a cost of £30,000); the Athenaeum Buildings; the Established East Church (erected in 1836–38 at a cost of £6,045 17s 4d); the North of Scotland Bank with its magnificent portico and columns (£15,000); the old Town and County Bank (now the offices of the Scottish Provincial Assurance Company); the Northern Assurance Office ; the Medical Hall (erected in 1818 at a cost of £2,000); the old Post Office ; the Mechanics Hall (costing £3,500 in 1846); the Lunatic Asylum (erected in 1819–20 at a cost of £7,000): Oldmachar Free Church, the group of the Free East, South and High Churches (costing £5,000 in 1844) with the spire which out of very unpromising material is so chaste in outline and exquisite in all its proportions. This it seems was his favourite work, and was introduced at his own request into the background of his well-known Gilies portrait. Simpson also planned and laid out Market Street, and was the architect of our much admired Market Buildings (costing £20,000 in 1841–42). He laid out Bon Accord Square and Terrace, Albyn Place and Ferryhill, and it is a great pity that his original plans for these have been so far departed from. His works out of Aberdeen are very numerous, and each of them almost has its own particular architectural beauty. Take the beautiful Established Church in Elgin; General Anderson's Institution there; the Mansion House at Newe; Rothesay Free Church ; the Duchess of Gordon's Schools at Huntly; the Mansion House of Craig; Haddo; Carnousie; Durris; Meldrum; Heathcot; Pittodrie; and any number of others, and each will be found to have some particular feature that not only receives but commands admiration.

Of Simpson, his friend, the late John Ramsay says, "He was imbued with the warmest enthusiasm and the finest feeling in art. He had great tact in the adaptation of his designs to any given circumstances, and where difficulties occurred, no man could display more adroitness in surmounting them. He was particularly happy in accommodating the style of his works to the purposes or which they were intended, and to the character of the situation in which they were placed."

Simpson died after a short illness on 23rd March, 1847 aged 57. His remains were interred in the City Churchyard; and it is hardly to the credit of the City that the only memorial to one who has so left his mark upon the Town should be the flat slab of granite above his grave.

A complete list of all of Archibald Simpson's known, attributed and "style of" works continues on the following pages together with a glossary of terms and some very necessary acknowledgements to all the various institutions and individuals who have been extremely generous and helpful in the research and compilation of this study.

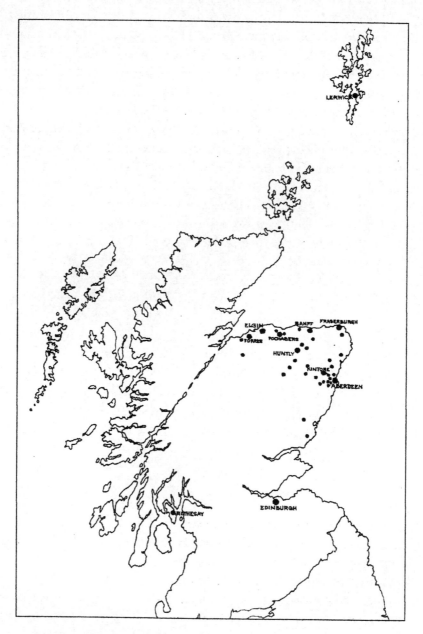

The distribution of Archibald Simpson's work throughout Scotland.

The Complete Works of Archibald Simpson

Note that Simpson's accredited buildings are in bold type; attributed and style of Simpson buildings are indicated in normal type.

1813 **UNION CHAMBERS**
At Nos. 46–50 Union Street, Aberdeen for the Duchess of Gordon.

MORRISON of AUCHINTOUL'S HOUSE
(Designed 1811) at 40–44 Union Street.

1815 **EXTENSION WING to DRUMINNOR**
The ancient Forbes Seat (demolished).

CASTLE FORBES, KEIG
New castle-style house for Lord Forbes, on Donside.

1816 **ST ANDREW'S CHAPEL**
(Now a Cathedral) King Street, Aberdeen (altered).

1817 **Nos. 136-144 UNION STREET**
Aberdeen; for the Aberdeen Hotel.

1818 **THE MEDICO CHIRURGICAL HALL**
King Street, Aberdeen: James McGrigor.

1819 **KINTORE PARISH CHURCH**
For his Uncle, the Revd. John Shand.

Nos. 23–25, GORDON STREET, Huntly
For George Lawson (probably by Simpson).

No. 13 GOLDEN SQUARE, Aberdeen:
Among possibly some others in the square.

LUNATIC ASYLUM, Barkmill:
1819–20 Aberdeen (largely overwhelmed later).

No. 19–21 UNION STREET
Bailie Galen's House
Phase one of Union Buildings.

THE PARISH CHURCH
Forgue, Aberdeenshire

No. 9 ALBYN PLACE, Aberdeen:
(Attr) now Royal Northern and University Club.

1820   **PUBLIC WATERHOUSE**
St Nicholas Street, Aberdeen (demolished).

THE COUNTY BUILDINGS or ASSEMBLY ROOMS:
Now the Music Hall.

1822   **Extension to HUNTLY LODGE,** Huntly
For the Duchess of Gordon.

HADDO HOUSE
Internal alterations, Stables, outbuildings etc., for Lord Aberdeen.

ATHENAEUM READING ROOM
For Alex Brown completing Union Buildings.

HEATHCOT HOUSE, Haugh of Ardoe, Aberdeen:
(Demolished in 1958).

PARK HOUSE, Drumoak:
For William Moir with also the West Lodge.

BOATH HOUSE, Auldearn:
For the Dunbar Family.

1823   **MURTLE HOUSE,** Beildside
For John Thorburn (now the Rudolf Steiner Schools).

BON-ACCORD SQUARE & CRESCENT ETC.,
For the Incorporated Tailors.

Probable involvement in the CROWN STREET development:
Various town houses.

PARK ESTATE
Completion of the Home Farm, steadings etc for William Moir.

1824   **DURRIS HOUSE**
Extensions to the original Scots house for John Innes.

SCOTSTOWN HOUSE, Bridge of Don:
For the Moirs of Scotstown and Spital.

1825   **CRIMONMOGATE HOUSE,** Lonmay
For Sir Charles Bannerman: outbuildings etc.

ST GILES CHURCH, Elgin:
Completed 1828 (his ecclesiastical masterpiece).

122–132, UNION STREET, Aberdeen
(Burnt, and rebuilt internally 1830).

95–99, and 101–105 UNION STREET, Aberdeen
(Almost certainly by Simpson).

1826   **TOWN & COUNTY BANK, 91–93 Union Street,** Aberdeen
(Demolished).

TILLERY HOUSE, Udny
For the Chambers-Hunter Family (fire damaged).

EAST LODGE, Gordon Castle
At 2 Castle Street, Fochabers.

1827   **STRACATHRO HOUSE**
For Alexander Cruickshank with various outbuildings

LETHAM GRANGE: Angus
(Much altered and considerably extended).

SCHEME: Proposed New Street, Broad Street , Aberdeen
(Unsuccessful)

1828   **HOUSE OF LEASK (PITLURG)**
For Gen. Gordon Cumming Skene (restored).

SCHEME
For the Damlands of Rubislaw prepared.

CASTLE GORDON, Fochabers
Restoration of the East Wing following a fire.

COTTAGE, No. 134–138 Crown Street, Aberdeen
(Probably by Simpson).

JOINT SCHEME
With Smith for a Chapel of Ease at Holburn Junction, Aberdeen.

1829   **BOGHEAD**
The Home Farm at Gordon Castle: Fochabers

TOWN HALL, Forres:
Extensions, (later became the Mechanics' Institute).

WOODSIDE CHAPEL OF EASE
Queen Street, Woodside, Aberdeen

Competition Scheme:
For the Bridge over the Dee at Craiglug
(Unsuccessful).

1830 **ANDERSON'S INSTITUTION,** Elgin
With Lodge: completed 1833.

EAST END SCHOOL, Elgin:
Completed 1833.

Nos. 18 and 20 ALBYN PL, Aberdeen
With probably Nos. 25 and 26 as well.

CASKIEBEN, Blackburn:
Estate buildings, etc. (1830–35) also Bendauch, Dyce etc.

GRANTON LODGE, Granton Place, Aberdeen:
(Probably by Simpson).

Commences design of the Ferryhill District for the Shoemaker's Incorporation.

1831 **Rebuilding the SPEY BRIDGE,** Fochabers
Along with the Toll House

FERRYHILL PLACE, Nos. 20–30 and Nos. 17–27
(Almost certainly by Simpson).

Nos. 3–11 BELVIDERE TERR.
(now Marine Terr). Begun 1837–completed 1877–82.

CASTLE NEWE, Donside:
For Sir Charles Forbes: (now demolished).

381–389 UNION STREET
(Most probably by Simpson).

MRS YEATS of AUQUHARNEY'S HOUSE:
Justice Mill Lanc, Abdn. (dem).

1832 **CASTLE CRAIG,** Lumsden:
Additions to the existing Castle.

NEW INFIRMARY BUILDINGS, Woolmanhill, Aberdeen:
Completed in 1839.

COMPETITION:
Unsuccessful design for the Hamilton Monument, Aberdeen.

1833 ST ANDREW'S EPISCOPAL CHURCH, Banff
THE EPISCOPAL CHAPEL, Fochabers
(Subsequently much modified).

1834 **Competition Scheme:**
Dr Bell's School, Frederick St, Aberdeen
(Successful).

Competition Scheme:
The East Church of St Nicholas, Aberdeen
(Successful).

1835 SCHEME for the Damlands of Rubislaw:
Reissued for Charles Gordon.

Designed 1–6 RUBISLAW PLACE:
21 & 23 WAVERLEY PLACE,
Built after 1849.

DR BELL'S SCHOOL, Frederick Street, Aberdeen
(Now demolished).

LINTON HOUSE, Midmar with Home Farm, Steadings & Funerary
Monument, etc.

EAST CHURCH OF ST NICHOLAS, Aberdeen:
Reconstruction of Medieval Choir.

NORTH OF SCOTLAND BANK, Fraserburgh
(Almost certainly a Simpson design).

DRUMOAK PARISH CHURCH, Drumoak, Aberdeenshire:
Manse built by Smith.

DURRIS HOUSE,
Extensions for A. Mactier, also in 1838 (dem):
Also Stable block.

Competition Scheme / Report:
For the widening of the Bridge of Dee
(Unsuccessful).

Competition Scheme:
Advocates Hall:
Simpson drops out of the Competition.

1836 **2–16 ALBYN PLACE**
(Modified in execution by Mackenzie and Matthews).

MELDRUM HOUSE,
Extensions and re-casting of original:
(Completed 1839).

HADDO HOUSE, Inverkeithney
(Almost certainly by Simpson).

1–7 ROTUNDA PLACE,
Now Polmuir Road, Ferryhill
(Almost certainly by Simpson).

NEW MARISCHAL COLLEGE, Aberdeen:
Quad Buildings
(Completed 1841).

North of Scotland Bank:
Alterations to premises 41– 45 Broad St., Aberdeen (dem).

1837 1–6 MARINE PLACE, Ferryhill: Aberdeen
(Almost certainly by Simpson).

LESSENDRUM HOUSE, Drumblade,
For the Bisset Family
(Burnt down).

MRS EMSLIE'S INSTITUTION, Albyn Place, Aberdeen
(Now Harlaw Academy).

1838 **No.28 ALBYN PLACE**
For Provost Leslie of Nethermuir
(Now the Albyn Club).

Re-erect OBELISK
To Sir John Forbes of Newe:
Lunatic Asylum grounds.

First Proposals for the **NEW MARKET:**
For Alexander Anderson (not built).

SCHEME:
Competition for the building of the New Town School
(Unsuccessful).

1839 **MURTLE COTTAGE,** Bieldside:
In the cottage-orné style.

WESTBURN HOUSE,
For the Proprietor of the *Aberdeen Journal*, David Chalmers.

NORTH OF SCOTLAND FIRE & LIFE,
Building at 1–5 King Street, Aberdeen.

COMPETITION:
NORTH OF SCOTLAND BANK,
Castle Street, Aberdeen.

GORDON SCHOOLS HUNTLY
For the Duchess of Gordon
(Completed 1841).

Designed 1–34 ALBERT TERRACE and 1 PRINCE ARTHUR STREET. Aberdeen (Built 1848–67)

1840   Designed 1–23 ALBERT STREET
(Built after 1849 by Mackenzie & Matthews).

Designed 2–18 ALBERT STREET
(Built after 1849 by Mackenzie & Matthews).

GLASSAUGH HOUSE,
Extensions for the Abercrombies
(Mostly ruinous).

CARNOUSIE HOUSE
(Probably not completed but now substantially demolished).

DEVANHA HOUSE, Ferryhill:
Extension & re-casting of 1813 house
For J. Blaikie.

No. 67 & Nos. 73–79 UNION STREET Aberdeen,
Terminals to Market Street.
(Demolished).

NEW MARKET BUILDINGS,
For A. Cruickshank: completed 1844
(Demolished).

THAINSTONE HOUSE, Port Elphinstone
For Duncan Forbes Mitchell.

THE MOIR MAUSOLEUM,
St Peter's Cemetery, Old Aberdeen.

LUNATIC ASYLUM:
Extension Kitchen wing added to original complex.

1841 SCHEME:
Competition entry for the Blind Workshops, Huntly Street
(Unsuccessful).

PITTODRIE HOUSE,
Extensions to the ancient Smith Ancestral home.

SCHEME:
New screen & street linking Marischal College with St Nicholas
Church.

1842 POST OFFICE,
5–9 Market Street, Aberdeen
(demolished).

NORTH OF SCOTLAND BANK,
Huntly.

1843 Designed 7–11 VICTORIA STREET
(Built around 1850: Mackenzie & Matthews).

Designed 21–59 VICTORIA STREET:
Actually begun in 1843.

Designed 18–56 VICTORIA STREET
and 2, 6, 8, 10 & 16 WAVERLEY PLACE.

LUNATIC ASYLUM:
Rear Extension to existing complex.

SCHEME:
For a new thoroughfare down to the Links
(Unsuccessful).

1844 TRIPLE CHURCHES:
'Cathedral of the Disruption', Aberdeen
(Partially ruinous).

FREE CHURCH, Rothesay:
Now Trinity Church, Isle of Bute.

GLENFERNESS HOUSE:
New Italianate house etc. in Nairnshire.

FEVER HOUSE and PORTER'S LODGE,
The old Infirmary, Woolmanhill, Aberdeen.

1845 **MECHANICS' INSTITUTE**
13–15 Market Street, Aberdeen:
(With William Ramage).

MORKEU HOUSE, Cults, Aberdeen
(Subsequently altered and much enlarged).

ST MARY'S CHURCH, Old Aberdeen:
(Now University Geography Dept).

NATURAL HISTORY MUSEUM,
Marischal College with fire damage repairs.

SCHEME:
Unsuccessful competition entry for the Incorporated Trades Hall.

PROPOSED RAILWAY TERMINUS, Market Street, Aberdeen
(Unrealised).

1846 **WOODSIDE NEW PARISH CHURCH:**
(Completed 1849 by William Ramage).

UNION BANK of SCOTLAND,
Lerwick, Shetland
(Destroyed by fire).

THE DUCHESS OF GORDON SCHOOL,
Holyrood, Edinburgh:
(Now altered).

CIVIC IMPROVEMENTS:
Numerous proposals throughout the City of Aberdeen.

LUNATIC ASYLUM:
Colonnade and Workshops extension with Chapel.

WEST PARISH CHURCH SCHOOL,
George Street, Aberdeen.
(Demolished).

1847 **SKENE HOUSE**
The house Simpson was working on at his death
(Completed 1850s).

NOTE: following Archibald Simpson's untimely death:

William Ramage went on to complete

THE MECHANICS' INSTITUTE

ALTERATIONS TO SKENE HOUSE.
CORNHILL MENTAL HOSPITA
ENLARGEMENT OF ELMHILL HOUSE.
MILITIA BARRACKS, King Street, Aberdeen.

In addition the firm of Mackenzie and Matthews succeeded in completing many of Simpson's initial street designs contemplated for the west end of Aberdeen, including the following:-

ALBERT STREET. (both sides)
VICTORIA STREET. (remaining parts)
ALBERT TERRACE. (remaining parts)

Mackenzie and Matthews also of course very significantly introduced a new era of Historical Revivalism into the City of Aberdeen with their magnificent RUBISLAW TERRACE development which commenced in 1852, in a design which virtually signalled the end of the neoclassical street in the City.

Glossary of Terms

Aisle: Lateral side portions of a Basilican Church arrangement separated from the central body by arcading or colonnades supporting the clearstorey.

Apse: semicircular of polygonal recess at the end of a Basilican Church.

Arcade: a range of arches carried on a row of columns or piers.

Architrave: the lowest of the divisions of an entablature resting on the column. It can also be used to refer to the lintels, jambs and mouldings round door and window openings in classical buildings.

Ashlar: very finely cut stonework with sharp right-angled arrises.

Astylar: a classical composition without the inclusion of columns or pilasters.

Attic: the storey in classical architecture placed above the main entablature and cornice. It must not be confused with a gablet or garret.

Balustrade: an upstand parapet composed of balusters, with coping, rail and occasional pedestals.

Band: a low flat square-faced string course running across a façade.

Basement: the lowest portion of a building nearest the ground. This can be a full basement or a half-basement and occasionally what might be a basement at the front could be a fully exposed floor at the rear.

Basilica: an interior designed in the old Roman fashion with a central higher nave section flanked by lower aisles on either side.

Battlement: a crenellated parapet formed at a wallhead.

Bay: properly used to describe a principal structural compartment or sub-division repeated throughout a building usually by piers, pilasters or columns. It is actually incorrect to refer to runs of windows as bays if there is no structural integrity behind.

Bay Window: a window projecting out of a room, rectangular, polygonal or semi-circular. A segmental bay may also be called a bow.

Bridge Street: an arrangement found particularly in Scotland, developed in response to the unevenness of the terrain in many of the ancient Burghs. The idea found its first expression in the Bridges in Edinburgh and in Marischal

Street in Aberdeen. Later Aberdeen would exploit this solution again in the construction of Union Street and Market Street, and also outwith Simpson's period in the building of both Bridge Street and Rosemount Viaduct.

Capital: the upper part of a column or pilaster, immediately placed under the lintol. In Greek inspired work they are either of Doric, Ionic or Corinthian in style and in Roman work there are a further two types, Roman Doric (Tuscan) and Composite orders.

Castellated or Crenellated: complete with battlemented parapets and turrets.

Coffer: The flat section of a ceiling where it may be enclosed by main beams and subsidiary cross beams. It may also refer to rectangular indentations within a ceiling or dome to both lighten the structure and create an effect.

Compartmented Ceiling: a ceiling broken up into areas by beams or bands.

Console: an S-shaped decorative bracket most usually found on either side at the head of a door or window opening supporting a cornice, pediment or lintel.

Corbel: a stone projecting out from the main face of a wall.

Corinthian Order: the most magnificent and elaborate of all the classical orders used by both the Greeks and Romans, based on the acanthus leaf.

Crescent: a series of connected buildings planned as part of the arc of a circle.

Crow-step, Corbie-step: end tabling at a gable where the blocks are left stepped.

Cupola: the drum or polygonal space or lantern on top of a dome or tower.

Cyma: a moulding hollow on its upper part.

Cyma Recta: an S-shaped moulding found at the top of a cornice.

Dado: a solid usually plain block forming the base pedestal or plinth on which a classical building sits. It can also be the base part of an internal wall, divided off by either a decorative timber or plaster plate or even a change of material.

Dance: The architect who in Britain did most to usher in the Greek neoclassical phase, following a visit to post revolution France. His first Greek portico at Stratton Park was extremely influential, as was his later London Work.

Distyle: a portico with two columns, often found in antis.

Dome: a usually hemispherical vault over a circular or elliptical opening or drum in a ceiling or roof.

Doric Order: the basic Greek and later Roman Order, with the simplest capital and no base to the column if used in a Greek context.

Dormer: a window inserted into the slope of a roof allowing the use of the attic or garret. In Aberdeen in the early period they were normally small, rectangular and flat on the face, but later developed into much larger canted-bay versions with inset half side windows at forty-five degrees. In some work, wide dormers incorporating two or more usually three windows can be found.

Dressings: mouldings, ornament or additional stone tooling around an opening.

Eaves: the lower edge and underside of a roof overhanging the wall face below.

Egyptian Style: a phase of Neoclassicism utilising basically Egyptian motifs and forms, particularly popularised following Napoleon's adventures there in the early nineteenth century.

Enrichment: any elaboration of mouldings in the classical style.

Entablature: the superstructure above a capital consisting usually of architrave, frieze and cornice over.

Fascia: a broad band or face usually used with other mouldings as part of a wall or the edge of a roof or projection.

Fenestration: the arrangement of windows within a façade.

Finial: a prominent terminal feature which may be spike, pyramid, ball, urn or even pineapple shaped.

Flute: concave channels in the shafts of classical columns – these are very rare in Aberdeen except internally or where the columns are made of wood.

Frieze: the middle division of an entablature and the upper portion of an internal wall below the cornice.

Gable: the end wall of a building which follows the basic shape of the roof.

Giant Order: a column or pilaster rising from the base over two or more storeys.

Greek Orders: Doric, Ionic and Corinthian, as distinct from Roman versions.

Greek Revival: the last phase of neoclassicism adopting archaeologically correct elements and arrangements from ancient Greece. The style was particularly suited to use in Aberdeen due to its inherent simplicity coupled with the hardness and difficulty of working the local granite.

Ground Floor: the storey of a building at ground level although it may be set over a basement below or behind.

Hexastyle: a portico with six columns in a line.

Ionic Order: the second Greek and third Roman classical Order with volutes.

Jamb: the side of a window or door opening within the thickness of a wall.

Lintel: the beam over an opening supporting the wall above.

Masonry: the craft of cutting, jointing and laying stonework.

Medallion: a square, rectangular, round, elliptical or oval tablet possibly with designs or busts carved in relief.

Module: a measure which by its multiplication or subdivision regulates proportion in a building.

Monument: an edifice erected to commemorate a person or event.

Monumental: an edifice or design which powerfully expresses the qualities of inherent strength, timelessness and scale. The use of granite in Aberdeen which imposed its own strength, simplicity and dignity, resulted in the construction of a City which is the epitome of the monumental.

Movement: the rise and fall, advance and recess of elements of building design.

Nave: the central part of a church, usually in front of the altar and flanked on either side by aisles. It can also be the western wing of a cruciform church.

Neoclassicism: an architectural period which was based on the increasingly archaeologically correct study of ancient Greek and Roman buildings at source. The style has a tendency towards purity of form which particularly appealed north of the border, but can be executed with a severity and seriousness which can be forbidding in less able hands. In Scotland the neoclassic period lasted longer than in England, dominated by William Playfair in Edinburgh and merging into the era of Greek Thomson in Glasgow. Smith and Simpson were the main protagonists of the style in Aberdeen and the North-East, where it was particularly suited to the use of granite.

Obelisk: a tall square tapering stone shaft used extensively in ancient Egypt and popular as a commemorative feature in the nineteenth century following the Egyptian phase of neoclassicism.

Order: Doric, Ionic, Corinthian in Greek work, with Doric, Ionic, Corinthian, Tuscan and Composite in Roman usage.

Pavilion: a small garden building or attached wing of a larger building, usually independently roofed.

Pavilion Roof: an independent roof, piended or hipped at all corners.

Pediment: the low pitched gable crowning a classical portico, attached or otherwise.

Picnded: a roof which is hipped on all corners, without gables.

Pilaster: a projecting feature from a wall treated as a flat column.

Pinnacle: a summit or apex or a terminating feature to a buttress or corner.

Plinth: the unadorned base of a wall or building on which the architecture proper usually sits.

Podium: a continuous pedestal or base usually supporting a colonnade.

Proportion: the proper magnitude of each and every part of a building within the overall classical whole.

Quadrangle: buildings arranged around a square or rectangular courtyard.

Regency: the classical style adopted in Britain from 1795–1830. The term is however less frequently used in Scotland than in England.

Rendering: a roughcast, drydash or stucco external finish to a building.

Return: the continuation of a cornice, string course or some other decorative element of a building in a different direction on an adjoining elevation.

Reveal: the side or jamb of a window or door opening.

Roundel: a circular decorative panel.

Soane: one of the leading neoclassical architects of the generation immediately following Robert Adam. A gifted architect and a free thinker, his work is as inspired as it is original. His designs for the Bank of England (now unfortunately hugely re-worked) is particularly interesting as is his own house in Lincoln Inn's Fields. He developed his own style of incised linear decoration, which he frequently used to actually highlight the smoothly sophisticated surfaces of his later interiors. The general vogue for this type of decoration is referred to as Soanean.

Serliana: or Venetian window, with a high central semicircular headed window arrangement flanked by lower half windows on either side, usually delineated by pilasters set between the windows.

Smith, John: Archibald Simpson's very gifted local rival (1781–1852). Having a head start on Simpson and good connections from his father's Architectural-Builders firm, he secured the post of Superintendent of the Works to the Trustees, following the retirement of Thomas Fletcher in 1807. By the 1820s this post had developed into that of the City Architect, and in this capacity he was responsible for the building of many new streets, bridges and civic buildings. He was often in direct competition with Simpson but overall their success was about equal. Among many notable neoclassical buildings in Aberdeen, the lower end of King Street, the North Church (his masterpiece), the Blind Workshops, the old Town School, the Wellington Suspension Bridge, and the Bridge of Don are very typical. However he progressed to earn the nickname "Tudor Johnny" and in this vein he was responsible for King's College Extension, the old Trades Hall in Union Street, and the widening of the Bridge of Dee among others. He also had a considerable ecclesiastical and domestic practice throughout the north-east, easily a match for Simpson's. On his death his practice continued in the hands of his son William, whose chief fame is the building of the new version of Balmoral Castle.

Soffit: the underside of any part of a building, arch or ceiling.

Stucco: a plaster or smooth cement rendering over stone or brickwork.

Terracotta: baked red clay, unglazed and frequently cast in moulds and often used as decoration.

Tetrastyle: a portico with four columns set in a row.

Tracery: the intersection of mullions and transoms in Gothic or Tudor windows.

Tuscan: based on the simple rustic style prevalent in northern Italy, usually associated with broad overhanging eaves.

Tuscan Order: the simplest of all the orders based on those of ancient Rome, with a plain architrave and columns never fluted.

Vault: an arched structure over a roof, chamber or bridge structure.

Veranda: an open gallery or terrace covered by a roof supported by columns, usually set along the garden front of a house.

Viaduct: a long bridge carrying either a road or railway.

Villa: originally a Roman Farmhouse, the word expanded to include eventually vast arrangements like Hadrian's Imperial Palace at Tivoli. The term became popular again following the success of Palladio's Villa Capra at Vicenza and could describe almost any mid-eighteenth century country house with a compact neoclassic centralised layout. In the nineteenth century the use of the word became completely debased to include any free-standing dwelling erected in the outskirts of a town or city, frequently usually quite small.

Volute: the spiral scrolls forming the main features of an Ionic capital.

Window: an aperture formed within a wall in order to admit light.

Wings: side portions to a building usually subordinate to the main central block.

Yard: a paved area or service area usually found at the rear of a house. In Town-houses of the early nineteenth century in Aberdeen, the service yard could be frequently found at the front of the property, at basement level, behind railings set at the back of the pavement

Acknowledgements

In the compilation of this study, particular thanks are due to the very considerable previous efforts of Bill Brogden, Ian Shepherd, Jane Geddes, Charles McKean, Edward Meldrum, Frank Walker, Fiona Sinclair, Mike Finnie, Cuthbert Graham, and of course the redoubtable G. M. Fraser, whose already available work on various aspects of Archibald Simpson's life and buildings has been of considerable assistance to me in terms of background, factual information, historical details and dates.

ARCHIBALD SIMPSON: Architect and His Times: G. M. Fraser.
ARCHIBALD SIMPSON: Architect of Aberdeen: by Cuthbert Graham.
ABERDEEN: An Illustrated Architectural Guide: by W. Brogden.
GORDON: An Illustrated Architectural Guide: by Ian Shepherd.
DEESIDE AND THE MEARNS: An Illustrated Architectural Guide: by Jane Geddes.
BANFF & BUCHAN: An Illustrated Architectural Guide: by Charles McKean.
MORAY: An Illustrated Architectural Guide: by Charles McKean.
NORTH CLYDE ESTUARY, An Architectural Guide: by Frank Walker and Fiona Sinclair.
SHETLAND: An Illustrated Architectural Guide: by Mike Finnie.
ABERDEEN OF OLD: by Edward Meldrum.

ROBERT GORDON UNIVERSITY.
SCOTT SUTHERLAND SCHOOL OF ARCHITECTURE
The Georgina Scott Sutherland Library.

Thanks are due to the Librarian, Mrs Elaine Dunphy, and in particular also Jim Fiddes and staff of the Georgina Scott Sutherland School of Architecture Library for their assistance in guiding me through their considerable archive book material and photographic collection on Archibald Simpson: most especially for the following sources which have been of very great assistance to me.

ARCHIBALD SIMPSON, His Classical Buildings in Aberdeen: by Robert W. Smyth.
THE HISTORY & ARCHITECTURE OF THE DAMLANDS (1802–1902): by Robert E. Morris.

THE EARLY HISTORY OF UNION STREET, ABERDEEN (1800–1824): by Frank Farmer.

COUNTRY HOUSES IN BANFF AND BUCHAN, (1790–1846): by Christine A. Souter.

The following local books and publications have also provided much essential background:

SIMPSON 1947 CENTENARY ORATION BOOKLET: W. Douglas Simpson.

ARCHIBALD SIMPSON: Notes by G. M. Fraser, Aberdeen Reference Library.

ABERDEEN 150 YEARS AGO: by James Rettie.

ABERDEEN ITS TRADITIONS AND HISTORY: by William Robbie.

ABERDEEN IN BYEGONE DAYS: 1910 published Edition.

A TALE OF TWO BURGHS: The Archaeology of Old and New Aberdeen 1987.

GEORGE WASHINGTON WILSON'S ABERDEEN: John S. Smith.

The LEOPARD MAGAZINE: 5th anniversary edition 1979.
Dec / Jan edition 1978 / 79.

ABERDEEN 1800-2000: A New History edited by W. H. Fraser and Clive H. Lee.

OLD ABERDEEN: Bishops Burghers and Buildings: edited by John S. Smith.

CITY BY THE GREY NORTH SEA: Fenton Wyness.

MORE SPOTS FROM THE LEOPARD: Fenton Wyness.

ABERDEEN ON RECORD: The H.M.Stationary Office.

THE NEO-CLASSICAL TOWN: Editor: W. A. Brogden.

LOST FERRYHILL: The Ferryhill Heritage Society.

A VISITORS GUIDE TO ABERDEEN: by R. E. H. Mellor and J. S. Smith.

ABERDEEN: WALKIN THE MAT: by Winram Cluer Publications.

THE LANDS OF LONACH: by Ron Winram.

THE COMING OF THE TURNPIKES TO ABERDEEN: by John Patrick.

THE GRANITE CITY: by Robert Smith.

THE ABERDEEN GRANITE INDUSTRY: by Ton Donnelly.

In addition to the local material the following more general books provided much valuable general background information on connected architectural subjects.

ARCHITECTURE IN BRITAIN: 1530–1830 by Sir John Summerson.

THE CLASSICAL LANGUAGE OF ARCHITECTURE by Sir John Summerson.

CLASSICAL ARCHITECTURE: by James Stevens Curl.

WILLIAM ADAM: Scotland's Universal Architect: by John Gifford.

ROBERT ADAM AND SCOTLAND: by Margaret H. B. Sanderson.

HISTORY OF SCOTTISH ARCHITECTURE Glendinning, MacInnes & MacKechnie.

Considerable thanks are also due to Aberdeen City Council, the staff of Aberdeen Public Library and Reference Library, the Robert Gordon University and Scott Sutherland School of Architecture, the Georgina Scott Sutherland Library, the University of Aberdeen, their Archive Department and the Queen Mother Library, RCHAMS, Historic Scotland, and Aberdeen Civic Society, all of whom were always of very great assistance to me in my various researches. In addition Lindy Cheyne, Bill Brogden, Mike Finnie, Norman Marr-Chairman of Aberdeen Civic Society, Paul Pillath of Aberdeen Planning Conservation Dept, and Judith Cripps, the City Archivist, have also all been particularly helpful in resolving many specific difficulties.

Illustrations Acknowledgements

I am also extremely grateful for the permission of the following sources and Institutions to reproduce the various prints, plans, maps, old photographs and old sketches which have been used as illustrations throughout the text of many buildings.

ABERDEEN CITY LIBRARY & INFORMATION SERVICES:

Sketch: Sketch of the Quadrangle of Simpson's New College building, Aberdeen.

Sketch: View of the City of Aberdeen from Torry Farm, 1845.

Sketch: View of Simpson's new Aberdeen Market Street Proposals of around 1840.

Photograph: Union Street, Aberdeen viewed from the Castlegate circa 1860.

Sketch: View of the Castlegate, Aberdeen circa 1840.

Sketch: Old St Nicholas Church, Aberdeen circa 1760.

Photograph: of E & W St Nicholas Church, Aberdeen circa 1850.

Sketch: View of the Union Bridge, Aberdeen viewed from the Denburn, 1805.

Abercrombie's original Proposals for the western extension of the City of Aberdeen.

Photographs outside and inside views of St Andrews Church, King Street, Aberdeen.

Sketch: View of the Lunatic Asylum, at Barkmill, Berryden Aberdeen.

Sketch: view of Old Marischal College, prior to its demolition.

Photographs: Marischal College Quadrangle and Greyfriars Church, Aberdeen.

Photograph of the interior of the Natural History Museum, Marischal College, Aberdeen.

Photograph: Mrs Auquharney's Villa, at Holburn Street – Justice Mill Lane corner, Aberdeen.

Photographs: externally and internally of the old Royal Infirmary Woolmanhill, Aberdeen.

Photographs: of the Triple Churches from the Denburn, and Union Terrace Aberdeen.

I would especially also wish to thank Catherine Taylor, Reference and Local Studies Librarian of the City Reference Library, for her very considerable help and assistance in researching and finding a great deal of material on this subject.

ROBERT GORDON UNIVERSITY
SCOTT SUTHERLAND SCHOOL OF ARCHITECTURE:
GEORGINA SCOTT SUTHERLAND: LIBRARY

I would thank the library for permission to reproduce various items from their archive.

The detailed historical information on the New Market development, Market Street, Aberdeen.

Information on the history of the Lunatic Asylum Barkmill, and the Royal Infirmary, Woolmanhill.

Background information on the design development of North of Scotland Bank, Castlegate, Aberdeen.

Permission also to reproduce the following prints from their Simpson collection. Simpson's initial sketch of the New Market Building proposals.

Simpson's competition entry for the Blind Asylum in Huntly Street, Aberdeen.

Simpson's proposals for a new Gothic Screen and new street, Marischal College

Simpson's competition entry for the Hamilton Monument, St Nicholas Churchyard, Aberdeen.

Sketch of Mrs Emslie's Institution in Albyn Place, Aberdeen.

Simpson's penultimate proposal for the North Bank premises in Castle Street, Aberdeen.

UNIVERSITY of ABERDEEN: ARCHIVES DEPT, King's College.
And the QUEEN MOTHER LIBRARY, the G. W. Wilson Collection.

Thanks are due to the University Archive Dept for their freely given assistance as well as the Library for their assistance with the G. W. Wilson Collection of photographs.

Mike Craig and his staff at the University Reprographics Department were also of considerable help and arranged permission for the reproduction both the Archibald Simpson portraits in the University's possession.

Also from the George Washington Wilson Collection:-

Their photograph of the lower end of Union Street, with the original Union Chambers building.

The early photograph of Union Street and the front of the Assembly Rooms, Aberdeen.

ABERDEEN CIVIC SOCIETY

For their very kind permission to reproduce the following photographic material from Archibald Simpson, Architect of Aberdeen 1790–1847, by Cuthbert Graham.

Internal photograph of the Chapel of Ease, Woodside, Aberdeen.

Internal photographs of the Round Room, Square Room & Foyer.within Aberdeen Music Hall.

Photograph of Simpson's New Market interior, Aberdeen (demolished).

Old photographs of Lessendrum, Newe, Carnousie, Durris, and Scotstown Houses (all long demolished).

Photograph of the west side of Victoria Street, Aberdeen.

ROYAL COMMISSION ON THE ANCIENT AND HISTORIC MONUMENTS OF SCOTLAND:

For the very considerable assistance of the staff on a number of instances with many queries on various Simpson buildings.

Also for permission to use their:-

Photograph: the Market Street frontage of the New Market, Aberdeen, by Archibald Simpson.

HISTORIC SCOTLAND:

Thanks are also due to the staff of Historic Scotland, who were on many occasions most generous with freely given help and information.

ADDITIONAL PHOTOGRAPHIC, PLAN & HISTORIC MATERIAL

I have been greatly encouraged and indeed also extremely grateful to the very keen interest shown by the following property owners who have all extended to me the greatest consideration and kindness in freely given information and plans. I am also indebted to them for their permission to take new photographs of their properties where necessary and to reproduce also their old photographs where more appropriate.

The University of Aberdeen, The G. Washington Wilson Collection: their photograph of Union Street, Aberdeen.

Mr Alexander Forbes, for use of his photographs of Drumminor extension wing (now demolished).

Malcolm, Master of Forbes for information, permission to photograph and for plans of Castle Forbes.

Aberdeen City Library Collection, St Andrew's Cathedral, for old external and internal photographs.

Session Clerk, St Andrews Cathedral Aberdeen: for information on the original plan form.

Aberdeen Hotel Building, Union Street: information from their files by Thomson Craig and Donald, Architects.

Medico Chirurgical Hall: Plans and information from their files by Thomson Craig and Donald, Architects.

The Revd. Alan Greig of Kintore Parish Church, for background information on the history of the church.

Aberdeen City Library Collection, for permission to copy their old print of the original Lunatic Asylum, Barkmill.

Aberdeen City Council, to allow the reproduction of copy plans of the Music Hall, (Assembly Rooms) Aberdeen.

and for permission also to take a number of internal photographs.

Aberdeen Civic Society for their kind permission to reuse their photographs of the Round and Square Rooms.

The University of Aberdeen, The G. Washington Wilson Collection: their photograph of the Music Hall, Aberdeen.

The Royal Northern and University Club for permission to reproduce their plan of No. 9 Albyn Place, Aberdeen.

The National Trust for Scotland, for information and permission to photograph Haddo House and Stables building.

The Earl of Haddo, Haddo House Estate, for information on Estate buildings and permission to photograph.

Thomson Craig and Donald, Architects, for information on the restoration of the Royal Athenaeum, Aberdeen.

Aberdeen City Library, for copies of Simpson's draft elevations of Union Buildings, Union St., Aberdeen.

Mr and Mrs M Dreelan for photographs and background information on Heathcot House (demolished).

Mr John Foster for permission to photograph, and his photographs, plans and history of Park House and the Estate.

Mrs Wendy Matheson for plans, permission to use photographs and website information on Boath House.

Mr Vincent D'Agostino and his Archive Staff for their information and plans on Murtle House and Estate.

Mr Friedwart Bock, Archivist and Mr Graham Donaldson, Camphill Architects for information & plans of Murtle.

Mr and Mrs I. Thomson of the Stable Block, Durris for their assistance and access to their home.

RCHAMS & South Aberdeenshire Planning Department for information on Durris Stable Block.

The Leopard Magazine for permission to reproduce their photograph of Durris House phase one.

The Leopard Magazine for permission to reproduce their photograph of Scotstown House.

The Hon. Mr and Mrs W. Stanhope for their information and kind permission to photograph Crimonmogate.

The Hon. Mr and Mrs C. Monckton for their kind permission to reproduce photographs of Crimonmogate.

Mr Donald & Iain Robertson, St Giles & St Columba's Church Elgin, for information & permission to photograph.

Ashley Bartlam Partnership, Architects for the use of their plan of St Giles Church, Elgin.

The Trustees and Manager of Anderson's Institute, for information and permission to photograph the property.

Mr D. M. Maccallum of Willetts, Architects, Elgin for copies of their plans of the Anderson Institute buildings.

122.–132 & 95–99 Union Street, general background information by Thomson Craig and Donald, Architects.

101–105 Union Street, plans and background information supplied by Grampian Design Associates.

Mr and Mr Moffat , for permission to photograph Tillery House, near Udny.

The Leopard Magazine, for permission to reproduce their photograph of Tillery House prior to the fire.

Tayside University Hospitals, NHS Trust, for their kind permission to reproduce the hall photograph of Stracathro.

Lickley Proctor, Chartered Surveyors and Property Consultants, Dundee, for their kind assistance.

Mr E. McIntosh, Site Manager, NHS Tayside, for plans and background information on Stracathro Mansion.

Lt. Col. W. J. Campbell Adamson, Careston Castle for background Family information on Stracathro Mansion

Mr F. Gemmell, Manager, for photographs and general information on Letham Grange Mansion House.

Mr and Mrs Gaucci for plans, information and permission to photograph the restored Leask (Pitlurg) House.

The Leopard Magazine for permission to reproduce their photograph of The House of Leask before the fire.

Major General Gordon Lennox for his assistance and permission to photograph Gordon Castle and Estate.

G.A..Duncan, Grain Ltd., Bogside Fochabers, for permission to photograph the Home Farm complex.

Dr Peter H. Reid, Robert Gordon's University for information on the Gordon Lennox Family and Estate.

Mr Charles Marshall for general information about Caskieben House and original Estate buildings.

Mr and Mrs David Grant, for access and permission to photograph Caskieben Stables building.

Mr and Mrs Youngson for their permission to photograph Bendauch near Caskieben.

Mr and Mrs Ross for permission to photograph Mains of Dyce, Aberdeen.

Caledonian Maps, Kyle of Lochalsh, for permission to reproduce part of their Aberdeen 1820 map.

The University of Aberdeen, The G Washington Wilson Collection: photograph of the Spey Bridge, Fochabers.

Mr and Mrs George Hardie, House of Newe, for information on the history of Castle Newe (demolished) and access to their considerable photographic archive of the house and its surrounding estate.

Mrs Margaret Davidson, Winram's Books, 32-36 Rosemount Place, Aberdeen, for a photograph of Castle Newe.

The Aberdeen Civic Society for permission to reuse their old photograph of Castle Newe.

Grampian University Hospital Trust, for information on the Old Royal Infirmary, Woolmanhill, Aberdeen.

Ms Fionna Watson, Archivist of Grampian University Trust, for her kind assistance.

Aberdeen City Library, for the use of old photographs, elevations and plan of Royal Infirmary, Woolmanhill.

Mr Jock Barles for information and permission to photograph Craig Castle, Lumsden.

The City of Aberdeen Reference Library, the Fraser Notes on Dr Bell's School, Frederick Street, Aberdeen.

Aberdeen City Library, for permission to use their photograph of old E & W St Nicholas Churches, Aberdeen.

The Session Clerk, East and West Church of St Nicholas, Aberdeen for permission to photograph the East Church

Mr and Mrs S. Ferguson for information and permission to photograph Linton House, Sauchen, Aberdeenshire.

Revd. Jim Scott for general information and permission to photograph Drumoak Parish Church.

Mr & Mrs D. Pearson, Meldrum House Hotel, for permission to reuse old photographs of the Simpson House.

The Leopard Magazine for permission to reuse their old photograph of Haddo, Inverkeithny.

The University of Aberdeen for permission to take internal photographs of Marischal College, Aberdeen.

The University of Aberdeen: Archives Department, for their historical information on Marischal New College.

Aberdeen City Library for permission to reuse old photographs and the plan of Marischal New College.

Aberdeen City Library, for preparatory sketches of the North of Scotland Bank, Castle Street, Aberdeen.

Mr Andrew Miller, Manager, Archibald Simpson's for information and permission to photograph the premises.

Aberdeenshire Council, Education & Recreation Dept, for plans of Gordon's Schools Huntly.

The Leopard Magazine for permission to reuse their photograph of Lessendrum house. (now ruinous).

School of Architecture Library for permission to reproduce their information on Simpson's New Market Scheme.

The Leopard Magazine for permission to reuse their photograph of Carnousie New House (demolished).

Macdonald Hotels for historical information on Pittodrie and Thainstone House Hotels, Aberdeenshire.

The General Manager, Mr S. Queen for permission to photograph the exterior of Pittodrie House Hotel

The General Manager Mrs Sylvia Simpson, and the Front of House Keeper, Mrs Mabel Sinclair for their assistance

Aberdeen City Library, for permission to use old photographs of the Triple Churches, Schoolhill, Aberdeen.

The Session Clerk, & Mr P. Linguard, Trinity Church, Rothesay, Isle of Bute, for information on the Church.

Mr Alan Marshall of Marshall Associates, Architects, Rothesay, for permission to copy their plan of the Church.

Lord Balgonie, Glenferness House, for historical information, plan, & permission to photograph the house.

BP, at Morkeu, (now Greenridge) Cults, for permission to photograph the house, and for the use of their plan.

Ms Judith Cripps, Aberdeen City Archivist, for details on Oldmachar Parish Church, Old Aberdeen.

The Revd. Alistair Murray, Woodside Parish Church, for background information on the church.

Mr Mike Finnie, for historical information on theUnion Bank, Lerwick, Shetland (demolished).

Mr Mike Finnie also for information and photographs of Alder Lodge, 6 Hillhead, Lerwick, Shetland.

The Rev. Alison Jaffrey and Mr Ewan Richardson for information on Forgue Parish Church, Aberdeenshire.

Mr Ian Shepherd for the use of his photograph of Forgue Parish Church.

I would also particularly wish to thank Grampian Design Associates for the very kind use of their offices, their photographic equipment and their photocopying facilities etc., which were of particular assistance in the preparation of the various house plans and layouts which have been reproduced and incorporated throughout the text.

While every effort has been made to obtain the necessary permissions to reproduce all the material and images used in this study, in a few instances it proved impossible to locate the appropriate source. Apologies are therefore offered in advance to any body or person who may consider themselves worthy of an acknowledgement, and have been inadvertently omitted from the list of acknowledgements through my ignorance.

I would also wish to acknowledge the considerable encouragement, patience and support of my wife Lesley in the creation of, and research for this book, together with the very invaluable computer skills of my daughter Louise whose expertise and freely given time has added immeasurably to the quality of all the illustrations and their reproduction throughout. I would also thank Andy Massie for his assistance, together with my readers, Lorna Jackson and Norman Marr for all their suggestions and special contributions to the text.

Index of Buildings

A START IS MADE 1813–1819   *pages 29–60*

Union Chambers, 46–50 Union Street, Aberdeen.

Morrison of Auchintoul's House, 40–44 Union Street, Aberdeen.

Druminnor: extension wing (removed) and alterations, Lumsden, Gordon District, Aberdeenshire.

Castle Forbes: enlargement, Keig, Gordon District, Aberdeenshire.

St Andrew's Chapel, (subsequently enlarged into St Andrew's Cathedral) King Street, Aberdeen.

The Aberdeen Hotel, 134–144 Union Street, Aberdeen.

Medico Chirurgical Hall, King Street, Aberdeen (now joined to Smith's County Records next door).

Kintore Parish Church, Kintore, Gordon District, Aberdeenshire.

Bank premises, 23–35 Gordon Street, Huntly, Gordon District, Aberdeenshire (now District Offices).

Town House No. 13 Golden Square, Aberdeen. (now used as offices).

The Lunatic Asylum, Barkmill (subsequently very considerably altered): Berryden, Aberdeen.

Bailey Galen's House No. 19–21 Union Street, Aberdeen (now offices).

ARCADIAN DREAMS 1819–1830   *pages 61–157*

Royal Northern and University Club premises, 9 Albyn Place, Aberdeen. (subsequently extended).

Public Waterhouse, St Nicholas Street, Aberdeen (demolished).

The County Buildings or Assembly Rooms, (the front part of the Music Hall) Union Street, Aberdeen.

Huntly Lodge: extensions, near Huntly, (now Huntly Castle Hotel) Gordon District, Aberdeenshire.

Haddo House: Alterations, Home Farm, and Stables. Methlick, Gordon District, Aberdeenshire.

Union Buildings (Royal Athenaeum) 1–17 Union Street, Aberdeen. (now commercial & office premises).

Heathcot House and Estate buildings, Haugh of Ardoe, Deeside, Kincardine. (House demolished).

Park House and Estate buildings, Drumoak, Deeside, Aberdeenshire.

Boath House, (now a Country House Hotel) Auldearn, Nairnshire.

Murtle House, (now offices of the Rudolph Stiener organisation) Murtle, Bieldside, Aberdeen.

Bon-Accord Square, Crescent and Terrace with East and West Craibstone Streets, Aberdeen.

Crown Street development, Aberdeen: possible involvement.

Durris House; first extension, Durris, Deeside, Kincardine (demolished).

Scotstown House and Estate buildings, Bridge of Don, Aberdeen. (demolished).

Crimonmogate House and Estate buildings, Lonmay, Aberdeenshire.

St Giles Church, High Street, Elgin, Moray.

Nos. 122–132, 95–99 and 101–105 Union Street, Aberdeen. (all now much altered internally).

Town and County Bank, 91–93 Union Street, Aberdeen. (demolished for B.H.S.).

Tillery House, Udny, Aberdeenshire (partly ruined).

East Lodge, 2 Castle Street, Fochabers, Moray.

Stracathro House and Estate buildings, near Brechin, Angus.

Letham Grange, near Arbroath, Angus (now a Golf and Leisure Complex).

New Cross-Street Scheme, Broad Street, Aberdeen. (unexecuted).

House of Leask, Pitlurg, Buchan, Aberdeenshire (destroyed but recently restored).

Scheme for the West End of Aberdeen (unexecuted).

East Wing, Castle Gordon: restored following a fire. Near Fochabers, Moray.

Cottage, 134–138 Crown Street, Aberdeen.

Church Scheme, Holburn Junction, Aberdeen. (unexecuted).

Home Farm, Boghead: Castle Gordon, near Fochabers, Moray.

Town Hall, High Street, Forres, Moray (now considerably altered internally and externally).

Woodside Chapel of Ease, Queen Street, Woodside, Aberdeen (now converted into flats).

Bridge over the River Dee at Craiglug, Competition Scheme (unsuccessful).

Anderson's Institution, South College Street, Elgin, Moray (modernised internally).

East End School, Institution Road, Elgin, Moray.

Nos. 18 & 20 Albyn Place, Aberdeen (now incorporated into Harlaw Academy).

Estate Buildings, Caskieben, Kinellar, Aberdeen.

Granton Lodge, Great Western Place, Aberdeen (sub-divided into flats).

First Proposals for the laying out of the Ferryhill District, Aberdeen.

A FAIR BODY OF WORK 1831–1840 *pages 159–256*

Restoration of the Spey Bridge, Fochabers, Moray.

Nos. 20–30 and 17–27, Ferryhill Place, Ferryhill, Aberdeen.

Nos. 3–11 Belvidere Terrace, (now Marine Terrace), Aberdeen, realised mainly in the 1880s.

Castle Newe, Strathdon, Aberdeenshire (demolished, stonework reused at King's College).

Town Houses, Nos. 381–389, Union Street, Aberdeen (now commercial properties).

House for Mrs Yeats of Auquharney, Justice Mill Lane, Aberdeen (demolished).

Castle Craig: alterations and additions, near Lumsden, Gordon District, Aberdeenshire.

Aberdeen Infirmary, Woolmanhill, Aberdeen.

Competition design for the Hamilton Monument, Aberdeen (unsuccessful).

St Andrew's Episcopal Chapel, High Street, Banff (extended).

Episcopal Chapel, Gordon Castle, Fochabers, Moray (subsequently altered).

Second Scheme for the West End of Aberdeen (unrealised).

Town Houses, Nos. 1–6 Rubislaw Place and 21–23 Waverley Place, Aberdeen.

Dr Bell's School, Frederick Street, Aberdeen (demolished).

Linton House and Estate buildings, Midmar, Gordon District, Aberdeenshire.

The East Church of St Nicholas, Aberdeen (subsequently restored following a fire).

North of Scotland Bank, Broad Street, Fraserburgh (now used as offices).

Drumoak Parish Church, Drumoak, Deeside, Aberdeenshire.

Stables and Durris House: (second extension). Kincardine (extension now demolished).

Competition Scheme for the Widening of the Bridge of Dee, Aberdeen (unsuccessful).

Competition design for the Advocates Hall, Aberdeen (declined).

Town Houses, Nos. 12–16 Albyn Place, Aberdeen (completed by Mackenzie & Matthews).

Meldrum House, extension. Old Meldrum, Aberdeenshire (now largely removed).

Haddo House, Inverkeithney, Aberdeenshire (currently dilapidated).

Town Houses, Nos. 1–7 Rotonda Place, Ferryhill, Aberdeen (now Polmuir Road).

New Marischal College (rear quadrangle range only) Broad Street, Aberdeen.

Terrace at Nos. 1–6 Marine Place, Ferryhill, Aberdeen.

Lessendrum House, alterations and extensions, Gordon District, Aberdeenshire (ruinous).

Mrs Emslie's Institution, 19 Albyn Place Aberdeen (now centrepiece of Harlaw Academy).

Provost Leslie's House, 18 Albyn Place, Aberdeen (now used as offices, etc).

Re-erect Smith's Obelisk at Barkmill, The Lunatic Asylum, Berryden, Aberdeen.

Scheme for a New Market Building for Aberdeen (unsuccessful).

Competition scheme for New Town School, Little Belmont Street, Aberdeen (unsuccessful).

Murtle Cottage, North Deeside Road, Bieldside, Aberdeen.

Westburn House, Westburn Park, Westburn Road, Aberdeen.

North of Scotland Fire and Life Offices, Nos. 1–5 King Street, Aberdeen.

North of Scotland Bank, Castle Street, Aberdeen (now the Archibald Simpson Bar).

Gordon Schools, Huntly, Gordon District, Aberdeenshire (much altered and extended).

Town Houses at Nos. 134 Albert Terrace and 1 Prince Arthur Street, (completed after 1850).

Town Houses at Nos. 1–23 and 2–18, Albert Street, Aberdeen, (erected after 1850).

Glassaugh House, near Fordyce, Banff (ruinous).

Carnousie House, Inverkeithney, Aberdeenshire (demolished, stones reused King's College).

Devanha House, Devanha Gardens, Ferryhill, Aberdeen. (now subdivided into flats).

Nos. 67 and 73–79 Union Street, Aberdeen (demolished).

The New Market, Market Street, Aberdeen (demolished).

Thainestone House, Port Elphinstone, Gordon District, Aberdeenshire (now a hotel).

The Moir Mausoleum, St Peter's Cemetery, the Spital, Old Aberdeen.

Lunatic Asylum, Kitchen extension wing, Barkmill: Berryden, Aberdeen.

A FAIR BODY OF WORK 1841–1847 *pages 257–305*

Competition design for the Blind Asylum, Huntly Street, Aberdeen (unsuccessful).

Pittodrie House: extensions, Chapel of Garioch, Gordon District, Aberdeenshire.

Cross street scheme, Broad Street, Aberdeen. (unsuccessful).

Post Office Building, 5–9 Market Street, Aberdeen (demolished).

North of Scotland Bank, the Square, Huntly, Gordon District, Aberdeenshire.

Town Houses, Nos. 7–11, 21–59, and 18–56, Victoria Street, Aberdeen.

Nos. 2, 6, 8, 10 & 16, Waverley Place, Aberdeen.

Lunatic Asylum: workshops extension wing, Barkmill, Berryden, Aberdeen.

East End of Aberdeen Proposals (unsuccessful).

The Triple Churches, Belmont Street / Schoolhill, Aberdeen (now partly ruinous).

The Free Church, Rothesay, Isle of Bute (much restored following collapse of the roof).

Glenferness House, & Estate buildings, etc., Ardclach, Nairnshire (the house much altered).

Fever Wing & Porter's Lodge, Infirmary, Woolmanhill, Aberdeen (Fever Wing removed).

The Mechanics Institute, 13–15 Market Street, Aberdeen. (now a nightclub).

Morkeu House, (Greenridge) Cults, Aberdeen (now the BP corporate entertainment centre).

St Mary's Church, High Street, Old Aberdeen (now the University Geography Department).

The Natural History Museum, Marischal College, Aberdeen (now refurbished).

Competition Design for the Incorporated Trades, Union Street, Aberdeen (unsuccessful).

Woodside New Parish Church, Woodside, Aberdeen (completed by W. Ramage).

Proposed Railway Terminus, Guild Street / Market Street, Aberdeen (unexecuted).

Union Bank of Scotland & Bank Manager's House, Lerwick, Shetland Isles.

Duchess of Gordon School, Holyrood, Edinburgh (now part of the Queen's Gallery).

Proposed Scheme for Civic Improvements, Aberdeen (unsuccessful).

Lunatic Asylum, Workshops and Chapel extension, Barkmill, Berryden, Aberdeen.

West Parish Church School, George Street, Aberdeen (demolished).

Skene House: alterations and extensions, Skene, Aberdeenshire (completed W. Ramage).